America

alexis de gheldere

Tu te diras, du haut de la montagne d'où
sont résolus tes problèmes: "Comment
n'ai-je pas d'abord compris?" comme s'il
était d'abord quelque chose à comprendre.
Car il suffit pour y voir clair de
changer de perspective."

ANTOINE DE SAINT-EXUPÉRY

*At the top of the mountain, when all of
your worries have melted away, you ask
yourself: "How could I not have reached
this understanding earlier?" As though it
were something to be understood, when it
is enough simply to see clearly and to
change your perspective.*

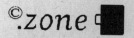

©.zone

AUTHOR
ALEXIS DE GHELDERE
SERIES DIRECTOR
DANIEL DESJARDINS
PRODUCTION SUPERVISOR
PASCALE COUTURE
PROJECT SUPERVISOR
DANIEL DESJARDINS
ASSISTANT PROJECT SUPERVISOR
CHRISTIAN ROY
CARTOGRAPHY AND GRAPHICS
ANDRÉ DUCHESNE
ASSISTANTS
PATRICK THIVIERGE
LINE MAGIER
ENGLISH EDITING
TARA SALMAN
STEPHANIE HEIDENREICH

ILLUSTRATIONS
LORETTE PIERSON
GRAPHICS AND COVER DESIGN
DOMINIQUE THIBODEAU
LAYOUT
STEPHANIE HEIDENREICH
PHOTOGRAPHY
CHANTALE DOYON
RESEARCH
DENIS FAUBERT
FRANCIS GIGUÈRE
ERIC HAMOVITCH
CLAUDE-VICTOR LANGLOIS
MARC RIGOLE
YVES SÉGUIN
CARLOS SOLDEVILA
CAROL WOOD

⏭ DISTRIBUTORS ⏮

AUSTRALIA: Little Hills Press, 11/37-43 Alexander St., Crows Nest NSW 2065, ☎ (612) 437-6995, Fax: (612) 438-5762

BELGIUM AND LUXEMBOURG: Vander, Vrijwilligerlaan 321, B-1150 Brussel, ☎ (02) 762 98 04, Fax: (02) 762 06 62

CANADA: Ulysses Books & Maps, 4176 Saint-Denis, Montréal, Québec, H2W 2M5, ☎ (514) 843-9882, ext.2232, 800-748-9171, Fax: 514-843-9448, www.ulysses.ca

GERMANY AND AUSTRIA: Brettschneider, Fernreisebedarf, Feldfirchner Strasse 2, D-85551 Heimstetten, München, ☎ 89-99 02 03 30, Fax: 89-99 02 03 31, Bretttschneider_Fernreisebedarf@t-online.de

GREAT BRITAIN AND IRELAND: World Leisure Marketing, Unit 11, Newmarket Court, Newmartket Drive, Derby DE24 8NW, ☎ 1 332 57 37 37, Fax: 1 332 57 33 99, office@wlmsales.co.uk

ITALY: Centro Cartografico del Riccio, Via di Soffiano 164/A, 50143 Firenze, ☎ (055) 71 33 33, Fax: (055) 71 63 50

NETHERLANDS: Nilsson & Lamm, Pampuslaan 212-214, 1380 AD Weesp (NL), ☎ 0294-494949, Fax: 0294-494455, E-mail: nilam@euronet.nl

PORTUGAL: Dinapress, Lg. Dr. Antonio de Sousa de Macedo, 2, Lisboa 1200, ☎ (1) 395 52 70, Fax: (1) 395 03 90

SCANDINAVIA: Scanvik, Esplanaden 8B, 1263 Copenhagen K, DK, ☎ (45) 33.12.77.66, Fax: (45) 33.91.28.82

SPAIN: Altaïr, Balmes 69, E-08007 Barcelona, ☎ 454 29 66, Fax: 451 25 59, altair@globalcom.es

SWITZERLAND: OLF, P.O. Box 1061, CH-1701 Fribourg, ☎ (026) 467.51.11, Fax: (026) 467.54.66

U.S.A.: The Globe Pequot Press, 6 Business Park Road, P.O. Box 833, Old Saybrook, CT 06475, ☎ 800-243-0495, Fax: 800-820-2329, sales@globe-pequot.com

⏮ TABLE OF CONTENTS ⏭

⏮ WRITE TO US ⏭

The information contained in this guide was correct at press time. However, mistakes can slip in, omissions are always possible, places can disappear, etc. The authors and publisher hereby disclaim any liability for loss or damage resulting from omissions or errors.

We value your comments, corrections and suggestions, as they allow us to keep each guide up to date. The best contributions will be rewarded with a free book from Ulysses Travel Publications. All you have to do is write us at the following address and indicate which title you would be interested in receiving (see the list at the end of guide).

Ulysses Travel Publications
4176 Rue Saint-Denis
Montréal, Québec
Canada H2W 2M5
www.zone.qc.ca
zone@zone.qc.ca

Canadian Cataloguing in Publication Data
Gheldere, Alexis de, 1975-
     Central America
     (Budget .zone)
     Translation of: Amérique centrale
     Includes index.
     ISBN 2-89464-182-6

1. Central America - Guidebooks. I. Title. II. Series.
F1429.G4313 1999 917.2804'53   C98-941526-0

⏮ LIST OF MAPS ⏭

⏮ SWEET DREAMS ⏭

All accommodations listed in this guide cost under US$13 for two people, unless otherwise indicated.

⏮ BON APPETIT ⏭

All restaurants listed in this guide cost under US$7 for two people, unless otherwise indicated.

We would like to thank SODEC for their financial support.

"We acknowledge the financial support of the Government of Canada through the Book Publishing Industry Development Program (BPIDP) for our publishing activities."

Canadä

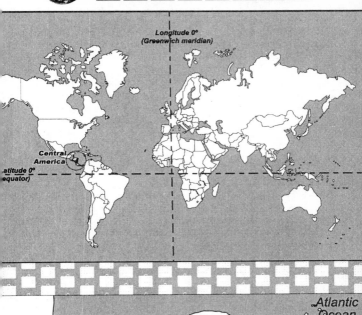

Longitude 0°
(Greenwich meridian)

Central
America

atitude 0°
equator)

Atlantic Ocean

Cuba

Gulf of Mexico

Haiti

México

Belize

Honduras

Jamaica

Dominican Republic

Guatemala

Caribbean Sea

El Salvador

Nicaragua

Panamá

Venezuela

Costa Rica

Colombia

Pacific Ocean

©zone

Ecuador   **Peru**   **Brazil**

▌▌▌▌▌ Land of a thousand contradictions, Central America is the long and narrow umbilical cord linking its northern and southern neighbours. Spanning seven countries over a distance of 2,500 kilometres between Mexico and Columbia, it is also bordered by the two largest oceans in the world. Its position between the Atlantic and Pacific oceans and the two neighbouring Americas is certainly striking, but this expanse harbours several other contrasts: huge volcanic mountains right near magnificent beaches; an intermixed Spanish, native (mestizo) and African population; political stability threatened by neighbours that have just emerged from civil wars; and so on. Welcome to the land of diversity!

▌▌▌▌▌ Spanish is the official language here, except for Belize, a former British colony nestled between Mexico, Guatemala and the Caribbean Sea. Colonization of Central America began in the 16th century, but was less intense than in Peru or Mexico, where there were more precious ores to mine and great civilizations to conquer. The famous Mayan pyramids, found deep in the Belizean and Guatemalan jungles, and to a lesser extent in Honduras, mark the pinnacle of this civilization which had already begun to decline 600 years before the arrival of Europeans. The Spanish only sped things up by engaging in genocide.

▌▌▌▌▌ In Central America, your position on the social ladder depends on the colour of your skin. The lighter you are, the easier it is to climb. The almost mythical violence that follows Central America like a bad action movie is directly linked to poverty, which is most apparent in shantytowns outside the major urban centres. Despite these woes, the people of Central America are extremely warm and friendly.

▶▶ GEOGRAPHY ◀◀

The Central American isthmus acts as a natural barrier separating the Atlantic and Pacific Oceans. Its narrowest point (70 kilometres) is in Panama, where a canal connects the two oceans. Despite its narrowness, the isthmus is an enormous wall of mountains that reach phenomenal heights. Several summits rise over 3,000 metres, even in very narrow Panama. Each country boasts a chain of mountains that forms a link between the North American Rockies and the South American Andes, and from whose lofty peaks the two oceans can often be seen. In Guatemala, most of the population resides in the high mountainous plateaus that can reach heights of 4,000 metres. Most of Central America is a jungle with a tropical climate, but temperatures can plummet dramatically as you reach higher altitudes. Some volcanoes are still active, notably in El Salvador, Nicaragua and Costa Rica.

From the summits, several waterways, only a few of which can be navigated, rush down the slopes toward one ocean or the other, most often the Atlantic. Most of the land thus receives an abundant rainfall and is home to billions of mosquitos which were one of the major obstacles in the construction of the Panama Canal. Take note that the rainy season lasts from about May to October.

⏭ FLORA ⏮

Three ecosystems are found in the Central American isthmus. The jungle (or forest of broad-leaved trees) boasts the largest variety of species. In fact, plants and animals are so numerous that human presence is scarce. In the mountainous regions, including those of Guatemala, a northern-type coniferous forest prevails. After all, if you think about it, latitude and altitude are similar: the higher you go, the colder it gets! Finally, there is also the narrow Pacific coastal plain, largely shaped by the massive deforestation carried out since the dawn of the century. Costa Rica is often lauded for its ecotourism: 12 percent of its territory has been converted into national parks and reserves. On the other hand, more than two thirds of the country's primal forest has been razed over the last fifty years.

⏭ FAUNA ⏮

Since it is located in the tropics, Central America has many different exotic animals: multicoloured parrots, jaguars, snakes, crocodiles, giant turtles, sea cows (like tiny dinosaurs that float to the surface to bask in the sun and greet sailors), as well as several species of monkeys, iguanas and other bizarrely named creatures such as agoutis and tapirs. As for birds, 10 percent of the world's species are found in Costa Rica, and the percentage of butterflies is even greater, as can be attested by the numerous farms in the region that breed them.

Swimming in fresh water in the tropics is definitely not a wise idea, because the hot and humid climate is a bona fide breeding ground for bacterial microorganisms. We have nonetheless cited the safest places for swimming where the water is clear, calm and clean; otherwise it's at your own risk.

⏭ HISTORY ⏮
before 1500 [before its (re)discovery]

Central America was home to two great Native American empires when the conquerors first arrived, namely the Inca Empire in the south and the Aztec Empire in the north. Only the latter civilization extended north of Central America, into Mexico. Human habitation of the region dates back 40,000 years ago when groups of nomads crossed the then-frozen Bering Strait between Siberia and Alaska. Central America did not have as many great civilizations as Mexico or Peru because it served merely as a transit point between North and South America. However, this region is still populated with descendants of the Mayan civilization, a civilization that left behind tombs, pyramids, hieroglyphic steles and other ruins in Guatemala, Belize and, to a lesser extent, in Honduras. Power struggles and the decline of agriculture probably caused the downfall of this culture, well before the arrival of Europeans. Moreover, the Inca and Aztec Empires were annihilated within about fifty years because their hegemony over the area was relatively recent and enemy tribes allied themselves with the European "saviours" — which proved to be a bitter alliance, indeed.

1500

Columbus "discovered" Central America on his last voyage, in 1502. A handful of Spaniards settled in the New World; they were given land by the Crown and used the Native Americans living there as slaves. This system of land division was known as *encomienda*. But the Crown largely left the area alone and focussed its attention on the quest for the elusive El Dorado in Peru, Bolivia and Mexico, where coveted precious metals were rumoured to be located. Thus, the region was primarily used as a bridge between two continents (especially Panama), and served as a base of exploration so that merchandise could be transported across the isthmus from the Pacific to the Atlantic.

1600-1850

For three centuries, the region experienced an economic boom, first in gold from the rivers, then in cacao, and finally in indigo, which is used as a natural dye. The Atlantic seaboard became a den of buccaneers, a base for pirates who looted Spanish galleons transporting South America's precious metals to Seville. Spain created the United Provinces of Central America in order to regain control of the area and protect its interests in Peru and Mexico. However, the union was only to last some fifteen years, since Great Britain refused to join it. In fact, the latter owned a few buccaneering and logging camps and was quite content with this balance of power. Despite its scarce natural resources, Central America was very worthwhile from a geopolitical point of view, and everyone wanted their piece of the pie.

1850-2000

Central American countries laid the foundations for and contin-ued working toward independence during the course of the 19th century. Colonial power slipped away from the Crown and into the hands of elitist governments, exporters and landowners.

With the 1930s came the repercussions of the Stock Market crash and conditions became ripe for dictatorships, military or otherwise. Elections were held, but were just for show.

In the sixties, shockwaves from the revolution in Cuba spread quickly to Central America and rocked its political foundation. Until then, economic growth had been proceeding at a good pace and the middle class was growing, as was the number of university graduates, some of whom led demonstrations and spawned political movements. One of these students was Carlos Fonseca Amador, who in 1961 founded the Frente Sandinista de Liberación Nacional, better known as the Sandinistas, to overthrow the Somoza dicta-torship which had been in power in Nicaragua since 1937. Amador's organization finally succeeded in doing this in 1979, three years after the assassination of its founder. At the same time, the Church was becoming divided in ideology. One of its factions was becoming increasingly aware of and horrified by the social inequities around them. They broke away from the established church and united around the *theología de la liberación*. This new perspective interpreted the Bible according within the context of liberating oppressed peoples (something that should perhaps be addressed by the G-7) by supporting the class struggle and the (armed) action to change society. It was the marriage between María-la-Virga and Karl-the-fundamentalist-Marx. People belonging to this faction preached the "good word" — much to the dismay of those in power, who saw it as a threat to their lifestyle. This probably explains why so many bishops have been assassinated in Central America in the past few decades. Recently, the Bishop of Ciudad Guatemala accused the state of having killed 200,000 people by repression and militarism since the 1950s. He was stoned to death in the middle of the night in April of 1998.

The struggle for power in Central America turned violent in the seventies, with the population resorting to arms. And so began the merry-go-round of military oligarchies that seized power but could not hold on to it for long: they tried to appease the populace with measly reforms, and were ousted by another junta soon after. (Certain specific instances will be discussed in the introductions to each country.) Even the United States, which considers Latin America (more like the whole world) their backyard, got involved. The best example of this is the Iran-Contra affair, in which the US sold arms to Iran to finance the *Contras* (a counter-revolutionary group) in Nicaragua. The Contras were backed by the Reagan administration and its ideological war against imaginary Communist bugbears. They were to topple the evil socialist Sandinistas, and turned a blind eye to the fact that this regime succeeded 40 years of despotism by a dictator-ship that had diverted most of the humanitarian aid sent from all over the world to help the country recover from the devastating earthquake of 1972 into its own pockets. Go figure.

Many books written over the last several decades deal with the political instability of Central America and give detailed accounts of such stories (a good one is *Open Veins of Latin America*, Eduardo Galeano, Press Pocket, 1981).

⏭ FAMOUS AND HISTORICAL FIGURES ⏮

CHRISTOPHER COLUMBUS

Italian navigator Christopher Columbus, with his crazy ideas of finding the route to Asia by heading west from Europe rather than south, finally came upon Central America on his very last voyage, in 1502. The previous three voyages had been to the West Indies, which had kept the expeditions sufficiently occupied. Though this fourth voyage was his very last, Columbus was convinced that the coast of Honduras was the Malaysian coast. He followed this coastline all the way to Panama, encountering Native American civilizations with impressive stocks of gold. But the great visionary's life was drawing to an end. He no longer had the stamina for adventure and had been shorn of glory after the Spanish Crown commissioned other explorers to head prestigious expeditions to these newly discovered lands. One by one his ships became damaged, morale broke down and Columbus soon returned to Spain for good. He died in obscurity in 1506, firmly believing that he had reached Asia.

VASCO NÚÑEZ DE BALBOA

Vasco Núñez de Balboa was born sometime between 1475 and 1477, probably in Badajoz, Galicia. Of noble but poor descent, he left for Seville, where he worked under explorer Rodrigo de Bastidas. At the end of 1501, he sailed for the *tierra incógnita*, where he discovered the Bay of Urabá (Colombia) and settled there for a while before reaching the island of Hispaniola (present-day Dominican Republic and Haiti). There he saw the potential for a colony based on the encomienda system (land and slaves were granted to colonists by the Crown) and founded Salvatierra de la Sabana. When the colony failed in 1510, he set off again and founded Santa María la Antigua del Darién, west of the Bay of Urabá. In 1511, after some clever manoeuvring, Balboa named himself provisional governor of the Darién province and headed up numerous gold-seeking expeditions. In August 1513, with the help of several natives, he began a long journey in search of a mysterious stretch of water known only to them. On September 25, 1513, after an arduous trek through the jungle, he finally reached the Pacific Ocean. Four days later, Balboa, only 38 years of age, officially claimed the South Sea in the name of King Ferdinand and Queen Juana of Spain. Francisco Pizarro, who had accompanied Balboa on his quest, had no idea of the extraordinary fate that awaited him. Indeed, it was he who, while sailing the "new" sea from Panama, would "discover" Ecuador and Peru. June of the following year saw the arrival of Pedro Arias Dávila, a new governor who had been appointed by the Court. Jealous of Balboa's popularity, he falsely charged his rival with treason and had him prosecuted so as to eliminate him. Thus, the great explorer was beheaded in the public square on January 22, 1519.

⏭ THE ECONOMY ⏮

The region's main economic activity is agriculture, which is very profitable thanks to the volcanic soil rich in natural fertilizer from the ashes. Yet, the soil is very vulnerable to erosion and can deteriorate when over-exploited, which is the case with 40 percent of the farmland. Export crops (cotton, coffee, bananas, sugar, beef) are grown in this region. Central American countries have endeavoured to diversify their crops so as to stop being dependent on international prices of a single commodity, whose value is set in London or New York. Cattle breeding also plays a considerable role in the region's economy, and a lot of the land had to be cleared for this purpose. The result is that forests now only cover 30 percent of the territory, as opposed to 70 percent a half-century ago.

The economy is thus unstable and still has a lot in common with a colonial one. Prominent families only prosper because they own huge properties and have a cheap pool of labourers with nowhere else to work. A good plot of land ensures a minimum of survival, but since a very small percentage of the population owns a very large share of the land, rich remain rolling in money while the poor work their fingers to the bone just to eke out a measly living. The economy and politics are common bedfellows, and a good number of landowners regularly meddle in the affairs of the country. Some governments have attempted to institute land reforms, but when these threaten the rich and powerful, a coup is staged or civil war breaks out. This is exactly what happened in Guatemala in 1954 when the Arbenz government redistributed 200-hectare plots of unused land among the rural peasantry. Compensation was even to be provided for landowners who were "robbed" of their land. The problem was that compensation was based on the owners' tax returns, which were practically nil. In short, the compensations were small and the US-based United Fruit Company saw 85 percent of its land expropriated, prompting it to put pressure on the United States. The CIA thus organized a coup from Honduras, and Arbenz resigned, leaving room for some thirty years of repression. This very repression would be responsible for 200,000 deaths, according to the Bishop of Ciudad Guatemala, who was assassinated in April 1998 for voicing his views. When members of the clergy get killed, something is very rotten in the state: the 'powers that be' don't want anyone going around preaching the "good word."

Since the population is mostly rural, the hundreds of thousands of landless people are at the mercy of the handful of owners. Even some poor farmers must rent land for themselves and their families on the owners' property. And because they never make enough to cover costs, they spend their lives reimbursing the debt to the owners, who are known to be all too generous in extending credit to peasants, thereby keeping them permanently indebted.

By and large, the gap between the rich and the poor is much greater than in the West. This poverty is most visible in the shantytowns. The West has long labelled these nations as "developing countries" while turning a blind eye to them. It is the kind of hypocrisy politically correct intellectuals love discussing over coffee — which comes from Central America.

⏭ THE ARTS ⏮

Land of refuge, land of exile. Central American culture has always drawn its inspiration from the hardships of adjusting to or leaving the land. Central Americans are a people in search of an identity, an identity that lies somewhere between their Spanish heritage, Native American past and the behemoth of the United States. Their mixed "native-Spanish-black" ancestry is evident in their artistic expression which shows influences from all these groups.

The harsh economic reality of these countries means that limited resources are allocated towards artistic endeavours. Literature and painting do not require enormous amounts of funding, but developing a national film industry does. It's cheaper to buy American films, just like everyone else!

Art and politics are inevitably connected, and Central America is no exception. In the 1980s, a socialist intellectual movement began to take shape in Latin America, particularly in Nicaragua. Intellectuals, artists and political refugees congregated in the cafés of the Barrio Martha Quesada (in Managua), where they held debates, exchanged ideas and displayed their art. In fact, this openness led many left-wing militants, who were being constantly harassed by the authorities of their countries, to seek refuge in Nicaragua. Today, things are less intense (and the socialists no longer in power), but the past remains palpable.

Central American artists draw on the political tensions in which they are immersed. This source of inspiration became that much more dominant in their works when artists and intellectuals became subject to censorship. Several went into exile, mostly to the West where they could express themselves more freely. Exodus brings new inspiration, which further shapes the region's identity.

▶▶ POPULATION ◀◀

Eighty percent of the population lives on the Pacific side of the rugged mountains that divide the subcontinent. The Spanish had little interest in the land on the Atlantic seaboard, which explains why the population there is mostly of Afro-Caribbean descent.

Since 50 percent of the population is rural, access to the land often means survival in Central America. The legacy of the colonial system, which is based on human exploitation, has yet to be surmounted. A small percentage of the population owns the greater part of the land and has instituted a kind of legal slavery where the peasantry is overworked and underpaid. In addition, work is sometimes seasonal or scarce, and in worst case scenarios, poorer farming families must pay rent for the land they occupy on the owner's property. Of course, because of the clear monopoly of the land, rental costs are exorbitant, which prevents these farmers from turning any profit. Their wages merely allow them to reimburse what they owe in rent.

Though these situations might not be the case everywhere in Central America, they are nevertheless very prevalent. The point is, the Central American peasant who strikes you as so placid and humble is not so by choice. Let's get real here!

Unsurprisingly, the governments trying to put through land reforms almost always have to suck up to American multinationals.

On top of these realities, recent political and military conflicts have driven thousands of families from their villages, mainly from El Salvador, Guatemala and Nicaragua. Considering all they have lived through, these people do not ask for much. This simplicity is what makes them beautiful, but the causes of it cannot be ignored.

⏭ HURRICANE MITCH ⏮

Christmas of 1998, Central America was hit by the worst storm ever to strike its shores. Hurricane Mitch was the most devastating in the region's recorded history. Was it a jolt from El Niño, or the result of climatic changes caused by pollution? Either way, the death toll rose to over 11,000. Mudslides caused by the heaviest rains in 20 years devastated the region, sweeping away hundreds of bridges, wiping out villages, 70 percent of crops and road infrastructure, especially in Honduras and Nicaragua. Some say the area had been set back 30 years within the space of a week. International aid was organized, but was slow in coming and shortages were widespread. Mitch primarily hit the Atlantic coasts of Honduras and Nicaragua, with winds gusting up to 290 kilometres per hour! Because of all the damage, the Atlantic coasts of these countries were temporarily isolated and could only be reached by boat or plane. With only a half-dozen old helicopters, one can readily imagine the urgent need for wealthier countries to provide the necessary supplies (food, clothing, etc.) to the three million homeless.

"The dead are not the problem. They are well and truly dead. The problem is the living. What jobs will they have? Where will they live? What will they eat?" exclaimed a former Costa Rican minister. Given that three-quarters of the population already lived below the poverty line, such concerns are understandable. With high unemployment at 53 percent and 30 percent respectively in Nicaragua and Honduras, these countries' troubles are not over yet. Moreover, a four-year drought had preceded the disaster. Many inhabitants had settled near the banks of the Rio Coco, which marks the border between the two countries. This waterway swelled from a width of 100 metres to 2 kilometres in three days, sweeping away everything in its wake, mixing the waste water with that of the river, thus creating conditions ripe for the outbreak of a cholera epidemic. It is said that the damage in Nicaragua is

greater than that caused by the earthquake of 1972 and the civil war that ravaged the country at the time. It is no doubt impossible to assess the extent of the damage. Don't be surprised to find that many homes and businesses don't exist any more because of the disaster, and, above all, keep in mind that the landscape and the people here have just suffered an(other) ordeal.

Even when faced with disaster, the population is generally welcoming, peace-loving and considerate. This is understandable. With so many natural disasters and other problems, the situation would quickly become intolerable if it were not the case.

Table of Distances (km/mi)
Via the shortest route

1 mile = 1.62 kilometres
1 kilometre = 0.62 miles

	Belize City (Belize)	Colón (Panamá)	Ciudad de Guatemala (Guatemala)	Managua (Nicaragua)	Ciudad de Panamá (Panamá)	San José (Costa Rica)	San Salvador (El Salvador)	
Belize City (Belize)								Belize City (Belize)
Colón (Panamá)	1139/706							Colón (Panamá)
Ciudad de Guatemala (Guatemala)	1293/802	262/162						Ciudad de Guatemala (Guatemala)
Managua (Nicaragua)	534/393	762/472	432268					Managua (Nicaragua)
Ciudad de Panamá (Panamá)	828/513	1359/843	66/41	1205/747				Ciudad de Panamá (Panamá)
San José (Costa Rica)	525/326	342/212	869/539	464/288	769/477			San José (Costa Rica)
San Salvador (El Salvador)	688/427	1179/731	353/219	181/112	1114/691	221/137		San Salvador (El Salvador)
Tegucigalpa (Honduras)	209/130	569/353	1018/631	234/145	362/224	952/590	200/124	Tegucigalpa (Honduras)

Example : The distance between Ciudad Guatemala and San José is 869km/539mi.

||||| It's a fact: the red tape involved in travelling to Central America can be annoying. To lessen the burden of it, this chapter provides you with all the details concerning money, customs, airports, etc.

⏯ ENTRANCE FORMALITIES ⏯

Each country has its own way of regulating who comes in and who goes out of it. And to make things more complicated, the travel documents required depend on the *gringo*'s country of origin. To speed up the process, we strongly suggest that you make several photocopies of all your official documents: one for yourself and one for your family or friends back home whom you can call in case you lose both the original and the photocopy — along with your luggage carrying them. Ouch!

Required Documents According to Your Country of Origin				
	Canada	United States	Britain	Length of Stay
Guatemala	passport tourist card	idem	idem	30 days
Belize	passport	idem	idem	30 days
Honduras	passport	idem	idem	180 days
El Salvador	passport visa tourist card	passport visa	passport	90 days
Nicaragua	passport visa	passport	passport	90 days
Costa Rica	passport	idem	idem	90 days
Panama	passport tourist card	idem	idem	30 days

Tourist cards are issued either on the spot or in advance from the embassy. If you are travelling to your destination by land, it is advisable to bring all the necessary documents with you. If you are taking a charter flight to Nicaragua, the tourist card is required instead of the visa, and it will be given to you either on the plane or upon your arrival at the airport. If you want to extend your visit, just go to another country for 72 hours, and then go through the whole process all over again. Another tip: If the customs officers in El Salvador find you too shabby-looking, they won't let you into the country.

Because these requirements change frequently, contact the embassy of the country you are going to for all the information you need before leaving. This way you won't encounter any surprises.

All the embassies are located in the capitals, except for Belize where the capital changed to Belmopan, but the embassies are still located in Belize City.

▶▶ FOREIGN EMBASSIES IN CENTRAL AMERICA ◀◀

Canada
(in Belize)
83 North Front St.
☎02-31-060

(in Guatemala)
71 Av. 71-59, Z-9
☎02/321-411

(in Honduras)
Edificio El Castano
Blvd. Morazán
☎31-4538

(in El Salvador)
Av. Las Palmas
Colonia San Benito
☎279-3290

(in Nicaragua)
Casa Nazareth Cortado Oeste
☎268-0433

(in Costa Rica)
Calle 3/Av. 1
☎55-35-22

(in Panamá)
Calle Manuel M. Icaza
Aero Peu, piso 5B
☎264-7014

United States
(in Belize)
29 Gabourel Lane
☎02/77-161

(in Guatemala)
Av. La Réforme
7-01, Z-10
☎02/311-541

(in Honduras)
Av. La Paz
☎32-3120

(in El Salvador)
25 Av. Norte 1230
☎226-7100

(in Nicaragua)
Km 4,5 Carretera Sur
☎02/660-010

(in Costa Rica)
Pavas
☎20-39-39

(in Panamá)
Calle 37/Av. Balboa
☎27-1777

Great Britain

(in Belize)
P.O. Box 91
Embassy Square,
Belmopan,
☎22146

(in Guatemala)
Edificio Centro Financiero
(7th Floor),
Tower Two,7a Avenida 5-10,
Zona 4
Guatemala City

(in Honduras)
Edificio Palmira, 3° piso,
Colonia Palmira,
Tegucigalpa,
☎325429 or 320618

(in El Salvador)
Paseo Escalón 4828
☎298-1763, 298-1769 or
298-1455

(in Nicaragua)
Los Robles,
Entrada Principal, No. 4
☎278-0014, 278-0087 or
278-4085

(in Costa Rica)
Edificio Centro Colón,
Paseo Colón,
Centro Colón,
☎258-2025

(in Panamá)
Calle 53 y Urb. Marbella,
☎269-0866

⏭ TOURIST INFO ⏮

There is no doubt that tourism plays an important role in the region's economy. But several countries are still slow in getting the message across. Usually the only way of finding out where to go is by word of mouth from other travellers in youth hostels or other popular tourist places.

Here are the main tourist information offices to begin your search:

Belize: Belize Tourism Industry Association, 99 Albert St., Belize City, ☎02/75-17 or the Belize Tourist Bureau, 83 North Front St., PO Box 325, ☎02/73-255.

Guatemala: INGUAT (Instituto Guatelmateco de Turismo). In the capital: ☎832-0763. They also have offices in the larger cities and at the airports.

El Salvador: ISTU (Instituto Salvadoreno de Turismo). They only have an office in the capital: Blvd. del Hipódromo 508, Col San Benito, ☎243-0427, ⊨278-7310.

Honduras: IHT (Instituto Hondureño de Turismo). They have offices in the main cities. Edificio Europa, Avenida Ramón E Cruz y Calle Rep. De México, Piso 3, ☎224-002, 📠382-102.

Nicaragua: Inturismo. They have offices in León and Managua. You can also buy a copy of the *Guía Facil*, a small publication that reports on what's going on in the country. The Ministry of Tourism is located one street west of the Intercontinental Hotel, ☎281-337, 📠381-187.

Costa Rica: ICT (Instituto Costarricense de Turismo), main office in San José: ☎800-012-3456. Very knowledgeable staff (rare) and free maps (same).

Panamá: IPAT (Instituto Panamenco Autonomo de Turismo) has its main office in the capital, but has very little useful informa- tion for budget travellers. ☎226-7000, 📠226-2544.

▶▶ AIRPORTS ◀◀

All Central American countries have an international airport near their capitals, which usually have a foreign exchange office and local and long-distance telephone booths. If there is no exchange office in the airport, you can usually get by with US dollars (isn't it interesting how you can use US money almost anywhere these days?).

Belize: 15 minutes from Belize City. There is an hourly shuttle service between the airport and the Belcan Bridge.

Guatemala: The 5 or 83 bus (cheap fare) runs between the Aurora Airport and downtown. Take the 5 or the 83 from the airport. From downtown, take either one from Avenidas 4A or 10A in Zona 1.

El Salvador: the Acaya minibus runs four times a day from the airport to the capital. The trip takes 45 minutes and costs much less than a taxi.

Honduras: Seven kilometres from the capital. The Rio Grande bus runs there from Avenida Gutemburg. To get to Tegucigalpa from the airport, take the Las Lomas bus.

Nicaragua: The Augusto Sandino Airport is located a dozen or so kilometres from the centre of the capital. Taking a taxi is the best way of getting there. The bus going there is cheaper, but the passengers are pretty much penniless and won't hesitate to somehow steal your bus fare — so don't take it! If you still want to risk it, it's safer to take one coming from a neighbouring city like Tipitapa.

Costa Rica: the Alajuela bus that goes from San José past the airport (stopping there) is the cheapest way of getting there. Taxis also cover the 16-kilometre distance, but are ten times more expensive.

Panamá: Tocumén International Airport is located 20 kilometres northeast of the capital. A slow shuttle bus makes the trip at regular intervals and is usually crowded. Another way of getting there is to share a *colectivos* taxi with other passengers, but make sure to set a group rate with the driver beforehand or he'll charge everyone full price.

Take note that, like everywhere else, city busses run during the day, and that some airports don't have baggage check, lockers or telephones for long-distance calls — even though these are international airports!

▶ CUSTOMS ◀

You need a permit to bring firearms or animals into the country. The laws vary from country to country, so to avoid any problems, it is best to leave any grenades, hamsters, etc. at home. For anything else you want to bring into the country, remember the following Latin-American proverb: *de lo bueno poco* or "everything is better in moderation."

▶ GETTING AROUND ◀

bus

The best form of transportation for budget travellers. Buses go everywhere, even into ravines, and will let you on, even if there's no room! There's nothing like an adventure through the jungle on the roof of an old orange Mercedes bus! Get ready for the minimum in comfort, animals sitting next to you, a driver who stops where he pleases (bus stop or not), over-airconditioning (if there is any at all), American movies playing at full blast, and paying the special — higher, of course — "tourist" fare. Ok, we're exaggerating here, but specify which class of bus you want because many places have two — and two different prices.

car

Going by car is expensive. Rental rates are better downtown than at the airport where there is usually only one company. You will also get better rates by calling international car rental companies two weeks in advance. Ask them to confirm your order by fax. Of course, 4X4s are the best vehicles since you can take them on the dirt roads (though even these can run into trouble during the rainy season), but they cost twice as much as a regular car.

train

Less expensive than the bus, but not the best way to travel in Central America. They're very slow and always late; it's a miracle that they run at all. If you're not in a rush, the train can be a pleasant ride and a different way of seeing the country. The rail network in Central America is rather short and doesn't exist at all in Belize or El Salvador. In other countries, trains are used only to transport bananas and plantation workers. And some countries only have one train in their "fleet."

motorcycle

The best rental rates are in the big cities. Make sure the engine works properly before renting one, because if it breaks down and you're far from the capital, you're very unlikely to find service stations that can fix it or replace the parts.

bicycle

The best form of transportation to keep your body and your wallet in good shape, bicycles also draw lots of attention. People are intrigued to see someone riding a bike in Central America, and will readily strike up a conversation with you. This is a great way of meeting people and exploring the region. Just bring spare parts with you and be extra careful in mountainous regions where the air is thinner. With a little planning, you should be fine. Biking through the jungle isn't a good idea because most of the trails are in poor condition.

boat

Ferries link certain villages where roads are nonexistent, mostly on the Atlantic coast between Belize and Panamá.

plane

This is an expensive but practical way of travelling, especially if you're in a rush but are absolutely determined to see the Tikal ruins in Guatemala or Bluefields on the Atlantic coast of Nicaragua. To find out how long a trip will take by plane, divide the number of hours it takes to get there by bus by 12. Here is a list of some national carriers and their phone numbers for flight fares and schedules:

Belize: Maya Airways, 6, Forth St., ☎02-357-945, ⚏02-305-85.
Guatemala: Aviateca, Calle 10, 6-30, Zona 1, ☎238-1415.
El Salvador: Transportes Aeroes de El Salvador, Edificio Caribe, Plaza Las Américas, ☎298-5066.
Honduras: Taca, Centro Comercial Prisa, Blvd. Morazán, ☎532-6469.
Nicaragua: Nica, Plaza España, ☎663-136.
Costa Rica: Sansa, Paseo Colón, Calle 24, ☎221-9414.
Panamá: Copa, Avenida Justo Arosemana and Calle 39, ☎227-5000, ⚏227-1952. Aeroperlas ☎263-5363, apflyap@aeroperlas.com.

If you're staying for a long time and want to travel by plane, the Visit Central America Airpass might be of interest. It consists of a complex zoning system between the United States and Central America. Depending on the length of your stay and the number of coupons you want, the pass costs between $300 and $1,400. Contact TACA *(North America: ☎800-255-8222, Great Britain: ☎1293-553-330)*, Lacsa, Nica or Copa for more information.

hitchhiking

Use your common sense if you do this. For example, a woman travelling alone shouldn't even bother. In some regions, hitch-hiking means an uncomfortable ride for miles on end in the back of a truck. In other regions such as Nicaragua, hitchhiking is common practice and drivers expect you to pay.

⏭ MONEY ⏮

US travellers' cheques are your best bet. They can be exchanged in the big banks (which charge a small commission), in certain touristy places (hotels, airports) and in foreign exchange offices.

Central American countries' currencies are divided into 100 cents. Here are the names of each country's currency and their value for $1 US on April 1st, 1999:

Belize: 1 Belizean Dollar = $0.50 US
Guatemala: 1 Quetzal = $0.14 US
Honduras: 1 Lempira = $0.07 US
El Salvador: 1 Colón = $0.11 US
Nicaragua: 1 Cordoba = $0.09 US
Costa Rica: 10 Colones = $0.04 US
Panamá: 1 Balboa = $1.00

If you are nowhere near a big city, make sure to bring enough local money with you to see you through until you get to the next big centre. Because of fraud, several banks may ask for your traveller's cheque receipts. Keep them in a separate bag from your cheques; this way, if you lose them, you will still have the receipts. If you want to be extra cautious, write down the serial numbers and also put them in a separate bag from your traveller's cheques and receipts in case these are lost or stolen. Street moneychangers will sometimes exchange your traveller's cheques, but if you choose to use them, check the exchange rates before making any transactions, or they can rip you off (some of them are real cons). The rates can change quickly, and many money-changers at the border take advantage of this by telling travellers that they'll give them the best rate (a rip-off rate). If you don't plan on returning to a country, it is better to change your money at the border, unless you are building a foreign currency collection.

⏭ CREDIT CARDS ⏮

Banks and automatic teller machines in big urban and tourist centres give Visa and MasterCard cash advances. American Express is less accepted despite what all the advertisements say. The most expensive hotels and restaurants only accept credit cards. Despite all these limitations, it is a good idea to have a credit card when you travel. You can withdraw money directly from your account with a bank card that works either with the Plus, Cirrus or Interac automatic bank machine networks.

⏭ TIME ZONE ⏮

All of Central America is in the same time zone, except Panamá which is one hour ahead. Therefore, if you are coming from eastern North America (Montréal, New York, etc.), you will have to advance your watch one hour or two, depending which country you visit. No big deal.

▶▶ INSURANCE ◀◀

Health insurance is the most important kind of insurance you can get if travelling to Central America. It is also important to get all the necessary vaccinations, but these still don't prevent you from getting other ailments. In most cases, if you get sick, you will have to pay for medical services up front. Check in advance if your insurance policy covers you for this and keep all the receipts and any other documents for insurance purposes. Also, always keep a copy of your insurance policy on your person.

▶▶ SAFETY ◀◀

Women shouldn't hitchhike or go out alone at night, especially in Panamá City, Colón and Belize City. Many countries have strict drug laws and even your country's embassy has no power to challenge them. Most important, don't buy drugs in the big cities or play *Midnight Run*.

▶▶ TELECOMMUNICATIONS ◀◀

Each country has a national or private mail and telephone company with branches in the larger cities. The rates are only available at the branches and are more expensive if you want to send something to another country. Mail service is slow and inefficient in certain countries, so don't be surprised if your letter gets to a friend after you've come back, if at all! As for telephones, you can always make operator-assisted long-distance calls, but this can be expensive and complicated. The Direct Dial service is offered everywhere around the world and lets you make less expensive long-distance calls by dialling a special number to reach your country's operator (for example, from Costa Rica: Canada Direct 0-800-015-1161; AT&T, Sprint, British Telecom offer similar services) followed by the number you are trying to reach. The Direct Dial access numbers are available at most branches of the telephone company and at some hotels. Sometimes you can make these calls from a phone booth without going through an operator.

⏭ TOURIST ATTRACTIONS ⏮

Ⓩ This icon indicates which parks or attractions shouldn't be missed.

⏭ ACCOMMODATIONS ⏮

small hotels

Perfect for budget travellers. You can find *hospedajes*, *pensiónes* and *posadas* in every town or city, near the central park, which is a great starting point for a tour. These establishments usually have a family atmosphere that will immerse you in the culture of the country you are visiting. The rates and comfort vary from one place to another, but make sure you get a screen (without any holes) and proper ventilation (fan or airconditioner) before renting a room. During high season (December to March), it is a good idea to make reservations for more upscale and popular hotels.

Warning: You'll quickly spot the difference between hotels and brothels by their extremely low prices. Brothels exist all over Central America and they are not comfortable places to stay.

youth hostels

Youth hostels exist, but not everywhere. Some are part of Hostelling International, whereas others aren't so they don't live up to the standards of the organization. But these hostels are generally decent, though they might not have a common room or an open kitchen. In both cases, you stay in dormitories that are usually co-ed. The whole point of staying in a youth hostel is to meet other travellers (from your country or another) and get firsthand accounts of where to go and what to see. Bulletin boards with postings for exchange or work abroad programs and excursions throughout the country are located near the reception desk where you pay for your bed.

camping

Obviously, this is the cheapest form of accommodation, but only outside the cities. Near the villages there is sometimes a piece of land where you can camp and be close enough to the village to do your shopping or go out to eat. Camping on the beach is also possible, but facilities are scarce. In this case, you can try to find a less secluded spot on someone's property and ask the owner if you can camp there. Be careful where you camp and never camp in a city park.

⏭ RESTAURANTS ⏮

There are Chinese restaurants everywhere around the world, even in Central America. In the capitals and big cities you'll find something for every taste. In the countryside, restaurants serve more traditional food, mostly beans and fried fish.

⏭ STUDYING IN CENTRAL AMERICA ⏮

There are many ways to study abroad in Central America. You can go directly to a university there and find out what they offer, but it's better to check this on the Internet first. Or you can go on an exchange program through your university. Finally, you can take an intensive Spanish course at a private language school. Antigua, a city in Guatemala, has more than 60 internationally renowned schools such as the Alianza Lingüística Cano, PO Box 366, ☎832-2377.

⏭ WORKING IN CENTRAL AMERICA ⏮

As you might have guessed, in order to work in Central America, you need (what a surprise!) a permit. And to get one, your employer there must confirm in writing that no one else in the country is qualified to do your job. Basically, if you can't find work with a foreign company, forget it. Many Westerners find work teaching English, but it pays very little. Some volunteer programs provide room and board for your labour. Check the bulletin boards or with the staff at youth hostels.

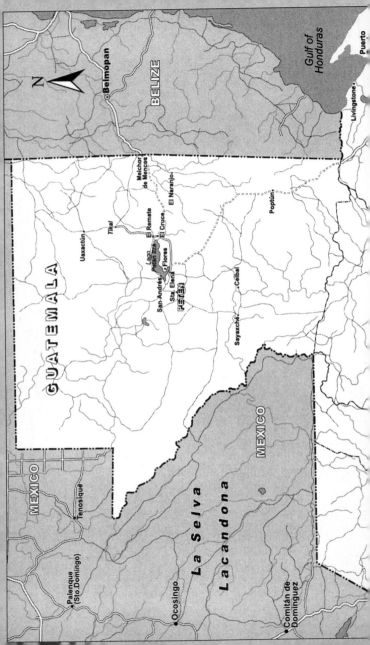

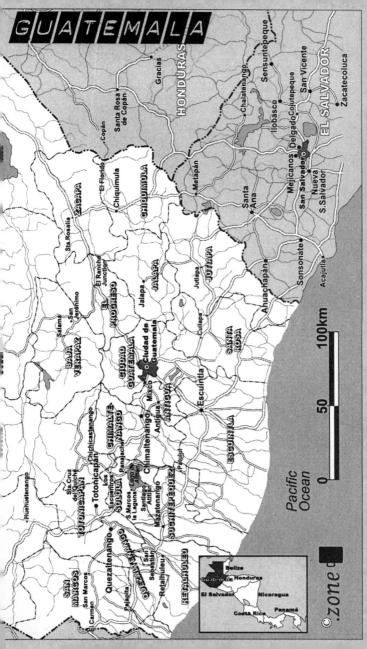

|||||| Diversity, you say? If Central America is a kingdom, then Guatemala is its capital. Indeed, it is a land of rather striking contrasts, starting with the population itself. Guatemala was the heartland of the Mayan Empire when the European explorers arrived, and half its population is still of indigenous descent, with its own particular language and customs. That these groups have managed to retain a much their cultural heritage is largely due to geographical factors: the high mountains of western Guatemala have kept it fairly isolated, though this has not always guaranteed peace. As elsewhere, the region's native people have been exploited from the outset, and their attempts to restore their rights and freedom have been quickly put down. In 1954, the country's president attempted to launch a vast land-redistribution campaign for the benefit of the less fortunate. He had cause to regret it, since the U.S.-based United Fruit company, a huge multinational seriously affected by the said reform, clamoured for help from the motherland, which responded by involving the good old CIA in overthrowing the elected democracy, thus paving the way for a succession of uncompromising dictators. The same stunt would be pulled in Chile some 20 years later. An ironic twist of fate, it was in Guatemala that Che Guavera took his first steps as a revolutionary. After the 1954 CIA-financed putsch swept away his dreams of social justice, Che headed for Mexico, where he first met the exiled Cuban revolutionary leader Fidel Castro. The latter was busy laying the groundwork for his second coup attempt in Cuba — which would work this time.

|||||| Because of these events, Guatemala's indigenous peoples have suffered greatly from the conflict between the military and the revolutionary groups hiding in the hills. Government-sponsored death squads stormed remote villages and literally wiped them off the map. More than 100,000 people died in 30 years, not to mention the several thousands of others who disappeared or became refugees. Such has been the political scene of the last few years. Things have calmed down since 1994, when a peace accord was signed by the chief participants. The gap between the rich and the poor remains monstrously wide, but at least people no longer live in fear of being shot in the back or burned alive in their own homes.

|||||| In northern Guatemala lies the vast Petén region, extensive jungle lowlands harbouring the most beautiful architectural creations of the Mayan civilization. Meanwhile, the high plateaus of the midwest exceed 4,000 metres, making them the highest summits in all of Central America. The long and narrow Pacific coastal plain is little developed and infested with mosquitos. In short, not very inviting. As for the small Atlantic coast, it is a world unto itself, separated from the rest, if for no other reason than that it can only be reached by boat. Oh, here's an

important detail for budget travellers: this country is the cheapest destination in Central America for everything from transportation to accommodation, food and attractions. So why not stay a while? Many do.

▶ CIUDAD GUATEMALA ◀

Guatemala City's architecture is very diverse and representative of the various eras the capital has lived through since its foundation. With three million inhabitants, Ciudad Guatemala is now the largest city in Central America. Its population has grown tenfold in only 50 years, forcing it to develop new areas farther south, where the *Zona Viva* is located, with the hottest night-life, shopping centres, art galleries and swanky shops. Guatemala City is an urban centre where cosmopolitan and traditional cultures live side by side, the latter surviving surprisingly well in the metropolis' old neighbourhoods. Ciudad Guatemala boasts an excessively modern, ritzy and urban environment that contrasts with the rural and rather quiet life of the rest of the republic. The city is divided into 13 zones: Zone 1 is the commercial and historic heart of the city, graced with both the oldest buildings and the modernity of the capital. It is the largest zone in the city and has the most attractions.

Parque Central *(Zona 1)*. The heart of the city, Parque Central (or the Main Plaza) is a primo starting point for immersing yourselves in the non-stop dynamism of the capital that is the country's driving force. The park is surrounded by umpteen vestiges of the past, including the cathedral, the National Palace and the old library. Moreover, right nearby is a huge bustling market bursting with Guatemalan treasures, which gives you a little idea of the wonders awaiting travellers here.

Parque Minerva *(Zona 2)*. Located on the grounds of Mariano Gálvez University in the north end of the city, the park's main tourist attraction is the impressive relief map of Guatemala, **Mapa en Relieve**. Designed by engineer Francisco Vela, it represents Guatemala's topography on a scale of 1:10,000 but, for greater effect, the height is calibrated at a scale of 1:2,000. Inaugurated in 1905 after nine months of work, the map gives newcomers an overall idea of the country's terrain.

Universitad de San Carlos *(Zona 10)*. Founded by royal decree on January 31 1676 in the city of Antigua Guatemala, the university moved into a neoclassical-style building in Ciudad Guatemala a century later. Its current home is made up of modern-style buildings. The museum of natural history is part of

PRACTICAL INFO

Transport: First District *(at Ave. 4 and Calle 7, Zona 4)*. In the heart of a huge hoppin' market. Buses leaving from this district serve the cities west and southwest of Ciudad Guatemala.

To Chichicastenango: Departures every half-hour from 5am to 6pm; 3-hour journey for $1.50.

To La Democracia: Departures every half-hour from 6am to 4:30pm; 2-hour journey for $1.

Second District: Several bus companies have their terminal at the corner of Avenida 10 and Calle 7.

To Cobán: The Escobar y Monja Blanca company, located at Avenida 8, 15-16, Zona 1, departs every hour from 4am to 5pm; 4-hour journey for $3.

To El Florido and Copán (Honduras): Take the Esquipulas-bound bus and transfer in Chiquimula. Departures from Chiquimula at 7am, 10am and 12:30pm; 2-hour journey.

To Esquipulas: This city is served by Rutas Orientales. Departures from Calle 19, 8-18, Zona 1, every half-hour from 4am to 5pm; 4-hour journey for $4.

To Flores (El Petén): Transportation provided by the Fuentes del Norte company. Departures from Calle 17a, 8-46, Zona 1, at 7:30am, 11am, noon, 1pm, 3pm, 5pm and 10pm; 12-hour journey for $12.

The La Petenera company (☎232-9658), located at Calle 16a, 10-55, Zona 1, offers daily trips aboard luxury buses. Fare: $23.

To Huehuetenango: Served by the Los Halcones company (☎238-1929), located at Avenida 7a, 15-27, Zona 1. Departures at 7am and 2pm; 5-hour journey for $3.

To Quetzaltenango: Served by the Galgos company (☎232-3661). Departures from Avenida 7, 19-44, Zona 1, at 5:30am, 8:30am, 11am, 2:30pm, 5pm and 7pm; 4-hour journey for $3.

Also served by the Transport Alamo company (☎253-2105): Departures from Calle 21a, Zona 1, at 8am, 3pm and 5:45pm.

To Río Dulce: The Flores-bound bus stops in Río Dulce; 5-hour journey for $6.

To Talismán and El Carmen (Mexico): Galgos (☎232-3661). Departures from Avenida 7, 19-44, Zona 1, at 5:30am, 10am, 3pm and 4:30pm; 5-hour journey for $4.

Third District: Calle 20 at Avenida Simón Bolívar. Right near the Asturias arts centre, in Zona 1.

To Amatitlán: Calle 20 at Avenida 2a. Departures every half hour from 7am to 7pm; 30-minute journey for $1.50.

To La Mesilla: Situated on the Mexican border, La Mesilla is served by the Transporte Velásquez company. Departure at 8:30am; 8-hour journey for $5.

To Panajachel: Served by the Rebulli company (*☎251-3521*). Departures from Calle 21, 1-34, Zona 1, every hour from 6am to 4pm; 3-hour journey for $1.30.

To Antigua: The point of departure for Antigua is a little removed from the three districts. The Transportes Unidos company (*☎232-4949, 253-6929*) makes its departures from Calle 15, between Avenidas 3a and 4a, Zona 1. Departures every 30 minutes between 7am and 8pm; 1-hour journey for 50¢.

Taxis: Few taxis roam the city. Calling one is therefore a better bet than flagging one down. Taxi Amarilla (*☎332-1515*) offers better fares than most other companies.

Money: Credomatic: Avenida 5a at Calle 11a, Zona 1. Gives cash advances on your MasterCard or Visa credit card and changes most foreign currency. **Banco del Café** (*Avenida La Reforma, 9-30, Zona 9*) serves American Express cardholders.

Tourist Info: INGUAT (Instituto Guatemalteco de Turismo): Avenida 7a, 1-17, Zona 4, ☎331-1333.

Mail: Oficina de Correos: Avenida 7a, 11-67, Zona 1.

Telephone: Guatel: Calle 12a at Avenida 8a, Zona 1.

Internet: Café Internet: Avenida 5a at Calle 16, Zona 10.

San Carlos University's biology department. A large botanical garden is open to everyone (*Calle Mariscal Cruz 1-56, Z.10*) and is a veritable oasis of tranquillity in a too-hectic city.

Museo Popol Vuh de Arqueología (*at Ave. 4 and 27 Calle 16, Z.10*). Located in the arts complex of the Francisco Marroquín University campus, this spectacular museum boasts a great pre-Colombian and colonial art collection, as well as a beautiful replica of the *Dresden Codex*, one of four Mayan books written in hieroglyphs. The Popol Vuh museum derives its name from the sacred book of the Quiché Maya, discovered in Chichicastenango by Dominican priest Francisco Ximénez sometime between 1701 and 1703. Popol Vuh means

"Book of Counsel." The visit is a good sequel to the Museo Nacional de Arqueología y Etnología.

Museo Nacional de Arqueología y Etnología *(at Ave. 7 and Calle 6, Z.13)*. Also known as the Guatemala City Museum, it is located in Aurora park and is easily reached by public transport. The national museum of archeology and ethnology of Guatemala inarguably boasts the greatest collection of sculptures, jade pieces and ceramics from the Mayan culture. Spanish colonial architecture went into the layout of the rooms, which are all arranged around an interior courtyard. Set up in a stylish building from the 1930s, the museum features models of the Quirigua, Zaculeu and Tikal sites. The latter is particularly impressive. A must for those who wish to really absorb Mayan culture.

The national museums of art and history as well as a zoo are located a stone's throw from the park.

Amatitlán *(40 min. south of the capital, on the Pacific-bound CA-9)*. This small town of some 33,000 inhabitants is situated 30 kilometres from Ciudad Guatemala, on Lago Amatitlán, at the foot of the Pacaya volcano. The lake vies with Lago de Atitlán as a popular seaside destination with residents of the capital. Though swimming in the lake is not the wisest idea, taking a dip in the hot springs of the natural pools nestled in the neighbouring hills is a treat. The view from Parque Naciones Unidas, located a few kilometres away on the slope of the still-active Pacaya volcano, is breathtaking. The city's Parque Morazán boasts a huge ceiba tree that is worth the trip. You can also feast your eyes on a small Mayan site 3 kilometres east of Amatitlán.

Chuarrancho and **San Pedro Ayampuc** *(21 km and 35 km north, respectively)* are two Cakchiquel villages, agricultural towns that have kept their cultural heritage intact, with traditional dress and typical musical instruments. Few tourists venture here. Other villages with the same cultural past line Mixco Viejo-bound Ruta Nacional 5. Noteworthy among these are **San Pedro Sacatepéquez** and **San Juan Sacatepéquez**, renowned for their handicrafts. **Mixco Viejo**, meanwhile, is an archaeological site perched in the mountains that boasted 50,000 inhabitants and wielded influence over the entire Pacific region at the time of the Conquest. Only for a short time did it hold out against Alvarado and the other conquistadors who torched the city and turfed out the entire population. Amazing ruins.

Ciudad
Guatemala

SWEET DREAMS

Pensión Meza *($12; Calle 10a, 10-17, Zona 1,
☎232-3177).* ▣ Basic comfort, but good ambiance
and unbeatable prices. The favourite haunt of
backpackers from the world over. A bulletin board
covered with messages and other useful info for
globetrotters.

Hotel Lessing House *($12; Calle 12, 4-35, Zona 1,
☎251-3891).* ▣ Spacious and cleaner-than-average
rooms. Some are also quite sunny. Less cosmopolitan than the Meza, but quieter.

Hotel Spring *($16; Ave. 8a, 12-65, Zona 1,
☎251-4207).* ▣ A good choice, but often full. Hot
water and good meals available.

Ciudad
Guatemala

BON APPETIT

The cheapest meals around are at the **Mercado**
(Avenida 5a, at Calle 14, Zona 1) in Parque
Centenario, where several small, typically Guatemalan food stands generally offer daily menus and
à-la-carte dishes. The best way to eat well while
enjoying the country's ambiance!

On the south side of Parque Centenario is the
small but popular **Delicatezas Hamburgo** *(Calle 15,
5-34, Zona 1),* which dishes out chicken, spaghetti, sandwiches and good fries.

Located right near Parque Centenario, **Productos
Integrales Rey Sol** *(Calle 8, 5-36, Zona 1)* is a
vegetarian restaurant. The daily menu features a
main dish that varies according to the season. A
good place for fruits and fruit juices.

the good life

Zona Viva is chock-full of café-terraces that are pleasant
enough, but hardly distinguishable from one another. Conversely,
Café de Oro *(the Avenida between Calles 12 and 13, Zona 10)* is a
veritable neighbourhood classic, featuring rock and alternative
music. A popular hangout with Guatemalan artists of all types.

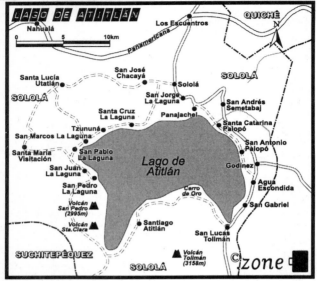

The **Jaguar Disco** of the **Camino Real Westin Guatemala** *(at Avenida La Reforma and Calle 14, Zona 10, ☎333-4633 or 337-4313)* boasts a great ambiance for all ages. A good place to "shake your groove thang" to Latin rhythms, pop and rock.

A must-attend in Zona 1, the **Bodeguita del Centro** *(Calle 12, 3-55, Zona 1 , ☎230-2976)* presents *trova* duos every night. *Trova* is a musical style from Cuba popularized throughout Central America by Sylvio Rodríguez and Pablo Milanés.

⏭ WESTERN GUATEMALA ⏮

Lago de Atitlán

The Atitlán region, perched at 1,560 metres in the midst of mountains, volcanoes and Mayan culture, is probably the most enchanting place in the country. West of the capital, the lake may seem easily accessible on a map, but make no mistake! The winding roads seem to go on forever, and it takes double the travel time than for the same distance on flat terrain. No matter, it is well worth it. Here, Mother Nature displays her splendour with enormous rolling waves of greenery that are, in

PRACTICAL INFO

Transport: A bus heads straight to **Ciudad Guatemala** from **Panajachel** at 10am, and from **Sololá** at 10:30am *($1,75)*.

Most **Panajachel**-bound buses run through **Los Encuentros** and **Sololá**.

Buses leave Panajachel from the road that runs to the town of Sololá, at the corner of Calle Real.

From Panajachel:

To Antigua: 3-hour journey for $1.50. Only one bus a day makes a non-stop trip. Your other option is to take a Ciudad Guatemala-bound bus and transfer at the bus station in the capital.

To Ciudad Guatemala: Departures every hour from 5:30am to 3pm; 3-hour journey for $1.50. If you miss the last bus, take a bus to the Los Encuentros roundabout, where you can transfer to the capital.

To Chichicastenango: Departures every hour from 7am to 4pm; 90-minute journey for $1.

To Quetzaltenango: Four to five daily departures from 5am to early afternoon; 2-hour journey for $1.50.

To San Lucas Tolimán: Numerous daily departures; 75-minute journey for 80¢.

To the Mexican Border (Cocales-El Carmen). To reach the Mexican border via the Pacific Route, take a bus to Cocales (2-hour journey for 80¢). Once there, take another bus to El Carmen. You can also go through Altiplano, via Quetzaltenango, to get to El Carmen.

By Boat: **Panajachel** boasts two piers for departures by boat to surrounding villages. At one end of Sololá's waterfront, a small dirt road leads to the first pier, the point of departure for the villages of Santa Cruz (20 min.), San Marcos (50 min.) and San Pedro (1 h, 10 min.). All boats leave once full and charge foreign tourists $1.75/person.

At the other end of the village of Panajachel, the second pier is the point of departure for Santiago Atitlán (1-hour journey for $1.75).

By Mini Bus: Several companies offer direct runs from Panajachel to the nation's major cities. Though a tad pricier than taking the bus, this service proves much faster and safer. The companies listed below offer similar rates.

Americo's Tours *(Avenida 3, 3-45 at Calle Santander, ☎/☎762-2021)* offers departures to Antigua, Chichicastenango, La Mesilla, Cobán, Puerto Barrios and Tikal aboard comfortable mini buses.

Americo's Prices are a little higher than those offered by **Panatours**, located right across the street. The latter accepts various credit cards and will even give you a cash advance on your card.

Servicios Turísticos Atitlán *(3-47 Avenida 3, Zona 2, Calle Santander, next to the Hotel Regis, ☎762-2075, ☎762-2246).*

Tourist Info: The staff at the INGUAT offices *(Edificio Rincón Sai, ☎762-1392)* in Panajachel is particularly efficient, providing all the necessary info for planning your jaunt to the various lakeside villages.

Bank: To change your currency, obtain cash advances on your Visa credit card and use an automatic teller machine (ATM) open 24 hours a day, head to Banco Immobiliaro *(at Calle Santander, corner of Calle Real).*

Telephone: The Guatel offices are located on Calle Santander.

Internet: **Cafénet Panajachel** *($1.50/hour; Calle Santander, next to Banco Industrial)* has Internet access and E-mail.

fact, countless valleys that contrast dramatically with the surrounding summits. Certain peaks exceed 4,000 metres, making them the highest in Central America. Mayan descendants make up 95 percent of the population scattered in pockets throughout the valleys. The majority still speak their own dialect and do not understand Spanish. In short, full-fledged cultural immersion awaits you here!

Panajachel is the point of entry for most travellers who venture into the region of Lago de Atitlán. This small lakeshore town is growing at a rapid pace, which means it is becoming increasingly touristy. On the whole, this is the place to change your travellers' cheques and get the skinny on the hot spots of the moment. At the end of Calle Santander stretches Lago de Atitlán, bordered by a lovely promenade. Turn left on the path to reach the main pier.

Santa Catarina Palopó *(5 km southeast of Panajachel).* The weavers of this picturesque little mountainside village, who are renowned for the quality of their hand-embroidered turquoise fabrics with geometric patterns, kindly open their studio doors to visitors.

The walk from Panajachel to Santa Catarina Palopó takes a good hour, which makes for a great half-day excursion.

Sololá *(8 km from Panajachel)* is the capital of the department of the same name, which encompasses the whole Lago de Atitlán region. This small town is especially prized for its market, held Tuesdays and Fridays. What sets this market apart is that it does not cater to *gringos*, but to the local population, the merchants and producers of the Altiplano. The road leading there abounds with breathtaking views over the lake. Those with a few hours to spare can walk there from **Santa Cruz**.

The **Catedral Nuestra Senora de la Asunción** is worth a stop. Inside are a few silver religious works and a stone bathtub for baptisms dating from the early days of the Spanish colony.

Panajachel

$

SWEET DREAMS

Panajachel is positively brimming with budget hotels. Upon your arrival, start by wandering through Calle Santander, lined with scads of such bargain establishments.

Run by a Cakchiquel family, the **Hospedaje Vista Hermosa** *($3 to $6; 3-35 Calle Monterey)* offers small and basic but generally clean rooms. Though not as frequented as the other inns in this price category, this *hospedaje* offers you a good opportunity to get acquainted with an aboriginal family.

Panajachel

$

BON APPETIT

As its Spanish name indicates, **Comedor Vista Hermosa** *(opposite the main pier)* affords a fabulous view over the lake. The place serves fish in a very tropical ambiance. Not bad at all, considering the price.

The small **Pizzería Florencia** *(Calle Santander)* food stand boasts a great little terrace. Try the *chorizo* (sausage) pizza. The place offers some fifteen choices of toppings and sells pizza by the slice. It also serves burgers, sandwiches and *empanadas*.

Panjachel

BON APPETIT

Deli Llama de Fuego *(on Calle Santander, next to Americo's Export)*. A terrific little café-terrace that dishes out yummy vegetarian (avocado, alfalfa sprouts, lettuce, tomato and onion) or ham-and-cheese sandwiches, as well as everything you could wish for in terms of tea, coffee, fruit juices...

San Marcos La Laguna

An enchanting and absolutely peaceful place offering wayfarers a relaxing rural environment. Small wonder then, to find a meditation centre (Las Piramides) here; a place well worth a stop, if only to check out its main pyramid.

San Marcos La Laguna

SWEET DREAMS

Paco Real *($6 to $11)* offers *cabañas* or dormitories, whichever best suits your budget.

Las Piramides *($20)* is a meditation centre where you can get some shut-eye and take part in daily group meditation sessions.

San Pedro La Laguna

Located on the other side of the lake, this village is very popular with hikers from all over the world, who flock here to tackle the San Pedro volcano (3,020 m) which can be scaled in one day. The village is smaller than Panajachel, which is all for the best as it is less swamped with tourists. The beauty and tranquillity of the place thus remains intact, and budget hotels abound. The village, which has a neo-hippie ambiance, is reached by boat.

Bolder hikers can reach the summit of the San Pedro volcano without a guide. To do so, take the trail at the village exit. Hang a left at the fork in the trail. The climb takes three to four hours via the most direct route. Unfortunately, there is no marked trail to guide you: ask for directions along the way or go with someone very familiar with the trail. The volcano boasts two summits: the second offers breathtaking views that are not to be missed. If you prefer to go with a guide, drop by the Fondeadero

PRACTICAL INFO

Transport: Boats leave the San Pedro pier for **Panajachel**, **San Marcos** and **Santa Cruz** at 5am, 6am, 7am, 8am, 10am, noon, 2pm, 3pm, 3:45pm and 5pm; 1-hour journey for $2.

To Santiago Atitlán: The Lancheros de Santiago company's boats leave the San Pedro pier every two hours (30-minute journey for $1.75 one way; $3.50 return).

restaurant, where José García and his son offer this service for 35 quetzals per person (3-person minimum).

San Pedro La Laguna

SWEET DREAMS

Familia Peneleu *($2)*. ▶ Clean cottages. Guests can cook on the premises. The warm welcome will make your stay here a very pleasant one.

The **Hospedaje Ti-Kaaj** *($3; on the small dirt trail parallel with the lake, near pier #2)* is much prized by hikers and has a bevy of tropical gardens peppered with hammocks in which you can get your forty winks at no charge.

Santiago Atitlán

This Tz'utujil village is the largest on Lago de Atitlán and sprawls over the sides of the Tolimán and Atitlán volcanoes on an old lava flow. On the other side of the bay, facing the village, stands the majestic San Pedro volcano. Mayan culture still reigns here, expressed in the vivid fabrics proudly worn by the locals. The village predates the arrival of the Spanish.

Today, this dusty village harbours many treasures and is particularly lively during the Semana Santa (Holy Week) processions. However, it is Maximón who will catch the attention of every visitor who ventures into the village. The cigar-smoking, hat-clad resident deity is inarguably one of Guatemala's wackiest saints. Maximón is highly revered by the Tz'utujil, who carry his wood-carved statue through the city streets alongside his traditional Catholic counterparts during Semana Santa.

PRACTICAL INFO

Transport: To get to Ciudad Guatemala by bus from Santiago Atitlán (departures at 3am, 4am, 5am, 7am, 11am, noon and 2pm; 4-hour journey for $2), head to the village centre, where two buses leave at the same time but take different routes. One skirts the coast and stops in Patulul, Santa Lucía, Esquintla, Palín and Amatitlán, while the other travels through the mountains and stops in Godínez, Agua Escondida, Tecpán and Chimaltenango.

By Boat: The **Lancheros de Santiago** (departures at 6:15am, 7:15am, 11:30am, 11:45am, 2pm, 3pm and 4:30pm; 1-hour journey for $1.75 one way; $3.50 return) company offers several daily departures for Panajachel. The boat travels straight there, without stopping in Santiago Atitlán.

Departures for San Pedro are at 7am, 9am, 10:30am, noon, 1pm, 3pm and 5:30pm; 30-minute one-way journey for $1.50, or $3.50 return.

Santiago Atitlán

$

SWEET DREAMS

Homestay (approx. $5). ▣ You can get the addresses of people who will put you up for the night at the **Boatwatch Café**.

The small **Pensión Rosita** ($9; Cantón Xechivoy, behind the market) has three rooms (Nos. 14-15-16) facing the San Pedro volcano. The tidy digs boast a small interior courtyard. Breakfast, lunch and dinner are served here.

Chichicastenango

With a 2,000-metre altitude, nights are chilly in "Chichi." Surrounded by majestic mountains and in the heart of Mayan culture, this village located 20 kilometres north of Panajachel and is especially renowned for its colourful market, held Thursdays and Sundays. On Sundays, the market is really too jam-packed and the busloads of tourists make haggling more complicated. The trick for getting the best deals is to show up at the end of the day, right before the stands are dismantled. The town itself is charming, particularly during the week, with its winding streets,

its central square and two old churches. Busses run here several
times a day, notably from **Ciudad Guatemala** and **Panajachel**.

Chichi-
casten-
ango

SWEET DREAMS

Posada Girón *($10; Calle 6, north of the park)*.
▶ Basic comfort and sure-fire cleanliness.

Posas Santa Marta *($10; Avenida 5, northward)*.
▶ Though the decor lacks charm, the place is
quiet and convenient.

Antigua

Ringed by three majestic volcanoes, Antigua has a dreamy,
enchanting setting. Visitors come to the city to admire relics of
what used to be the nation's capital from 1543 to 1773, when two
earthquakes destroyed it. Legacies of this era, including the
numerous colonial ruins and a "sepulchral" aura, still mark the
city, which now has half the population it did 300 years ago.
Most tourists here are students who have come for a few weeks of
Spanish immersion thanks to the umpteen schools offering courses
that include room and board with local families. During Semana
Santa, Antigua becomes a non-stop celebration.

The Ruins *(Parque Central)*. Once again, the park is the perfect
starting point for a tour of the city, which is easily covered on
foot as it is not too spread out. No matter what direction you
head in, you are sure to come upon old treasures, be they old
convents, churches or villas, but there are a few more interesting monuments north of the park.

The Museums *(closed Mondays)*. The **Museo de Arte Colonial** *(Calle
5 Oriente, one block west of the park)* boasts a fine collection
of furniture and other household items from 17th- to 19th-century
Antigua. On one side of the park also stands the **Museo del Libro
Antiguo**, where a replica of Guatemala's first printing press, as
well as ancient books and documents, is on display.

Cerro de la Cruz *(Avenida 1 Norte)*. This small summit, which
offers a great view over the whole city, is about a half-hour's
walk north. Do not go alone.

Language Schools. Antigua is world-famous for its Spanish-language schools and boasts several dozen. Most packages
include about twenty hours of private classes. It costs about
$100 a week, including room and board with a local family — the
best way to learn and practice your newly acquired skills. Here

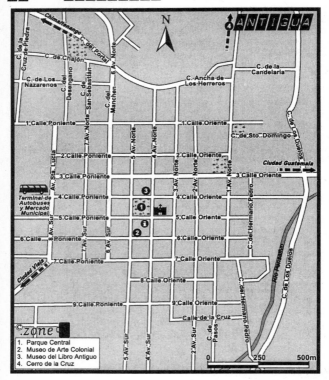

1. Parque Central
2. Museo de Arte Colonial
3. Museo del Libro Antiguo
4. Cerro de la Cruz

area a few popular schools: **Projecto Lingüístico Francisco Marroquín** *(4 Avenida 4 Sur)*; **Centro Lingüístico Maya** *(20 Calle 5 Poniente, ☎832-0656)*; **Instituto Antigüeño** *(24 Calle 1 Poniente, ☎832-2682)*.

Ciudad Vieja *(6 km southeast of Antigua)*. The first capital of Guatemala, from 1527 to 1541, it was completely destroyed by a landslide and resulting floods. The city now boasts few attractions other than a handful of ruins and one of the oldest churches in all of Central America. Buses leave throughout the day from Antigua.

Volcanoes. The region's three volcanoes are over 3,500 metres high, so climbing them is no picnic. The trails are sometimes very hard to follow, occasional *bandidos* sometimes prey on hapless tourists (even groups with tour guides), and the long and arduous trek will discourage a fair share of would-be climbers. Of course, the panoramas are breathtaking, particularly as you approach the smoking craters. Gutsier types can go on a night hike to the **Volcán Agua** or even a two-day adventure to the **Acatenango** and **Fuego volcanoes**, which are much harder to reach. Head to the tourist office for the latest news and to hire a guide.

PRACTICAL INFO

Transport: Buses leave for **Ciudad Guatemala** from the corner of Alameda Santa Lucía and Calle 4 Poniente every 45 minutes until nightfall; $1. Several buses leave for **Panajachel** throughout the day; 2-hour journey for $2.

Money: The banks are on Calle 4 Poniente, opposite or right near the park. Changing your money or travellers' cheques here is no problem.

Tourist Info: INGUAT: Calle 4 Oriente, ☎832-0763. The staff speaks English and will answer any questions you may have. Assorted info and maps available.

Mail: Opposite the bus station, at Calle 4 Poniente and Alameda de Santa Lucía.

Telephone: At Avenida 5 Sur and Calle 5 Poniente.

Internet: A few places offer E-mail service. Inquire at INGUAT.

Antigua

$

SWEET DREAMS

Hospedaje El Pasaje *($5; at Alameda de Santa Lucía and Calle 5 Poniente)*. ▶ A nice, clean and friendly place, though sometimes noisy. Another bonus is the rooftop terrace.

Pensión El Arco *($8; 32 Avenida 5 Norte)*. ▶ In a quieter area, this boarding house's small rooms are always spick n' span. Hot water.

Casa de Santa Lucía *($10; at Calle 5 Poniente and Alameda de Santa Lucía)*. ▶ Pricier, but stylin' with its pseudo-colonial decor. Private bathrooms.

Antigua

$

BON APPETIT

Comedores *(at the market opposite the bus station).* ▶ Food stands dishing out typical fare at unbeatable prices. For strong stomachs only.

Jardín *(on one side of Parque Central).* ▶ North American and local fare for a pittance in the midst of the urban bustle.

Capri *(24 Calle Poniente 4).* ▶ Cheap but unfortunately rather meagre dishes. Good ambiance and popular with the younger set.

Quetzaltenango

The biggest town in western Guatemala sits 2,400 metres high on its throne in a very hilly agricultural region. This, too, is aboriginal land. The (still-active) Volcán Santa María looks down on the tiny city of 130,000 from its lofty 3,772 metres. The city was in fact utterly ravaged by a volcanic eruption at the turn of the century. Up until then, life in Quetzaltenango had revolved around coffee plantations that were its pride as well as its sustenance. The city was soon rebuilt, but lost its title of metropolis. It is thus quieter, with less hustle and bustle than the capital. But few will complain. With many language schools and fewer tourists than Antigua, Xela (as the Quiché Maya call it) is just the place to learn Spanish, as visitors cannot get by without speaking the language which, with a little effort, they will learn in record time.

Parque Centroamérica. This central park is one of the most interesting in the country, with its old neoclassical buildings, and its cathedral. Plans for a shopping-centre were abandoned because it could not attract enough of a clientele.

Language Schools. Prices are the same as those in Antigua, and since there are less tourists here, you will have no choice but to speak Spanish. Two recommended schools: **Projecto Lingüístico Santa María** *(☎761-2570)* and **Projecto Lingüístico Quetzalteco de Español** *(☎761-2620).*

Baños Los Vahos *(take an Almolonga-bound bus and ask the driver to stop in Los Vahos).* Lovely small natural hot springs in the mountains.

San Francisco El Alto *(a few km north; take the bus very early in the morning).* A tiny Mayan town that still follows the old

260-day calendar. A good place for those who still find Xela too big. A market is held every Friday. In **Momostenango**, Sunday is market day. The village is a little farther north, but still closer to the authentic cultural heritage.

PRACTICAL INFO

Transport: Located by Parque Minerva, the budget bus station is a little ways from the town centre *(Calle 6, Zona 3)*. To get there, take a bus marked "Parque." Buses leave the station about every hour for all major destinations such as the capital, Panajachel, Chichicastenango and the small northern Maya villages.

Money: The banks are near Parque Central.

Mail: At Avenida 15 and Calle 4, Zona 1.

Telephone: At Avenida 12 and Calle 7.

Tourist Info: INGUAT, located at the south end of the park, has the usual maps available.

Quetzal-tenango

$

SWEET DREAMS

Radar 99 *($5; Avenida 13, near the park)*. ▣ Hot water on request and sometimes questionable cleanliness, but very practical for its location.

Hotel Capri *($7; Calle 8, 11-39)*. ▣ Shared bathrooms and rooms that lack charm but are clean and comfy.

Casa Kaehler *($9; next to Radar 99)*. ▣ Lovely and spotless, this old hotel has few rooms. Get there early.

Quetzal-tenango

$

BON APPETIT

Utz' Hua *(at Avenida 12 and Calle 3)*. A very standard menu offering nothing special, but cheap and filling food.

Pizza Ricca *(2-42 Avenida 14)*. ▣ Good and cheap pizza with choice of every topping imaginable.

Quetzal-
tenango

BON APPETIT

Restaurante Shanghai *(12-22 Calle 4, near the park)*. ▶ THE Chinese restaurant in Xela. Good prices and good grub prepared by local chefs.

Huehuetenango

Huehuetenango is the last major city before the Chiapas border. Small wonder, then, that the Mexican influence is felt here. In other respects, the department is situated in the loftiest region of Guatemala, with summits over 4,000 metres high. Spanish-language courses are offered here, as well. This city is even less touristy than Quetzaltenango, which makes learning the language that much easier. A market is held every day. To penetrate deeper into the high plateaus, you must travel to **Todos Santos Cuchumatán**, 20 kilometres north; market day (more traditional than most) is Saturday. The village still keeps to the old Mayan ways. Those who wish to stay in Huehuetenango for a while can put up at one of the following hotels.

Huehue-
tenango

SWEET DREAMS

Hotel Central *($6; Avenida 5, 1-33, north of Parque Central)*. ▶ Safe, quiet and clean.

Hotel Maya *($6; Avenida 3, 3-55)*. ▶ A good place open all day long. Shared bathrooms and hot water.

▶▶ EASTERN GUATEMALA ◀◀

Heading toward the Atlantic will reveal another face of Guatemala. Perhaps also a less contrived face as it is off the typical tourist-beaten path. Eastern Guatemala abounds with coffee and banana plantations, a frontier atmosphere alternating with the immutable calm of a vast misty forest and the ever-present Afro-Caribbean heritage, increasingly felt the closer one gets to the ocean.

Cobán

Well established in its lush valley, Cobán is an old Mayan city.
Its inhabitants are all of Native American descent. This is also
the region in which the *monja blanca*, the national flower, is
cultivated. Speaking of national symbols, the quetzal, a crested
bird with brilliant plumage, is a regular visitor to the Cobán
area. The city primarily owes its expansion to the German
colonizers who established vast *fincas de café* at the turn of the
20th century. Their presence faded a half-century later, when
World War II broke out and the United States pressured the
Guatemalan government to send them packing. Several were avowed
Nazi sympathizers. Parks, caves and rivers are not-to-be-missed
sights in the region.

Parque Central. This triangular-shaped park is Cobán's centre,
just the starting point from which to explore the city and
discover its wonders. Once you've had your fill of the colonial
architecture around the park, head north and wander through the
old cobblestone streets. You will soon reach the **El Calvario**
church, which offers a fabulous panorama of the city and the
surrounding area.

(Z) **Parque Nacional Las Victorias** *(a little west of El
Calvario)*. Located on the land of a former German *finca*,
this park now boasts an extensive network of trails that climb
toward the mountains behind the city. A nice 'n simple way to
spend the day. Get there early!

Biotopo del Quetzal *(50 km south)*. Take a bus and ask the driver
to drop you off here. The quetzal is an endangered species, so a
biologist created this park to protect part of the bird's
territory. There are two small trails that can be covered in a
few hours and on which you may get a lucky break and spot the
famous bird. To improve your chances, hit the trail at sunrise or
in the late afternoon. Camping is permitted just outside the
park.

(Z) **Lanquín** *(60 km east)* boasts the two most fantastic attractions in the country. First, there is the cave *($2; bring a
flashlight)*, located one kilometre before the village. The
Lanquín river gushes up from the ground, and moseying your way
through its underground passages is a real treat (allow for a
good 2 hours). In the afternoon, the sight of bats flitting out
by the hundreds is quite simply surreal. Camping is permitted at
no charge next to the cave entrance. Be careful not to fall, and
wear non-skid shoes. The second not-to-be-missed attraction is
Semuc Champey *(10 km south of Lanquín)*, though it's a two-hour
walk away (try hitching a ride from a passing car). This enchant-

ing place consists of natural pools flowing into one another, right in the middle of the forest, before disappearing underground after the last pool (be careful!). This is a great place to swim, of course, and those who can't bare to leave can pitch their tent right nearby.

PRACTICAL INFO

Transport: Capital-bound buses leave every hour from the corner of Avenida 8 and Calle 15. To reach **Lanquín**, take one of the buses that leaves several times a day for **Cahabón**. Those wishing to go all the way to **El Petén** have a long journey ahead of them; there are two to three buses a day that depart at different times and run though **Sebol** on the way to the vast northern jungle.

Money: The banks are concentrated around Parque Central.

Tourist Info: Next to the park, the tourist office suggests other activities and organizes outings to Lanquín. Contact the **Acuña** family, which organizes very good expeditions to Lanquín, as well as other destinations.

Mail and Telephone: Right near the park.

Cobán

SWEET DREAMS

Hotel La Paz *($6; Avenida 6, Zona 1, ☎951-1358)*. ▶ Small but spick n' span, with a little garden out back. Peaceful, too.

Hotel Monterey *($10; 1-12 Avenida 6, ☎951-1131)*. ▶ Spacious, clean and quiet.

Hotel Central *($10; 1-79 Calle 1, ☎951-1442)*. ▶ Peaceful and clean. Boasts a fabulous yard and a good restaurant.

Cobán

BON APPETIT

Café El Tirol *(next to the park)*. ▶ Decent meals and a mind-boggling selection of coffees. The German colonizers' influence can be smelled here!

Café Santa Rita *(opposite the park)*. ▶ Good menu of Guatemalan dishes for a pittance. Very popular.

Livingston

Ⓩ In a somewhat anomalous tropical-island setting, this remote spot is cut off from the rest of the country and is only accessible by ferry. The population is clearly Garifuna, which is to say that it originates from a mix of African slaves and Caribs, namely Native Americans from the Caribbean islands. These peoples were rudely expatriated from St-Vincent by the British Crown 200 years ago and relocated to the islands in the Bay of Honduras, from which they reached the coastal mainland populating it from Belize to Honduras. Culturally speaking, this Garifuna outpost is light-years away from the official image of Guatemala: a black English-speaking population, a laid-back Jamaican-style ambiance and palm trees galore. Life is quiet in Livingston, so head elsewhere for more action.

Los Siete Altares *(6 km north)*. Although it lies on the coast, there are no real places to swim in Livingston. Go figure. But don't despair; by walking north along the coast for an hour, you will arrive at this swimming paradise of waterfalls and natural pools. You can also inquire in Livingston about getting there by boat. Don't walk there alone, especially if you are a woman.

Lago Izabal and **Castillo de San Felipe** *(30 km inland, on the Río Dulce)*. Take a boat excursion to the biggest lake in the country, where several high-ranking Guatemalan officials have their secondary residence. Though the lake is large enough to be the reason to go, the boat ride there is what truly makes the trip worthwhile (see "Biotopo" below). The Castillo is an old fort built in the 17th century to defend Spanish cargoes against recurrent raids by English pirates. The excursion starts from either Livingston or Fronteras.

Biotopo Chocón Machacas and **Biotopo de Manatí** *(between Livingston and Lago Izabal)*. Both these nature reserves are accessible by boat. The best thing is to organize a one-day excursion from Livingston, an adventure that will lead you through a network of rivers where the many birds can be seen in all their glory. The Río Dulce is particularly impressive when its banks rise up and suddenly form cliffs carved out of the rock and covered with the thick canopy of the jungle. It costs about $10 for the trip from Livingston to Fronteras. The boat stops at every attraction along the way.

PRACTICAL INFO

Transport: Livingston is only accessible by boat, and schedules change on a regular basis. Boats leave from **Río Dulce** and **Puerto Barrios**. From the latter city, the boat left every day at 10:30am and 5pm (get there an hour in advance to be sure to get a seat) and returned from Livingston at 5am and 2pm. The private boats will take you anytime, but are only worth it for groups of six or more. Another good option is to make the journey up or down the Río Dulce: **Río Dulce-Livingston,** Tuesdays and Fridays at 6:30am. The return trip leaves around noon. The journey is fabulous either way.

Money: Last we heard, the bank changed travellers' cheques but, if this isn't right, you can change US dollars in several businesses.

Mail and Telephone: Up the street from the pier.

Livingston

SWEET DREAMS

Weary globetrotters seeking total peace and quiet can stay in one of the bungalows available for $3 per person on the way to Siete Altares. You can also hang your hammock on the beach. Make sure the area is safe.

Hotel Río Dulce *($5; on the street leading to the pier).* ▶ Minimal comfort but reasonably clean rooms in an old wooden building.

El Vajero *($6; on the left when coming from the pier).* ▶ Welcoming and clean. Rooms are spacious and comfortable.

Livingston

BON APPETIT

Cafetería Coni serves typical Creole fare at unbeatable prices. Same goes for **Restaurant Lili**.

⏮ PETÉN AND TIKAL ⏭

Surrounded by dense vegetation in a humid climate, the tiny village is crisscrossed by muddy streets where rich and poor live side by side. Completely isolated from the rest of the country despite the road built here in 1970, the Petén region accounts for close to a third of Guatemala's territory. These lowlands harbour dense, primal forests and many lakes and rivers, as well as the largest number of Mayan ruins in the country, including Tikal, Uaxactún and Ceibal.

Ⓩ **Flores** and **Santa Elena** are the two biggest cities in the enormous Petén region. The former was the last aboriginal bastion of this border territory ultimately conquered by the Spanish in 1697. Flores is a charming little island 500 metres from the shore and Santa Elena. Its old narrow streets are pleasant to stroll along, especially for anyone who has just spent dozens of hours on the bus, as is often the case. Santa Elena, meanwhile, is much bigger and offers all the convenient services, but really has no particular charm. In short, for a memorable trip, stay in Flores and take a jaunt to Tikal.

PRACTICAL INFO

Transport by Plane: Tikal Jets and **Aerovias de Guatemala** offer roughly the same rates and several daily flights to the nation's capital, Ciudad Guatemala. Taking the plane is by far the best way to reach El Petén (if you can afford it), as road transport is very long and exhausting. The Ciudad Guatemala-Flores return trip costs between $80 and $120.

Both **Tropic Air** (☎02-4567, ✈02-62338; US and Canada ☎800-22-3435; tropicair@btl.net) and **Aerovias de Guatemala** offer daily flights to **Belize City**.

By Bus: The bus station is located in the middle of the **Santa Elena** market, an ultimately chaotic place. To find the right bus, just look for the destinations displayed on their windshields.

Three bus companies, **Tikal Express, Máxima** and **Fuente del Norte,** have had their terminals in the same place since 1997, next to the bus station, on Calle Principal.

If at all possible, try to reserve your seat a day in advance with any of the three companies. Otherwise, you may well be left standing in the aisle.

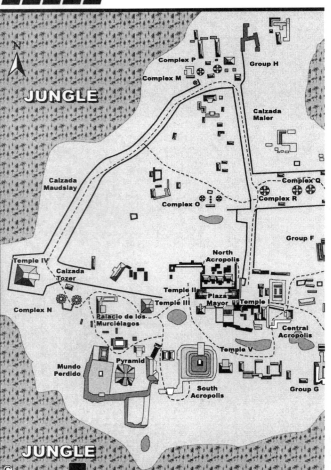

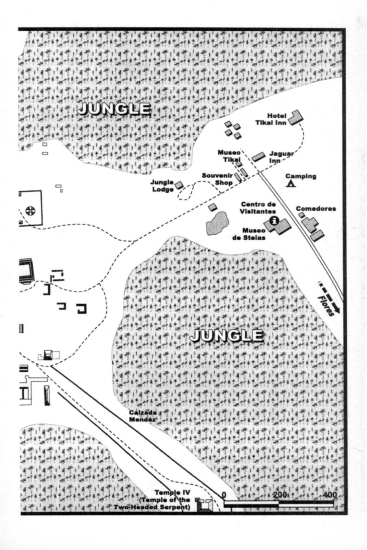

JUNGLE

Hotel
Tikal Inn

Museo
Tikal

Jaguar
Inn

Camping

Souvenir
Shop

Jungle
Lodge

Centro de
Visitantes

Comedores

Museo
de Stelas

to Flores

JUNGLE

Calzada
Mendéz

Temple IV
(Temple of the
Two-Headed Serpent)

0   200   400

Santa Elena – Ciudad Guatemala: 12-hour journey for $10; departures at 8:30am, 9:30am, 10:30am, 11:30am, 3:30pm, 4pm, 5pm, 6pm, 7pm, 8pm and 8:30pm.

To Poptún: 3-hour journey for $3; same schedule and buses as those for Ciudad Guatemala.

To Río Dulce: 7-hour journey for $8; same schedules and buses as those for Ciudad Guatemala.

To Chiquimula (at the Honduran border). Departure at 5:30am: 9-hour journey for $10.

To El Naranjo: Departures at 5am, 7am and 9am; 5-hour journey for $3.

To Tikal and Uaxactún: Departure at 1pm; Tikal: travel time: 2 hours, 30 minutes; fare: $1.50; Uaxactún: 4-hour journey for $2.50. This same bus leaves Uaxactún for Santa Elena at 6am and stops in Tikal at around 7:30am.

To Belize (Melchor de Menchos): Departures at 5am and 8am; 3-hour journey for $1.50.

Transporte Rosita. To Belize (Melchor de Menchos) **from Flores:** Departures at 11am, 2pm and 6pm; travel time: 2 hours, 30 minutes; fare: $1.50.

Boats: Many small boats shuttle back and forth between Santa Elena, Flores and the small villages on the shores of Lago de Petén-Itzá.

To San Benito: $1.

To San Andrés: 50¢.

Money: Flores and Santa Elena have their own financial institutions that cash travellers' cheques. Many hotels and shops also exchange money and travellers' cheques.

Mail: The post office is located in the heart of Santa Elena, on Pasaje Progreso, east of the park *(Mon to Fri 9am to noon and 2pm to 4pm)*.

Telephone: Guatel *(7am to 10pm;* ☎926-1299*)*, on the road leading to Santa Helena, in Flores.

Tourist Info: the **CINCAP** (Centro de Información de la Naturaleza, Cultura y Artesanía del Petén) offices *(Tue to Sat 9am to 1pm and 2pm to 8pm, Sun 2pm to 6pm; east of the police station, Parque Central)* gives visitors the scoop on the region's eco trails.

The **Centro de Visitantes de Tikal** *(8:30am to 5pm)* also boasts a tourist info centre.

Internet: Tikal Net *($2/message; 15¢/min.; Calle Centroamérica,* ☎926-0655,*tikalnet@guate.net)* offers Internet access.

Language Schools: Eco-Escuela de Español *(in Flores ☎928-8106, →926-1370, in the US ☎202-973-2264)* offers excellent private Spanish classes in the small village of San Andrés, on Lago de Petén-Itzá. The rate is $70 a week, which includes five hours of classes a day. It costs $50 more a week to rent a room in someone's house, which includes all three meals.

Flores

SWEET DREAMS

Some rooms at the **Hospedaje Dona Goya** *($7 to $10; Calle de la Unión)* have private bathrooms and balconies. It is by far the best budget hotel in Flores and Santa Elena. Lots of info and maps are posted so that visitors may find their way around the city. The hotel also boasts a great little restaurant.

Clean and cheap, the **Posada Toucán** *($7; 2 Calle 15 Septiembre)* offers a great view of the lake. Lounging in the pleasant common room will make you forget how small the rooms are.

Santa Elena

SWEET DREAMS

For a memorable stay, head to **Hotel Alonzo** *($5 to $10)*, located right near the offices of the Guatel phone company. Hot water in the bathrooms on the main floor. Ceiling fans relieve the sometimes stifling heat that rages through this lovely country. Note that you can change your travellers' cheques here. If there are no vacancies, try the **Hotel San Juan**.

Flores

BON APPETIT

The **Hospedaje Dona Goya**'s restaurant has a dining room where continental breakfasts (with muesli, fruit and salads) starting at $2.50 are served. You can also scoff down sandwiches and burgers at this eatery whose cleanliness is one its trademarks.

Flores

$

BON APPETIT

Restaurant Chaltunha, southwest of the island, boasts a lakeside terrace with a fabulous view of the little island of Santa Barbara. Typical and scrumptious fare — especially the fish dishes.

Pizzería Picasso is inside an old colonial house in the heart of Flores. Try the vegetarian or all-dressed pizza, both served in bountiful portions.

Lago de Petén-Itzá Villages

A few small, under-appreciated Lago de Petén-Itzá villages are worth a stop, at the very least as part of a one-day boat excursion. All boats leave from the various piers of Flores and Santa Elena. The village of **San Andrés**, sprawled at the foot of a mountain, is renowned for its superb sunrises. There are many travellers here, most of whom have come as part of the program offered by Eco-Escuela. Less than 2 kilometres from San Andrés, the small village of **San José** is one of the few Itzá-speaking towns in the region. You can rent a room in someone's house here. **El Remate** is the most visited village on the lake, because the road leading to the ruins of Tikal runs through it. It has a few small restaurants and inns.

Tikal

Ⓩ **Tikal** *($8; 5am to 8pm; 65 km north)*. Tikal is inarguably on one of the most fascinating places on earth. From atop a pyramid, you will be mesmerized by the flight of toucans, captivated by the cries of howler monkeys and the mysterious rustlings of the jungle. Although this ceremonial centre was abandoned over a thousand years ago, Tikal has remained singularly intact. The ghosts of the ancient Maya seems to haunt this place. Tikal almost seems to transcend the Maya's specific history, taking us beyond cultures, race and borders.

The Ruins. The beginning of the road leading to the Tikal ruins is easily recognizable by its gate, set up beneath a large tree at the junction of the trail leading to the Jungle Lodge hotel. On this westbound road, you will notice a large *ceiba*, the national tree of Guatemala, on your right. The *ceiba* was sacred to the Maya: the lower part of the tree, where the roots begin, represented night; its trunk symbolized human life as well as day; and, ultimately, its branches were said to epitomize the sky. This particular tree has parasitic plants wrapped around its branches.

The checkpoint to access the site is a few metres past the *ceiba*. Since most visitors purchase their ticket at the border, they have only to present it to the guard here. If you plan on staying at the site for more than a day, however, you must pay additional charges for each extra day of your stay *($8 US; 5am to 8pm)*.

Once past the checkpoint, you will find yourself at the starting point of an overwhelming maze of trails that crisscross the park. The first trail, to the south, leads to **Temple VI**, known as the Temple of the Inscriptions. The middle trail (southwest) leads to Calzada Méndez (causeway) and to Temple VI, then to Plaza Mayor. Finally, the trail on the right runs to Complexes Q and R, as well as to Plaza Mayor.

The shortest trail to Plaza Mayor, the "Great Plaza," is the middle trail, which runs through Complex F. If you have only one day to see the ruins, though, take the trail that begins on your right. This route will lead you to **Complex Q** (AD 771), which boasts a very well-preserved pyramid made up of five terraces that are perfectly aligned east to west. Most complexes consist of twin pyramids facing each other across vast plazas. In the case of this particular complex, only one of the two pyramids has been unearthed; the second, farther west, remains buried beneath the vegetation. Before the uncovered pyramid are nine smooth, upright steles; at the foot of each one is an altar, an oval stone monument on which animals and humans were sacrificed. These altars, much like the lime-coated steles on which the priests painted descriptions of the traditional ceremonies, were primarily used to celebrate the end of the Catún (20-year period) and the beginning of a new temporal cycle.

South of Complex Q stands a nine-entrance structure that was used to shelter members of the elite from the sun during ceremonies. To the north, an enclosure contains a carved stele depicting a god or ruler. Notice the Mayan arch that marks the enclosure's entrance.

Inside the structure stand **Stele 22** and **Altar 10**. Stele 22 boasts a bas relief depicting the god of the forest or corn. The figure, whose hand sets down what appear to be kernels of corn, carries a scepter, the symbol of power. The hieroglyphs adorning the stele have not been deciphered. At the foot of Stele 22 is Altar 10, whose flat surface depicts a sacrifice in bas relief.

Head west between the two pyramids. A few metres to your left is the first pyramid of **Complex R**. This complex hasn't been touched by archaeologists since Tikal was discovered in 1878: the steles lie on the ground, covered in tree roots, and the pyramid (AD 790) hasn't been restored.

Go up the small slope to **Calzada Maler**, a causeway that runs between Plaza Mayor and groups P and H. This road dates from the time of the ancient Maya, at which point it was 40 metres wide and used for commercial and ceremonial purposes. Take Calzada Maler on your left to Plaza Mayor, about 500 metres farther.

Plaza Mayor, or the central plaza. You can reach it from both the south (Calzada Maler) and the northeast (Calzada Méndez).

Temple I (Temple of the Great Jaguar). The consummate symbol of Tikal and, by extension, of all Guatemala, Temple I towers 45 metres above plaza level and dates from AD 700 (Classic Period). At the time of its construction, Tikal was ruled by Ha Cacau, whose tomb was discovered by American archaeologist Aubrey S. Trik. It was found level with the first terrace of the temple, though close to 6 metres below the surface of the plaza. A replica of this magnificent relic (Tomb 116) can be viewed at the Museo Tikal.

The temple consists of nine platforms, at the top of which a group of Mayan vaults and arches link three chambers. Also on its summit is the carving of a ruler surrounded by what appear to be serpents, though it can only be discerned in late afternoon, when the light creates shadows on the bas relief.

Archaeologists have found magnificent wood-carved lintels here, including one depicting Ha Cacau sitting on his throne with the figure of a crawling jaguar, the ruler's protector, at his feet. These pieces are now in museums outside Guatemala; in London, New York and Basel.

Temple II (Temple of the Masks). Temple II, which stands 38 metres tall, is in several respects a reduced version of Temple I, which faces it across the plaza. Built in the same period (AD 700) and by order of the same ruler, it consists of three terraces to which a smaller one is appended to support the crest. Much like Temple I, it has three chambers, one of which contains a mural depicting a ceremony in which an arrow flies toward a sacrificial victim. The temple has been dubbed the "Temple of the Masks" because of the masks adorning its façade on the upper part of the third terrace, which can be seen through binoculars around 8am when the light is good.

North Acropolis. The North Acropolis encompasses three main structures and seems to have mainly served as a cemetery, because it contains numerous mausoleums, undoubtedly erected for the ruling class. This section boasts the most masks sculpted in high relief, including that of Chac, the rain god, and Kinitch Acau, the Sun God, as well as a zoomorphic sculpture.

After scaling the first level, go down one storey, beneath the thatched roof, to view the **Mask of Chac**. It is recognizable by its large nose and ears. Human sacrifices by decapitation were performed at its base; the victim's blood was sprinkled onto the mask, after which the body was burned on the spot. From here, take the small tunnel, to the east, that leads to another mask of Chac. A little higher is the **Mask of the Sun God**, recognizable by the serpent emerging from its ears. The zoomorphic high reliefs are on the next terrace.

Central Acropolis. Located on the south side of Plaza Mayor, the Central Acropolis over 210 metres long and is so named because it stands between Temple V and Temple I. At its summit are six small courtyards surrounded by one- to two-storey buildings.

Behind Temple II (to the west) is a **rest area**, with public washrooms and a refreshment stand. Head west (to the left) along the path to Temple III then on to Temple IV.

Temple III (Temple of the Jaguar Priest). The highlight of this temple, built in AD 810 and almost 55 metres tall, is the frieze at its summit. At the foot of the temple is **Stele 24**, whose inscriptions mark the year of the temple's construction. Although it is in a bad state of repair, **Altar 6**, before the stele, depicts a goddess reclining on a three-legged pedestal.

The climb to the temple's summit is rather difficult, so be cautious. If you persevere, however, you will be amply rewarded at the top! One of the two skylit chambers contains a carved lintel with a scene depicting a priest clothed in a jaguar pelt — hence the temple's name.

On the way to Temple IV, the path skirts around Temple III, then crosses the **Palacio de las Ventanas** (Palace of Windows), also known as the **Palacio de los Murciélagos** (Palace of Bats). The various chambers of the unexcavated two-storey temple are interconnected and bare numerous inscriptions.

Midway between the "Palace of Bats" and Temple IV are the twin pyramids of **Complex N**. Dating from AD 711, these rectangular-shaped pyramids each have two side stairways, but no structures on their summits. They are separated by a plaza containing numerous steles, including **Stele 16**, which stands out for its very well-preserved inscriptions. **Altar 5**, at its base, is also magnificent.

Temple IV (Temple of the Two-Headed Serpent). Built in AD 741, Temple IV rises to a height of 65 metres and ranks among the tallest structures in the Mayan world; indeed, it is only surpassed by that of Caracol, in Belize. It is estimated that close to 90,000 cubic metres of building materials were used to construct this towering pyramid.

To reach the top of the temple, you must climb a series of wooden ladders on the north side of the pyramid (those on the south side having been blocked off). Before, too many visitors climbed right onto the crest that it is now off-limits so as to preserve it. You can, however, walk around the temple on the last terrace of the upper level, and thus admire the crest right up close. This temple offers the best views of the entire Tikal ruins at sunrise.

Built for the ruler Ha Cacau, the god of cocoa, Temple IV is also called "Temple of the Two-Headed Serpent," because a lintel depicting a throne resting on a two-headed serpent was uncovered here. The wooden figures found in the chambers of Temple IV are now in museums in Basel (Switzerland), London and New York.

Temple IV also has three chambers similar to those of Temples I, II and III. Archaeologists believe that the last chamber was used to store the priest's ceremonial instruments, notably sacred objects such as censers and obsidian blades.

Retrace your steps and take the path leading to the ruins of El Mundo Perdido.

El Mundo Perdido. Climb the large Mundo Perdido (Lost World) too see one of the most beautiful sunsets over Tikal and the surrounding jungle. This 30-metre-high pyramid was built around AD 600 (Late Classic Period). It was probably one of the largest pyramids in the Mayan world at the time, and it is similar in construction to the pyramid at Teotihuacán, Mexico.

Temple V. Measuring 57 metres in height, Temple V was built circa AD 700 and has only one small chamber at its summit. During our visit, this pyramid was undergoing major restoration work by the Spanish government, and was therefore closed to visitors.

Temple VI (Temple of the Inscriptions). This temple, which stands at the end of Calzada Méndez, was built in AD 766 for the ruler Yaxkin Caan Chac. It boasts the longest glyph in Tikal, inscribed in its 12-metre-high crest. There are two chambers at the summit, and at its base stand **Stele 21** and **Altar 9**. Although both monuments are rather damaged, their glyphs can still be made out. The figure of a prisoner lying on his back is engraved on the upper part of the altar.

The **Parque Nacional de Tikal** has two museums that display archaeological artifacts found at the site, and relate the history of the Maya, the discovery of the Tikal ruins and the work carried out by archaeologists over the years. Both are worth checking out, even if you have only a day to spare.

Tikal	**SWEET DREAMS**

Generally speaking, the hotels in Tikal have the bad habit of losing reservations, so confirm your reservation the same day you arrive or the day before.

The **Jaguar Inn** *($5 to $48; ☎502-926-0002)* is popular with hikers and offers several types of accommodation: a *cabaña* with shared bathroom for $25, camping, or a hammock with mosquito netting for $5. The Jaguar Inn has a relaxed family ambiance.

Tikal	**BON APPETIT**

The restaurant of the **Jaguar Inn** is very inviting and offers a laid-back ambiance as well as a cheap menu.

Uaxactún

Located some 40 kilometres north of Tikal, Uaxactún is a mid-size Mayan archaeological site dating from the Classic Period. You should visit these ruins if you're a hard-core archaeology buff, otherwise you may be disappointed, since they hardly compare with the grandeur of Tikal. But the visit is an adventure in itself, as the road leading there runs through about 24 kilometres of jungle.

Uaxactún	**SWEET DREAMS**

You can camp in the small village next to the ruins and snooze in hammocks (with mosquito netting) at **EcoCampamento** *($4/person; ☎926-0077 in Flores)*. The tents, supplied by the establishment, and the hammocks are set up under a palm-thatched roof to shelter guests in case of rain.

Uxactún

SWEET DREAMS

Located right in front of the village bus stop, **Hotel y Campamento El Chiclero** *($7)* has rooms that are clean and decent, but have no private bathrooms. The very affable owners offer excursions in the region.

Sayaxché

Located 60 kilometres southwest of Flores, by the Río de la Pasión, the village of Sayaxché is an interesting starting point for a tour of the region's archaeological sites. Not the most happening spot in Guatemala, the quiet village is no more interesting thanits frontier-town appearance. Beyond Sayaxché is nothing but the dense jungle and a few farmers. The excursion to the ruins of **El Ceibal** is particularly interesting, as the site is reached by boat followed by a walk along a rather steep trail.

Sayaxché

SWEET DREAMS

The rooms at the **Hospedaje Mayapán** *($4)* don't have a lot to offer other than their rock-bottom price. Another bonus: all rooms have a fan.

Located three blocks from the Hospedaje Guayacán, the cute little rooms of the **Hospedaje Margot** *($5)* will suit travellers only in Sayaxché for the night. Guests have to share the bathroom, but have access to the terrace out back.

El Ceibal

SWEET DREAMS

Though a little far from Sayaxché, El Ceibal has camping and as you walk there you can hear the sounds of tropical birds and (sometimes roaring) mammals. On the way there, you will also be able to see the El Ceibal ruins, which, though not as grandiose as those of Tikal, are also not as swamped with craning tourists.

Poptún

In **Poptún** *(halfway between Flores and Livingston)*, lovers of the great outdoors will be delighted with the packages offered by the **Finca Ixobel**. Indeed, owner Carol Divine offers a whole range of activities deep in the jungle. Guests can horse-back ride *($4/h)*, sleep in a cave and kick back in hammocks, all for $95 (4-day package). Other activities include tubing on the Machiquila river *($10)* and, equipped with a candle and a flash-light, exploring a nearby cave *($5; bring good shoes and a flashlight; the latter are sold here for $2)*, which is also a great place for climbing and swimming. The last part of this excursion will faze even the coolest of cucumbers, when only a few metres stand between them and the inky waters below. Even the bravest souls will hesitate a moment before jumping in!

Poptún	SWEET DREAMS
$	**Finca Ixobel** *($4; half an hour's walk south of the village)*. Stop here for the many activities offered and to stretch your legs a bit before continuing the long trip to El Petén. You can sleep in either hammocks or cabins.

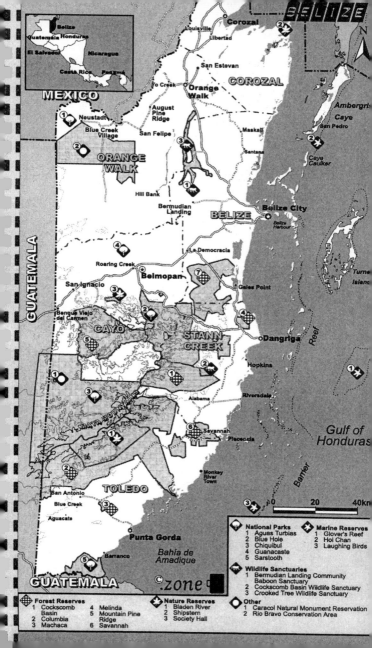

||||| In most Central American countries, regions are distinguished by their affiliation with a particular ocean. Belize, however, is an exception to the rule in that its shores lie exclusively on the Caribbean Sea. Nevertheless, Belize has several regions, each associated with a different ethnic group. *Mestizos*, who are of mixed Mayan and Spanish descent, live in the north and west. In Belize City and the coastal villages, Creoles form the majority, while the south is populated by Garifunas, descendants of African slaves and Carib Indians who found refuge here after having been uprooted from St. Vincent by the British Crown in the late 18th century. Moreover, Mayan culture is very widespread here, and a few groups in the west of the country have managed to keep their culture intact without having to defend themselves against merciless death squads, as is the case in Guatemala.

||||| However, Belize is exceptional in other ways, as well. Colonized by the British and its corsairs back in the 17th century, its territory has always been hard to reach due to the world's second largest coral barrier reef, whose expanse forms a natural obstacle only twenty-odd kilometres offshore. It is said that the country's colonizers ran aground on these reefs and had no choice but to remain on this hostile land. English is thus the official language, though Spanish and Creole patois are widely spoken throughout the country. Belize has about 200,000 inhabitants spread out over a territory just a little bigger than El Salvador, which boasts 6,000,000! Belize's population is by far the smallest of any Central American country. Ultimately, Belize only gained full independence in 1981, the year in which it dropped the name British Honduras and took charge of its own destiny.

||||| With its mountains, its fabulous little islands strewn along the coral barrier reef, its banana and sugarcane plantations, its dense tropical forests and Mayan ruins, Belize is typical of the subcontinent, while also boasting a distinct Caribbean flavour. It is, however, less visited than its neighbours, so budget travellers can enjoy beautiful tourist-oriented places that have still retained much of their character and charm, as they have not yet become tourist meccas. Make the most of it while it's there, because nothing lasts forever, at least not in this civilization!

⏭ BELIZE CITY ⏮

If all roads lead to Rome, all those in Belize lead to Belize City. A veritable crossroads and maritime junction, Belize City is unavoidable for anyone crossing the country. This city is

PRACTICAL INFO

Transportation by bus: Departures to **Corozal, Orange Walk** and **Mexico** (*Batty Brothers, located at 54 East Collet Canal, ☎027-7146*) all day long. Two-hour journey or more for $3 to $4.

To **Belmopan** (*$2; 1 hour 15 minutes' travelling*) and **Dangriga** (*$5; 3 hours 30 minutes' travelling; Z-Line, Magazine Rd., ☎027-3937*): Departures at 8am, 10am, noon, 2pm, 3pm, 4pm and 5pm. Travelling to **Punta Gorda** costs $11 and takes eight hours; call for departure times. Another company, **James Bus Line** (*West Collet Canal St.*), runs to Punta Gorda at 7am every day except Wednesday and Friday. To reach **San Ignacio** and the **Guatemalan border**, change buses in Belmopan.

By Boat: Marine Terminal & Museum (*10 North Front St., ☎023-1969*). Reserve one day in advance for weekends. Departures for **Caye Caulker** every two hours between 9am and 5pm; 40-minute boat ride costs $7.50. Have a raincoat and insect repellent on hand. A boat leaves for **San Pedro** at 9am; the fare is $15. However, San Pedro is pricy and draws highfalutin upper class tourists.

Money: Belize Bank, Barclay's Bank and the **Bank of Nova Scotia** are all on Albert Street. You can get a cash advance on your Visa card and change travellers' cheques here. Closed afternoons, except Friday.

Mail: At Queen Street and North Front Street; 8am to 4:30pm.

Telephone: 1 Church Street, next to the park. Open from 8am to 8pm.

Tourist Info: 83 North Front Street. Maps and brochures available.

also the starting point for boat expeditions to the Cayes and the coral barrier reef. It is the ideal place to go shopping or stock up on supplies, as it is the only real "big" city in the country, and has all necessary products and services. However, its tourist attractions are quickly explored before setting off for other horizons, unless you wish to see the sights located a little farther inland.

A metropolis on the Caribbean Sea, Belize City has much in common with the Caribbean countries. Its population is a medley of black, white, and many variations in between, and a buccaneer-like ambiance is clearly felt in its lively streets. Old wooden houses stand closely huddled together along canals where all-too-apparent poverty rears its ugly head. And while safety problems seem to have abated with the years, don't take any chances: arrive during the day.

The **Swing Bridge** *(last bridge to the south, over Haulover Creek)* spans the waterway that runs through the city. It is the perfect starting point if you want to explore the city. You have two options here: follow either side of the river to the Caribbean Sea (this will give you the opportunity to see certain important monuments such as the former governor's house and several central parks), or quite simply lose yourselves in the maze of alleyways, each narrower than the last.

Belize Zoo and Tropical Education Center *($6; 9am to 4:30pm; Western Hwy., ☎081-3004)*. Located 40 kilometres north of the city, this 400-hectare zoo lets you observe the country's indigenous animals in their respective natural habitats. Unfortunately, the animals and their re-created environments are caged. On the plus side — for humans, at any rate — this enables visitors to see a few of their fellow creatures. Real animal lovers may well prefer the two reserves listed below. To reach them, take a bus on the Western Highway and ask the driver to drop you off at the entrance.

Altun Ha *($2.50; 9am to 5pm; 48 km north of the city)*. If you're sick and tired of archaeological sites that all look the same: you are in for a pleasant surprise! Not that these ruins are dramatically different from the likes of Chichén Itza, Palenque or Copán, but they are located deep in the jungle, and many trails lead through the area, giving you the chance to also see some wildilfe while you're there. Discovered in 1957, Altun Ha is the cemetery in which the high priests of the Mayan civilization were buried. The temple of the Sun God rises to a height of 18 metres. To reach the site, take a northbound bus and ask the driver to stop at the junction for Rockstone Pond. You will then have to hitchhike the remaining fifteen-odd kilometres.

The **Bermudian Landing Community Baboon Sanctuary** *($5; 8am to 5pm; 33 km northwest of Belize City)* is the realm of howler monkeys, who will respond in kind to your attempts to "ape" them. You can ask the guides to help you coax them down from the treetops, and even rent a canoe and paddle on the adjacent river. This 32-square-kilometre reserve is also home to scads of other animals. To get there, take a northbound bus for about 20 kilometres and ask the driver to stop at the Bermudian Landing intersection, from which you'll have to hitchhike.

Crooked Tree Wildlife Sanctuary *($4; 8am to 4pm; ☎022-2084)*. This reserve is primarily home to rare birds who wing their way over the swamps and the lagoon. Visitors are in for a magical experience, though the cost of making special excursions and sleeping in the neat little village on site is steep, unless you camp. The entrance to the reserve is 4 kilometres from the Northern Highway and 50 kilometres from Belize City. To get there, take a north-bound bus and walk or hitchhike the rest of the way.

Belize City

SWEET DREAMS

Bon Aventure Hotel *($120; 122 North Front St., ☎024-4248 or 024-4134)* ▶ Small, clean rooms. Well-situated and run by a friendly and helpful Chinese-born family. Right next door, the **North Front St. Guesthouse** is a tad more expensive and a big draw for backpackers. Large clean rooms.

Mira Rio *($13.50; 59 North Front St., ☎023-4147)* ▶ On the other side of the street and by the river. Simple and quieter if your room faces the water. Bar, terrace and pool table.

Seaside Guesthouse *($20 in dormitory; 3 Prince St., ☎027-8339)* ▶ Run by Quakers, the establishment donates its profits to socio-environmental and charitable organizations. The staff can fill you in on the specific issues and also give you some tips on how to get involved. Oh yes — the rooms are clean and simple, and you can get advice about your trip.

Belize City

BON APPETIT

Dit's Restaurant *(at King St. and Albert St.)* ▶ A favourite with the locals. The place serves reasonably priced and bountiful portions of rice & beans and makes good desserts, too. Laid-back and down-to-earth.

GG's Café & Patio *(2-B King St., ☎027-4378)* ▶ Pleasant decor, varied menu and the best burgers in town.

Macy's Café *(18 Bishop St., ☎027-3419)* ▶ Varied menu and local as well international grub. Draws many adventurers. Laid-back ambiance.

◄► THE CAYES ◄►

The largest chunk of the second largest coral barrier reef in the world flanks Belize, and is one the country's most famous attractions. Scattered along the reef are small islands, or islets, known as the Cayes. People come here to scuba dive and relax in the shade of palm trees. If you can't afford a scuba-diving course (it's cheaper in Útila, Honduras), there's always snorkelling. A few islands have tourist facilities. The two most popular among them are Ambergris Caye and Caye Caulker, though only the latter is worth checking out, since it's far more affordable and less overrun with "Yankees" than its big sister to the north. It is also the mellower of the two, with very welcoming *Mestizo* and *Garifuna* residents.

Caye Caulker

ⓩ Everything here is within easy walking distance as the island is only 7 kilometres long. This is fortunate, given that Caye Caulker has no more than a dozen vehicles. A roadsign says it all: *Go Slow*. This, in a nutshell, sums up the carefree, if not downright dreamy, ambiance of the island. It's the kind of place where you can see yourself bringing a case of books and spending a month reading – with alternate days of snorkelling, of course! Watch the sunset from indoors, or come armed with powerful insect repellent to fend off the sand fleas that come out in droves at that time.

ⓩ **Snorkelling** *(Dolphin Bay Travel, Front St., ☎022-2214)*. This company makes arrangements for all local excursion organizers and offers retail prices, which range from $5 to $20 for one day of snorkelling. Special excursions farther away will cost you more. Your Rasta guide Johnny has the inside scoop on the various places where you can observe the incredible marine life. What is special about this tour is that Johnny takes you in his little sailboat, which adds to the serenity of the adventure. Those staying at the Ignacio Beach Cabins can make an excursion with Ignacio and, if the weather is gloomy and you get too chilly after an hour, he will supply bait so you can fish. At night there is, of course, a feast. Snorkelling gear can also be rented on the island. Scuba-diving courses are really overpriced here, so you're better off waiting until you've reached Útila, in Honduras, where it costs a third of the price.

The Cut *(north of the village)*. A hurricane left its mark in a rather unusual way, to say the least, when it hit the island – cutting it right in two! This is the only place on the island with a real beach where you can swim. Otherwise, you must go on a scuba-diving excursion off the coast and swim in the ocean.

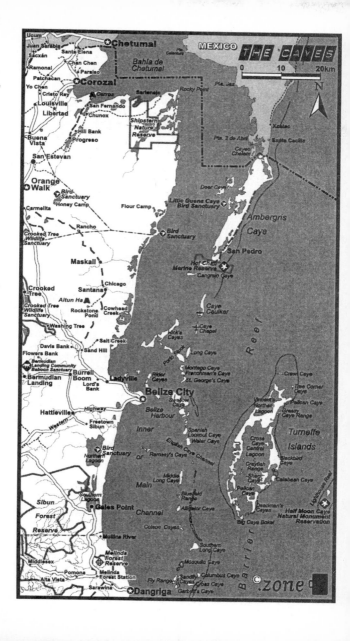

PRACTICAL INFO

Transportation by boat: It is best to reserve a day in advance for weekends. Daily departures for **Belize City** at 6:45am, 8am, 10am and 3pm. The 40-minute ride costs $7.50. Tickets are purchased at the foot of the pier, at the **Caye Caulker Water Taxi Association** (☎022-2992). On the other side of the island, on the Back Pier, you can catch one of the boats coming back from **Ambergris Caye** by flailing your arms about at 10:30am or 1:30pm.

Money: Atlantic Bank *(weekdays 8am to 2pm, Sat 8am to noon, Middle St.)* is the best place to exchange your travellers' cheques and currency or get a cash advance on your credit card.

Tourist Info: Dolphin Bay Travel *(Front St., north of the pier, ☎022-2214)*. The staff here takes the time to answer your questions. This is also the place to buy tickets for excursions to the coral barrier reef. Lower rates are available for groups.

Mail: Post Office *(open weekdays 8am to 5pm, except Fri afternoon; Back St. South)*.

Telephone: The **BTL** offices are on Front Street, near the pier.

Internet: Island Girl Productions *(9am to noon and 4pm to 7pm; Front St., north of the pier, ☎022-2309; islandgirl@btl.net)* not only offers E-mail service at 50¢/2 minutes, but puts out a local biweekly newspaper, the *Village Voice*, offering info about the island that is sometimes useful to travellers.

Caye Caulker

SWEET DREAMS

Miramar Hotel *($10; Front St.)*. ▶ Popular with backpackers due to its unbeatable price, the hotel is often full and offers decent rooms.

Caye Caulker

$

SWEET DREAMS

Castaways Hotel & Restaurant *($11; Front St., ☎022-2294)* ▶ Cheap, centrally located, good grub, simple and comfy rooms.

② **Ignacio Beach Cabins** *($15; on the beach to the south, ☎022-2212)* ▶ Small charming cabins surrounded by palm trees on the beach. Great pier at your disposal and a bathroom in every room. Excursions to the coral barrier reef with Ignacio are available.

Caye Caulker

$

BON APPETIT

Glenda's Restaurant *(Back St., ☎022-2148)* ▶ Located on a less touristy street than Front Street, Glenda's serves good and hearty breakfasts and lunches. Cinnamon buns and *burritos*. Yum!

I&I Resto-Bar *(between Front and Back St., to the south)* ▶ Vegetarian and assorted dishes served to non-stop reggae music on a terrace bursting with greenery.

Marin's Restaurant *(Back St.)* ▶ Prices here are a little steeper, but worth it for the huge servings and good meat and grilled fish dishes.

▶▶ NORTHERN BELIZE ◀◀

What sets this region apart is its relatively even landscape, which makes it extremely favourable for agriculture. This area yields the country's greatest output of citrus, not to mention sugarcane, fields of which you are sure to drive by while on the bus. The stream of trucks carrying sugarcane to the processing plant is constant and can sometimes cause traffic jams on the highway. With regard to the local attractions, there is always nature, most splendid at the **Rio Bravo Conservation Area**, bordered by Guatemala and Mexico. Unfortunately, this conservation area is hard to reach unless you're willing to pay big money.

A good way to get the best of both worlds is to take part in an expedition to one of the many Mayan sites in the area, most of which are located deep in the jungle. The region boasts a rich Mayan past, and has some of the civilization's oldest sites, dating back to 2500 BC. A little more recently, northern Belize served as a land of exile for many Mexican *Mestizos* fleeing the Caste War that ravaged the Yucatán in the 19th century. This explains why you will hear more Spanish spoken here than English, and encounter fewer Garifunas.

Orange Walk

Set right smack in the middle of sugarcane fields, Orange Walk was also the scene of the last Mayan uprising from 1866 to 1872. Later, a few Mennonite colonies settled near this town of 10,000. Apparently farmers have no qualms about growing marijuana plants in the thick of the fields so they can be less dependent on a single crop whose price is set by Western speculators who control the market.

Ⓩ **Lamanaí** *(35 km south of Orange Walk, via the New River)*. The one-day expedition to Lamanaí is probably the best reason to pass through Orange Walk. The boat trip leading you there safe and sound gives you the chance to see lots of flora and fauna. You will also drift by the Mennonite community of **Shipyard** along the way. Two hours into the journey, the river and swamps give way to a lagoon, and the first hills appear. These hills are crowned with temples still engulfed in vegetation. The site was founded as early as 1,500 BC, seven centuries before the founda-tion of the grand city of Tikal! Boasting 783 structures, of which barely 10 percent have been restored, Lamanaí is the country's second largest site (after Caracol), and its highest temple towers 32 metres above plaza level. The site is also unique because it was home to 3,500 Maya when the first Francis-can missionaries arrived. In fact, Lamanaí got its name from these very missionaries. Taking the boat from Orange Walk costs $30 per person if you manage to round up a party of five. Contact **Jungle River Tours** *(20 Lovers' Lane, ☎032-2293, Orange Walk)*. It's pricy, but worth it. Moreover, lunch is included. Reserve one day in advance.

Cuello *(free admission; 5 km west of Orange Walk)*. These more modest ruins hold the record for the oldest Mayan site, dating back to 2,500 BC. They are now on the property of a rum distill-ery. You can take a bus there from the corner of Aurora and Santa Ana Streets.

Corozal *(50 km north of Orange Walk)*. A slightly smaller village with a few good hotels for travellers on a shoestring budget (notably the **Hotel Maya** and the **Capri Hotel**). The Mayan ruins of **Cerros** are easily reached from here by taking one of the boats

PRACTICAL INFO

Transport: Buses tend to be more frequent in the morning, but the waiting period never exceeds an hour, whether you're going to **Belize City** or **Corozal**. The fare is about $2. You can also take a bus to the ruins of **Lamanaí** on Tuesday and Thursday afternoons from the market, but the trip by boat is far more spectacular.

Money: Both the **Belize Bank** and the **Scotia Bank** are located opposite the central park on the main street. Open from 8am to 1pm and 3pm to 6pm.

Tourist Info: Jungle River Tours *(20 Lovers' Lane, ☎032-2293)*. Have a drink at the bar next to the tourist office while chatting about the many faces of Belize with the staff. They are very friendly and know the region like the backs of their hands.

Mail: Opposite the market; on Hospital Crescent. Open weekdays from 8am to 1pm and 3pm to 5pm.

waiting at the port. A few kilometres north of town is the **4-Mile Lagoon**, the best place on the north coast to go swim and chill out. Buses heading to the border will drop you off there.

Orange Walk $	### SWEET DREAMS
	Jane's *($13; Market Lane)* ▶ Attractive double rooms in a pleasant but none-too-clean house.
	Hotel Taisán *($15; downtown, ☎032-2752)* ▶ Shared bathrooms and small, simple and clean rooms. Sometimes noisy.

Orange Walk $	### BON APPETIT
	There is an impressive number of affordable **Chinese restaurants** scattered throughout the town. Two good choices are the **Hong Kong** and **Lee's**.

Orange
Walk

$

BON APPETIT

Juanita's Guesthouse & Restaurant *(8 Santa Ana St., ☎032-2677)* ▶ National specialties and unrivalled neighbourhood-restaurant ambiance. All kinds of food is served here.

⏭ SOUTHERN BELIZE ⏮

This is where you literally and figuratively get off the beaten path. Truth be told, the road deteriorates and gives average tourists an excuse to stop their Homeric journey. Consequently, the local attractions retain their pristine beauty and the locals are friendlier toward tourists, whose presence has not become as run-of-the-mill as it has in the rest of the country. So hotfoot it to pleasant Garifuna villages, dense jungles that harbour the Mayan secrets, less populated Cayes and beaches. Travelling the extra miles can cost a bit more, but it is worth keeping in mind is that the further you go, the more fabulous the experience. Visit the region on Garifuna Settlement Day, November 18 and 19, when the arrival of the first Garifunas is celebrated in a festive carnival ambiance.

Dangriga

Dangriga boasts the largest population of Garifunas, who founded the town in 1823 after having been unceremoniously expatriated from the island of St. Vincent. Garifuna culture evolved from the union between Carib Indians and the descendants of African slaves who ended up on St. Vincent in the 17th century and were befriended by the Caribs. The commingling lasted a century before the British, bolstered by the Treaty of Paris, attempted to reinstitute the heinous yoke of slavery. Needless to say, the free Garifuna people were violently opposed to this, and as a result were sent off to islands in the Bay of Honduras. Discontent, they later migrated along the Caribbean coast, from Honduras to Belize. This culture is present throughout Dangriga, which is also the region's main centre of commercial development. This town where wooden shacks stand alongside a few colonial-style structures is quickly explored.

Gales Point *(40 km north of Dangriga)*. This is not a beach, but rather a small village smack in the middle of a lush coastal environment. Though you can swim or rent a kayak here, the main attraction remains the observation of flora and fauna (manatees,

PRACTICAL INFO

Transport: Z-Line *(Commerce St.,* ☎052-2160*)* is the region's main bus company.

Belmopan: $3; departures at 5am, 6am, 8am, 2pm and 5pm; 2-hour journey. These buses go all the way to **Belize City** in four hours.

Belize City: $4.50; departures at 5:15am and 8:15am; 2-hour journey.

Placencia: $4; departures at 12:15pm and 4:30pm; 2-hour journey.

Punta Gorda: $6.50; departures at noon, 4pm and 7pm; 5-hour journey.

Money: The banks are on Commerce Street.

Tourist Info: The **New River Café** is a popular hang-out with travellers, which makes it *the* place to get the lowdown on the region. The food here, however, is a tad pricy.

Mail: 16 Caney Street.

Telephone: Commerce Street, opposite the police station.

crocodiles, sea turtles, iguanas, tapirs, jaguars...). To get there, catch the 6am or 9am bus for Belize City for $2.50. The bus returns at 3:45pm and 5:30pm.

Hopkins *(13 km south of Dangriga)*. Divide the size of Dangriga by 10, move it to a small bay and you get Hopkins. Here, the term Garifuna takes on its full meaning, and most inhabitants will greet you as you go by. This small unspoiled town is not exactly your run-of-the-mill modern luxury resort and is bound to throw a few people off. To give you an idea of this, Hopkins on ly got electricity and television 10 years ago! Take a lovely promenade on the beach where you can swim in an enchanting setting of small cabins alternating with a bevy of palm trees. The overall effect is a quiet setting in a friendly ambiance, great for meeting the locals who will introduce you to their unique culture. A bus travels there every day. Information provided on site. As far as accommodation is concerned, many options are available. Close by, south of Hopkins, is the village of **Sittee River**, the starting point for **Glover's Reef**. Every Sunday morning at 8am, a boat travels to this archipelago located more than 60 kilometres from the coast. The five-hour trip costs $40. The boat returns on Saturday. There are a good number of *cabañas* where you can stay for about $100 a week. Camping, a much cheaper alternative, is permitted on these idyllic islands. Bring a mask and snorkel, sunscreen lotion and insect repellent.

Ⓩ **Maya Center and the Cockscomb Basin Jaguar Reserve** *(a little farther than Hopkins, inland)*. For true nature lovers not afraid of getting bitten: this is the only jaguar reserve in Central America. A visit to Maya Center, a very typical village where people still wear traditional dress and located right at the entrance of the reserve, is not to be missed. One of the village's highlights is the **Hmen Herbal Center & Medicine Trail** (☎05-2266), where you can enter into the mysterious world of Mayan medicinal herbs. The centre can arrange hikes in the park for you, as well as a visit to its botanical garden *($2)*. Meanwhile, the reserve itself is the wildest park in the country and should be jotted down on every adventurer's to-visit list. Besides jaguars, you can spot brilliantly coloured frogs as well as pumas. To get there, take one of the buses for Punta Gorda and get off at Maya Center, then hitch a ride or join an expedition from the village. Hikes of more than one day can be made, but having a guide tag along is a must since the trails sometimes end in the middle of nowhere.

Placencia *(50 km south of Dangriga)*. Another village with a resolutely Caribbean atmosphere that gives you the feeling of being on an island somewhere in the West Indies. Placencia lies at the southern tip of an idyllic sandy peninsula that extends over 17 kilometres. Its beaches are among the most stunning on Belize's mainland. Swim in the limpid waters and dive down to admire the coral, or simply stroll along the shore that seems to go on forever. Outings to the coral barrier reef can be organized. Bus timetables change constantly, but there is at least one bus a day from Dangriga; inquire in Dangriga.

Punta Gorda *(115 km south of Dangriga)*. Guatemala and Honduras can be reached from this port (the southernmost one in the country) by means of a car ferry. Boats leave every morning for Puerto Barrios, Guatemala, at 9am *(Requenas Charter Services; $10; 12 Front St., ☎05-2070)*. Other boats may leave as well if there are enough passengers. Otherwise, Punta Gorda is a small, quiet and very multicultural village from which you can reach the fabulous Mayan ruins of Lubaantun, some twenty kilometres away. There is no bus to this neck of the woods, so you must find another means of transport to San Miguel. Only worth it for true admirers of Mayan culture. For information about home-stay programs with families in Mayan villages contact the **Toledo's Visitor's Information Centre** at ☎07-2470. **Z-Line** and **James Bus Line** offer departures to the north of Belize at 4:30am and 11am, depending on the day. No service on Thursdays and Fridays.

Cayes of Southern Belize *(islands reached by boat from Dangriga)*. Several of the southern Cayes can be pleasant places for a longer stay, depending on your finances. From **Placencia, Kitty's Place** (☎06-2327, ✆06-2326, info@kittysplace.com) organizes camping excursions to **French Louis Caye,** a tiny island that is home to a few fishing families. The $60 price includes sea-kayaking and snorkelling activities. You can also go to **Southwater Caye,** a bigger island than the former, made up of palm trees and white sand. The island is isolated in the middle of the coral barrier reef, which makes it just the place if you like lots of peace and quiet. Arrangements can be made from **Dangriga** with the staff at the **Pelican Resort** (☎05-2044, ⊷05-2570, *pelican-beach@btl.net*): $150 for one week and a double room in a desert-island paradise.

Dangriga

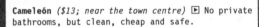

Cameleón *($13; near the town centre)* ▶ No private bathrooms, but clean, cheap and safe.

Bluefield Lodge *($19; 6 Bluefield Rd., ☎05-2742)* ▶ The place to go, even if the price is a little steeper. Rooms are attractive and airy, and you can get one with or without a bathroom, which can save you a few bucks.

Gales Point

SWEET DREAMS

The small unpretentious inn named **A Jentings** *($20, brkfst incl.)* is a good place to crash.

Hopkins

SWEET DREAMS

Budgetwise, the **Caribbean View Hotel** *($15)* is your best bet for the price and its location right on the beach.

Placencia

SWEET DREAMS

The charming **Paradise Vacation Hotel** *($20; at the southern tip of the village)* is not the cheapest place in the village, but it offers above-average comfort and can organize all kinds of excursions, be it to the barrier reef or through the jungle to check out buried Mayan sites.

Punta Gorda 	## SWEET DREAMS You can spend the night at the **Nature's Way Guesthouse** *($13; 65 Front St., ☎07-2119)* in simple rooms with a family ambiance. They also offer excursions in the area.

Dangriga $	## BON APPETIT **Burger King** (not part of the multinational chain) *(Commerce St.)* ▣ Excellent breakfasts. Traditional and American food. Both the **Starlight Restaurant** and **Alida's Restaurant** *(on the same street)* dish up Chinese food and traditional fare.

▶▶ WESTERN BELIZE ◀◀

Western Belize is inland Belize. Though it is no more than 150 kilometres from the sea, it feels light-years away from the cayes. The jungle reigns supreme here, and makes you wonder how the Maya managed to erect their many temples in places devoid of any waterways. The westbound road runs through Belmopan, the new capital where civil servants come only to work for the day before returning to the "real city," that is Belize City. But the heart of Western Belize is truly San Ignacio, situated a little farther away, smack in the middle of the region's riches, and only 25 kilometres from Guatemala.

San Ignacio

(Z) A real must, San Ignacio is the place for both action-seekers and those in search of peace and quiet. The city boasts umpteen attractions, and the landscape is simply fantastic. Depending on how much time you have and what your scene is, San Ignacio is the perfect starting point for daily expeditions in the area. Situated on a slightly elevated, hilly terrain, the city boasts a pleasant climate and is a great place to roam. San Ignacio is not too spread out and walking is the best way of getting around. Doing so is not only very cheap, but will get you in tip-top shape, as well.

PRACTICAL INFO

Transport: Buses leave for **Belmopan, Belize City, Benque Viejo** and the **Guatemalan border** from the market every half-hour as of 8am. The fare ranges from 75¢ to $2.50, depending on your destination. **Tikal** is 150 kilometres from San Ignacio. The return fare with Mini Transporte Miaita (☎092-2253) is $20.

Money: The banks are located on Burns Avenue and offer all services.

Tourist Info: Its walls plastered with all kinds of tourist info, **Eva's Restaurant** is a gold mine for travellers who want to meet other travellers to chat or share excursion expenses (and save a few bucks). Postings, maps as well as good grub.

Mail: Post Office, above the police station.

Telephone: The **BTL** is located a little farther along Burns Avenue.

Internet: You can surf the Net at **Eva's** (what a great place!).

Cahal Pech *($2,50; closed Mon and Sun afternoon)*. These Mayan ruins are located next to the city, on the highway leading to Guatemala, a little beyond the San Ignacio Hotel. The one-hectare site offers great views over the region. A small museum will complete your enlightenment on Mayan culture.

El Pilar *(25 km northwest of town)*. Inquire about organized excursions at **Eva's Restaurant**. The passage of time can really be felt in this city. Contrary to most sites in the country, this one has yet to be excavated and restored, and new grass has yet to be planted between its 25 plazas. Move over Indiana Jones — this is where it's at! You will feel like you're the first one to have set foot here since the downfall of El Pilar, 1,000 years ago. There is also a lot of wildlife to be seen on the paths that run through the site.

Pantí Medicine Trail *($5; 12 km southwest of town)*. The apprentice of an old Mayan healer who died a few years ago decided to lay out this trail to pay homage to her mentor, who had taught her a few secrets about the medicinal properties of plants in the primal forest. The trail identifies more than 4,000 genera and is truly fascinating. It can be reached by canoe or with one of the excursions organized in town.

Ⓩ **Xunantunich** *($2; 12 km west of town)*. Probably the most accessible site in the area. You have only to take one of the many buses bound for the border on the hour and get off in the village of **San José Succotz**. Undergoing major restoration work for several years now, Xunantunich's 40-metre-high pyramid, *El Castillo*, is the tallest Mayan structure after the one at Caracol. The views over the region's various horizons are breathtaking.

② **Mountain Pine Ridge** and **Caracol** *(20 km and 100 km south of town, respectively)*. Gateway to the unspoiled country stretching to the Maya Mountains, the region is a huge territory that has of yet been relatively untouched by colonization and clear cutting. This makes the place all the more beautiful, and you will almost feel as if you've just landed in Belize in 1502, except there are roads, of course. Go to **Eva's** to see when the next affordable expeditions are leaving. A day of swimming and exploring at the incredible **Hidden Valley Falls,** cascading from over 1,000 metres into the verdant wilderness, is one option. The same day, you will be taken to the **Rio Frio Caves,** a network of caves and underground rivers where you can play speleologist. You will feel smaller and smaller as you penetrate deeper into the jungle whose giant trees get increasingly taller. The other expedition is more ambitious and requires at least another day. It goes to **Caracol**, *the* Mayan city in Belize (the equivalent of Copán in Honduras and Tikal in Guatemala). Not only is Caracol more extensive than Tikal, but uncovered here were more elaborate hieroglyphs describing Caracol's military victories over neighbouring Petén. In its heyday, Caracol numbered 35,000 structures and 150,000 inhabitants spread over 8 square kilometres. Its size is quite incredible for a site that is nowhere near a waterway: you wonder just how the Mayas managed to transport all their building material here. Caracol is quite a way's away, and getting there costs a pretty penny. And the farther you go, the deeper you penetrate into a "no man's land" where the wildlife moves around with greater ease than do the less well-adapted *Homo sapiens*. You can observe live jaguars here; they are definitely a prettier sight than the roadkills you may see on the way here!

San Ignacio

SWEET DREAMS

 Cosmos Camping (*$3 to $8; a half-hour's walk to the north, along the river*). ▶ The advantage (or disadvantage) of being in a remote spot: This oasis of greenery boasts four rooms so basic that the chirping of crickets will put you to sleep. Daub your skin with aloe hand-picked in a shower full of plants. If you have a tent, this is the place to pitch it. The river runs along the foot of the property, and guests should rent the owners' **canoe** for $10 and paddle up the river, past the city, to the jungle, with its motionless iguanas and mysterious aura.

The Budget Hotel (*$10; 17 Burns Ave., ☎092-2024*). ▶ Centrally located and clean. Two shared bathrooms. The street noise and the morning hurly-burly will wake you up early so you can make the most of your day (Rise and shine!).

Tropicool Hotel (*$12.50; 30 Burns Ave., ☎092-3052*). ▶ Clean and safe with a family ambiance. A great place.

San Ignacio

BON APPETIT

Martha's Kitchen (*10 West St., ☎092-3647*). ▶ Typical fare, burritos, sandwiches and vegetarian dishes. The perfect place to relax at sundown.

 Original Eva's Restaurant (*22 Burns Ave., ☎092-2267*). ▶ More than a bar-restaurant, Eva's is the rallying point of travellers. Very diverse and always scrumptious menu. People come here for breakfast, dinner or to wash down a beer – but any reason will do!

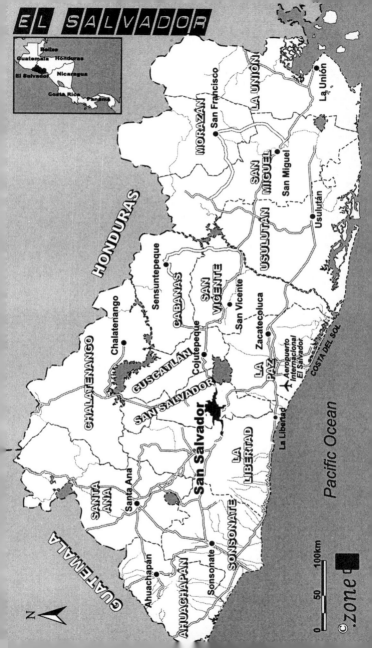

||||| El Salvador, a tiny tract of land clinging to the Pacific coast, lies between Honduras and Guatemala. It's the smallest country in Central America, and the most densely populated on the entire continent with six million inhabitants living in an area the size of Massachusetts.

||||| Unfortunately, this country is better known for its violent conflicts than for its spectacular beauty. Because 75 percent of the economy is geared towards coffee, sugar and cotton production, there has been almost constant rivalry for control of this rich volcanic land. Since the beginning of the last century, a dozen families, known as "oligarchies," have exercised a monopoly on land ownership (40% of the land for 2% of the population) and political control. Before 1850, El Salvador had less than half a million inhabitants, but the country began to prosper when coffee became so immensely popular in Europe. A well-known sociologist recently stated that the Industrial Revolution couldn't have happened without coffee, which became essential to the morale of the workers! It's not surprising that enterprising individuals seized a large portion of this lucrative pie when its value first became known.

||||| Since the 1930s, civil war in El Salvador has claimed the lives of some 100,000 people (the "Saviour" was on holiday, they say). The last conflicts were settled barely 10 years ago when a peace agreement was reached through UN mediation. This turmoil has discouraged tourists who didn't want to contemplate the beautiful countryside in the midst of gunfire. For the past few years, tensions have relaxed; the last two governments were elected (unlike the preceding ones!), signalling an important step for this nation. Nevertheless, poverty is still very visible, and the gap between the rich and the poor is far from bridged.

||||| Today, travellers can visit the country without feeling like a gun is being pointed at their backs. Military controls are still frequent, but they are more a matter of routine, and are not threatening to the globetrotter. Do take care of your appearance though, as the customs officials and other officers have a tendency to be less sympathetic to people looking dishevelled and unkempt, whether it's the clothing or physical appearance (long, unwashed hair, beard, etc.). In short, go to El Salvador now while it is peaceful, and admire its numerous attractions: mountains, beaches, volcanos and coffee plantations.

⏭ SAN SALVADOR ⏮

Buried deep in a valley, the capital San Salvador is certainly
not the most beautiful place to visit. In this city of more than
a million inhabitants, green spaces are rare and fumes from
diesel engines linger over it. Recently the city-centre has
become a lot less lively since the mass exodus of the city's
elite which moved to the surrounding hilltops in search of
fresher air and a better life. Therefore, the older quarters are
only maintained as well as their occupants can afford to.
Climbing the hillsides from the valley floor, you'll see rein-
forced concrete luxury hotels next to shacks made of cardboard
and plastic panels that are home to entire families.

All the same, a visit the old part of the city is worthwhile, if
only to glimpse the other side of life in this country. Other
than that, the city is pretty much a wasteland as far as attractions are concerned. On the other hand, because it is so well
situated in the centre of the country, the capital is the most
appropriate point of departure for trips to distant regions where
the country's many stunning attractions are found.

City-centre. Anyone expecting to find lots of elaborate vestiges
of the colonial era can dream on, because the centre of town is
quite distressing. Its central square (**Plaza Barrios**), has just
enough trees to shade a few pigeons, and the immense **Catedral
Metropolitana**, next to the park, is a large cavernous, concrete
structure topped with a high dome. In fact, it was never finished
because the creditors who financed the project had a falling out
with the religious authorities who, they believed, were getting
along too well with the poor. On the west side of the square,
Palacio Nacional is where the government held sway before the
building was damaged by the earthquake of 1986.

Markets. To dig up handicrafts at a good price (if you're ready
to bargain a little), go to the **Mercado Ex-Cuartel** *(three blocks
south of Calle Delgado and Avenida 8 Norte)*. **Mercado Central**
(Calle Rubén Darío, three streets south between Avenidas 7 and 9)
is the place to buy food and household items.

Panchimalco *(14 km south: take bus 17)*. This little village,
whose population is almost exclusively Amerindian, is situated in
the heart of a green area. Walking through the narrow cobblestone
streets in front of the little colonial church is just one of
those little pleasures in life.

Parque Balboa *(60¢, bus 12 "Mil Cumbres")*. Many paths cross the
luxuriant gardens of this park. A visit to the **Puerta del Diablo,**

PRACTICAL INFO

Transportation by bus: To go west: **Terminal de Occidente** (*Boulevard Venezuela and Avenida 49 Sur; take lines 4, 27 or 34 to get there*) serves destinations such as **La Libertad, San Juan Opico, Santa Ana, Ahuachapán** and **Sonsonate**.

To go east, towards the centre or north: **Terminal de Oriente** (*Boulevard Ejército and Avenida 38 Norte; take lines 7, 29, 33 or 34 to get there*) serves **San Sebastián, Ilobasco, Cojutepeque, San Vicente, El Poy, Chalatenango, San Miguel, Usulután, La Unión** and **Santa Rosa de Lima**.

To go south: **Terminal del Sur** (*Autopista del Sur; take bus 11-B*) serves **Zacatecoluca, La Herradura** and the **Costa del Sol**. Service begins at daybreak and stops in the afternoon. Prices vary according to the destination but are not expensive.

Money: The **Banco Agricolo Commercial** exchanges dollars. For travellers' cheques it's better to use the *casas de cambio* found just about everywhere.

Tourist Information: **Instituto Salvadorño de Turismo** (*619 Calle Rubén Darío between Avenidas 9 and 11 Sur*) has information in English and Spanish on the city's attractions as well as useful maps. They give suggestions and directions for sights you may want to see.

Mail and Telephone: Centro de Gobierno on Rubén Darío between the Calles 5 and 7 Sur.

a series of ridges at the southern tip of the park, is a must (by bus or a 45 minute walk); from here you have an impressive view of the whole region.

Lago de Llopango (*16 km east of San Salvador*). The largest lake in the country, 8 kilometres wide by 12 kilometres long, is in the crater of an extinct volcano. You can swim here but avoid going on the weekends, when everyone from miles around seems to have the same idea. To get here take bus 15.

Los Chorros (*60¢, 18 km northwest of the city*). Take bus 201 "Ordinario" in the direction of Santa Ana. Los Chorros is made up of natural ponds and waterfalls surrounded by magnificent green hills. This is an enchanting place to swim and walk, although weekends are to be avoided, when this paradise becomes positively jam-packed.

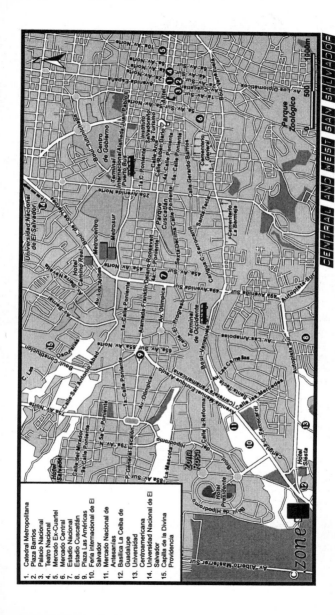

CENTRAL AND WEST SAN SALVADOR

1. Catedral Metropolitana
2. Plaza Barrios
3. Palacio Nacional
4. Teatro Nacional
5. Mercado Ex-Cuartel
6. Mercado Central
7. Estadio Nacional
8. Estadio Cuscatlán
9. Plaza Las Américas
10. Feria Internacional de El Salvador
11. Mercado Nacional de Antesanías
12. Basílica La Ceiba de Guadalupe
13. Universidad Centroamericana
14. Universidad Nacional de El Salvador
15. Capilla de la Divina Providencia

Ⓩ **Volcán San Salvador** (*Santa Tecla*). This mountaintop rises to about 2,000 metres, is visible from the city, and can be climbed quite easily. Bus 101 goes to **Santa Tecla**, from where you take bus 103 which goes to the foot of the volcano every hour. It takes a few hours to climb the volcano, but also (and especially) to travel around the rim of the two craters situated on the trail. The **El Boquerón** crater is particularly breathtaking, but be careful not to fall as the sides are very steep in places.

La Libertad (*31 km south of the capital*). A fishing port and the country's main seaside resort, La Libertad has only so-so beaches. The neighbouring **Playa El Sunzal** and **Playa El Tunco** are much better, being more sandy and having great waves for surfing. These two beaches are 8 kilometres west of La Libertad, and you take the local bus 80 to get there, after taking bus 103 from Terminal de Occidente in San Salvador. Bring along something to eat, since the beaches are far from town.

San Salvador

$

SWEET DREAMS

Hotel Yucatán (*$6; 673 Calle Concepción*). ▣ Not a safe neighbourhood at night but the best hotel in this area. Shared bathrooms.

Hotel San Carlos (*$10; 121 Calle Concepción and Avenida 2 Norte*). ▣ Its main asset is that it's where the Trica bus stops. Otherwise, the place is a bit of a dive and in a disreputable neighbourhood.

Hotel Panamericano (*$10; 133 Avenida 8 Sur and Calle Delgado, ☎222-2959*). ▣ The size of the rooms varies, but they're comfortable. An unsafe area at night.

La Libertad

$

SWEET DREAMS

Porto Bello (*$6; Av. 1 Sur and Calle 2 Poniente, ☎335-3013*). ▣ Dark and uninviting, its only advantage is that it's inexpensive.

El Retiro Familial (*$11; towards the point*). ▣ A pleasant little hotel; a bit more expensive.

BON APPETIT

Los Entremeses de Federico (*$2; Calle Ponient, between Avenidas 13 and 15*). ▶ A restaurant with a varied menu in the crumbling city-centre. The meals are often buffet style. Open for lunch only.

La Zanahoria (*$4; 1144 Calle Arce, between Avenidas 19 and 21*). ▶ Vegetarian dishes are the speciality of this open-air restaurant.

▶▶ NORTHERN EL SALVADOR ◀◀

This region has been severely affected by the civil war, which left the area with widespread poverty. Today the territory is free, the fighting having stopped long ago. The temperature is not as hot as in the capital because the region is dotted with many mountains, some of the highest in the country. If you're looking for a refreshing change from the noxious fumes of San Salvador, this is the place.

La Palma

Imagine a road winding through the mountains, leading to a little town of 6,000 inhabitants perched at an altitude of 1,100 metres right in the middle of a pine forest. From this village you can climb the highest mountain, and just a few minutes' walk brings you to superb waterfalls. The town's main activity is making handicrafts such as wood sculpture and brightly-coloured wall-hangings. You'll find this mix of attractions quite pleasant and life will seem good in La Palma! Plan on staying here a few days because after spending more than three hours and 80 kilometres on a jam-packed bus travelling up the winding roads between the capital and this village, you'll probably want to stay put awhile. But look on the bright side: when you know what lies at the end, the journey just whets the appetite! The village is only a few kilometres from the Honduran border.

Ⓩ **Casa de la Cultura** (*Parque Central*). Several workshops (*talleres*) are spread around the centre of town. The Casa de la Cultura can give you information and direct you to the kind of handicrafts that interest you. La Palma is where almost all of the country's craft-work such as sculptures, ceramics, wood carvings, and painting is produced.

PRACTICAL INFO

Transportation: Buses to **San Salvador** (119) leave all day long and take between three and four hours to make the journey. You can also take a bus to Honduras, passing through **Copán** and **San Pedro Sula**.

Tourist Information: at the Hotel La Palma.

Ⓩ Cerro El Pital (*Bus 119 towards San Ignacio, then a 4X4 to the village of Chiquito*). You made it! At 2,730 metres, this is the highest point in San Salvador. Unlike most of the mountains in this country, it isn't a volcano so it doesn't have the characteristic cone-shaped form. Climbing it takes about an hour and a half on an unmarked, but visible, path. The panorama is impressive — you can see as far as Honduras, a few kilometres to the north. Another mountain, **Miramundo**, not quite as high, can be climbed from Chiquito.

Los Tecomates (*90 min. walk from La Palma*). This hike takes you directly to the foot of a spectacular waterfall deep in the mountains. It is recommended to go with a guide. Information available at Hotel La Palma.

La Palma	SWEET DREAMS
	Hotel La Palma (*$20, on the main street, at the entrance to town*, ☎335-9012). ▣ It's expensive, but there is no other alternative and you will enjoy staying in one of its beautiful rooms with wooden ceilings. There is a pleasant terrace and garden.

La Palma	BON APPETIT
	Cafetería La Terraza (*Parque Central*). ▣ A friendly place where you eat on the terrace. The food is authentic and not expensive.
	Cafetería La Estancia (*next to La Tarraza*). ▣ The same kind of meal in a less attractive spot that is dark and enclosed.

⏭ EASTERN EL SALVADOR ⏮

It's difficult to believe that this was a war zone up until 1992. In a supposedly civilised world, it's incredible such atrocities still exist. This isn't a sociological treatise, and there is no need for one because you can see the signs of war for yourself — they are still visible here in eastern El Salvador, the former rebel stronghold. Of all the Salvadorian territory, this region was probably the most affected by the fighting. People are now re-building their lives in the calm that is too easily taken for granted in peacetime and so precious after years of conflict. Like the rest of the country, the eastern part is a medley of beaches, mountains, colonial villages — and of frayed memories.

San Miguel

San Miguel, in the centre of the eastern region, is home to 240,000 people who live in the shadow of the Chaparrastique Volcano. Again, the town itself has nothing special to offer. Even colonial ruins have been wiped out by volcanic eruptions, the last dating from 1976. However, it's the ideal place from which to venture north, south or even further east in the country.

Chinameca (*20 km west of the town, take bus 333*). This little colonial village with cobblestone streets and an old church straddles hilly terrain. It's very pleasant to walk here, deep in the mountains close to the volcano. Sulphurous vapours and boiling mud pots (**Los Ausoles de la Viejona**) are visible one kilometre from the outskirts of the town, next to the cemetery.

Ⓩ **Perquín** (*180 km north, take bus 332B, 3 hours travelling*). All fans of Che Guevara, or of other revolutionary figures should come to this town that was the centre of the FMLN resistance between 1980 and 1992. The town never yielded to the many government bombardments, but these attacks have left obvious scars. Seeing this mountainous countryside, one can easily imagine the crazy game of hide-and-seek that the guerrillas played here. Most of the population left town during the war and are now slowly returning, trying to rebuild their lives and the town. Situated 300 metres up, the **Museo de la Revolución Salvadoreña** (*$1.20; Tue to Sat 9am to 4pm*) overlooks the central square. This museum, created by the FMLN in 1992, presents their viewpoint of the revolution by displaying the conditions of unimaginable poverty in which the population lived — the conditions that necessitated revolutionary action. Behind the museum is a huge crater left by a 230-kilogram bomb. And inside the museum, an incredible aerial photograph shows the atrocities of a neighbouring village, El Mozote, a massacre in which

---

PRACTICAL INFO

Transportation: When coming from **San Salvador**, take the 301 that leaves frequently from Terminal de Oriente: a three-hour trip for $2.50. Terminal de San Miguel is located in the centre of town (*Calle 6 Oriente between Avenidas 8 and 10 Norte*) and, in addition to the capital, serves **Playa El Cuco** (320),

La Unión (324), **Perquín** (332-B) and **Playa El Tamarindo** (385).

Money: Travellers' cheques can be difficult to cash. The banks and the *casas de cambio* are near the cathedral.

Mail and Telephone: near the central square.

---

500 civilians were slaughtered. And it doesn't end there — this incredibly interesting museum is sure to raise your political consciousness.

Les Playas (*between 40 km and 60 km south of San Miguel*). Several beaches whose volcanic sands vary in colour from light grey to a deep black, are spread out along the coast. Most are quite rocky. To reach them, take bus 385 from San Miguel. For food and accommodations, your best bet is without question on **Playa El Tamarindo** — but even there you must be content to spend the night in a small hut sleeping in a hammock.

(Z) **Volcán Chaparrastique or Volcán San Miguel** (*at the southwest end of town*). The hike to the top of this volcano, which last erupted in 1976, takes three hours. However, you can take a 4X4 for much of the distance, leaving you with only one hour of walking to reach the summit. At 2,130 metres, the crater is fabulous, and you can go inside it by following a series of steps. The path isn't always visible and if you're not the adventurous type, its best to hire a guide. Ask for Tereso de Jesús Ventura by leaving a message with Marío Cruz, ☎661-4210.

San Miguel

$

SWEET DREAMS

Hotel San Rafael (*$8; Calle 6 near the bus station*, ☎661-4113). ▣ Very plain, but quite clean with fans and bathrooms.

Hotel Caleta (*$8; Avenida 3 Sur*, ☎661-3233). ▣ A beautiful little hotel with many clean, well-kept rooms with bathrooms.

Perquín

SWEET DREAMS

You can sleep at the (not always very clean) **Casa de Huéspedes Gigante** (*$5; easy to find in this little town*). Dark and gloomy.

⏭ WESTERN EL SALVADOR ⏮

Thousands of bags of coffee beans are produced in this mountainous region which is the joy of outdoor enthusiasts. Other than the mountains and the wonderful Cerro Verde park, there are panoramic views of lakes and lovely little colonial villages not too damaged by the recent conflict. The FMLN had a much smaller presence in the western part of the country.

Santa Ana

Santa Ana is to western El Salvador what San Miguel is to the eastern part of the country. It's the main city and commercial centre. Coffee and sugar are the two staples of the local economy, since the fertile hills surrounding the town are ideal for growing these prized crops. In fact, most of its rapid development can be attributed to coffee, which has been in high demand for a century and a half now. Santa Ana is very close to San Salvador (just 60 km away), but it has managed to retain its its olden-days charm while the capital has absorbed most of the "progress" of modern development. It's still the ideal departure point to explore more distant regions where it's difficult to find accommodations. In the town itself, near the **Parque Central**, you will find old restored colonial buildings as well as a theatre, the cathedral and churches. Further west, **Parque Menéndez** is dominated by the beautiful **Iglesia del Calvario**.

Lago de Coatepeque (*13 km south of Santa Ana, take bus 220*). Situated at the foot of the local volcanos, the water in this crater lake is at a comfortable temperature, perfect for swimming and sailing. Unfortunately, several developments have ruined the scenery, but even so the place is still very beautiful.

Parque Nacional de Cerro Verde (*50 km south, take bus 248 which does not run very often*). This park has three peaks rising up some 2,000 metres in altitude. Besides **Cerro Verde**, there is the **Santa Ana Volcano**, the highest volcano in the country at 2,365 metres, and **Itzaco Volcano**, whose last eruption was in 1957. All hikes leave from the parking lot of Cerro Verde and take between one and three hours to reach the summits. Making

PRACTICAL INFO

Transportation: The station is at the corner of Avenida 10 Sur and Calle 15 Poniente. Bus 201, 60¢, leaves for **San Salvador** throughout the day, and takes one hour. The *directo* bus is faster. For **Sansonate**, bus 205 runs all day long. And for **Metapán**, bus 235. Some of these buses continue on to the border of Guatemala.

Money: **Banco Salvadoreño** (*near Parque Central*) changes traveller's checks.

Mail and Telephone: Avenida 2 Sur and Calle 7 Poniente for mail. You can make telephone calls at the Antel building next to the cathedral.

your way up the two volcanos is worth the effort, not only for a fantastic view of the region, but for the incredible craters and their sulphurous lagoons.

Reserva Natural de Montecristo (*200 km north, bus 235*). The reserve is one of the most unspoiled areas in the country, and the animals are still wild. Thus, it's difficult for humans to get there without a 4X4. Stop in Metapán and ask for information at **Hotel San José de Metapán**.

To visit **Lago de Güija**, get off the bus a little before Metapán (Km 97, ask the bus driver). Surrounded by lush vegetation and rolling hills, it's a great place just to walk, and you can even ask the local fishermen if they can give you a tour by boat.

Santa Ana	SWEET DREAMS

Hotel Livingston (*$7; Avenida 10 Sur and Calle 9 Ponient, ☎441-1801*). ▣ Clean, which is the basic minimum to sleep well, and not expensive. You can choose a room with or without a bathroom.

Pensión Monterrey (*$8; same area as Livingston, ☎441-2755*). ▣ Smaller, but always clean.

Hotel Libertad (*$12; Avenida 1 Norte and Calle 4 Oriente, ☎441-2358*). ▣ More expensive, but better situated, this hotel has rooms that are clean but not incredibly charming. The rooftop terrace has a beautiful panoramic view of the city.

Lago de Coatepeque

$

SWEET DREAMS

Amacuilco Guest House (*$15; 200 m from the Antel office, ☎441-0608*). ▶ Plain rooms in a laid-back environment. Very bohemian.

Santa Ana

$

BON APPETIT

Los Horcones (*next to the cathedral*). ▶ Hamburgers and tacos in a lovely room filled with greenery and beautiful furniture. And a little expensive.

Kyomi (*Avenida 4 Sur between Calles 3 and 5*). ▶ Fish, steaks and sandwiches in a setting less charming than the average, especially in comparison with Los Horcones.

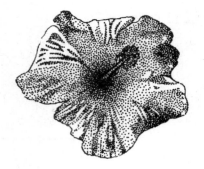

▐▐▐▐▐ At first glance, it might shock you to see a gun hanging from the waist of every man you meet. But you'll get used to it: people here are educated and most of them leave their guns with the guards before entering a bank. Like in all Central American countries, urban Honduras is very different from rural Honduras, the latter sometimes resembling a Western movie with its cowboys and copious amounts of alcohol. In the interior of the country there are fabulous mountains which take several days to climb. Because the paths here are not marked like in Costa Rica, having a guide is essential. Few tourists visit these mountains and you will certainly experience a change of scenery. What's more, there won't be any surprise eruptions because Honduras doesn't have any active volcanoes.

▐▐▐▐▐ For a long time, most tourists to Honduras flocked to the Islas de la Bahía in the Caribbean Sea for the bright blue water surrounding these islands of palm trees, where the pace of life is laid back. If you visit Honduras, you absolutely must go to Útila, the smallest and least expensive of the three large islands of the Bahía, whether it's to take a scuba-diving course (the best and least expensive in these tropical waters), or just to relax in an enchanting environment. In fact, once you get here, it's hard to leave.

▐▐▐▐▐ The Caribbean coast of Honduras is much more populated than those of its neighbours. Several larger cities are found here, which makes it easier for *gringos* to access the coast. The roads vary in quality; the best one runs to San Pedro Sula.

▐▐▐▐▐ One more thing — the country has been politically stable for the last several decades, and has not been shaken by armed conflict during the eighties like all its immediate neighbours. In fact, this banana-producing country served as a base for United States interventions in Guatemala in 1954, and more recently in Nicaragua, via the Río Coco. And what's more, US army veterans have decided to retire here, widening the gap between rich and the poor. A recent study by independent economists concluded that the neoliberal model introduced to the country in 1990 has dramatically accentuated these disparities, and that between 1988 and 1998 the poverty rate rose from 68 to 80 percent. The study also showed that violence and depression are on the rise: between 1994 and 1997, psychiatric care in the country increased 25 percent.

▐▐▐▐▐ In short, don't walk on the beach in the evening, avoid poor neighbourhoods, and keep your camera hidden as much as possible.

▶▶ TEGUCIGALPA ◀◀

If you arrive by plane, you will have an amazing view of an
expanse of houses spreading out like a great wave breaking
between green crests. Tegucigalpa is a large, sprawling city, but
the centre of town can be visited very easily on foot. A band of
poor, rundown areas surrounds the centre and it's not advisable
to walk there. The city has the usual colonial-style churches and
public squares. However, the traffic is terrible (and the
pollution even worse), and taxis have three or four different
types of horns — as if one weren't enough! The streets are
narrow, and it seems that the urban planners were asleep on the
job, about 300 years ago. In some places there are stairways
instead of streets, because the city is spread across several
hills. Tegucigalpa is a place of transit more than it is anything
else, but enjoy the cool air while you're here; you're at an
altitude of about 1,000 metres.

Plaza Morazán (Parque Central). The 24-hour centre of urban
life: during the day, you'll find several lottery sellers with
their tickets displayed at their feet, and thousands of pigeons
fly back and forth from the roof of the cathedral and the bread
crumbs thrown to them on the ground. On the east side is the
whitewashed **Catedral San Miguel**, whose architectural splendour
contrasts dramatically with the neighbouring buildings and even
more with the houses in the winding streets just a little to the
north. The **Iglesia Los Dolores,** two streets west and two more to
the north, is in better condition than the cathedral, and away
from the racket cause by the traffic horns.

Parque La Leona (*Av. 7 and Calle La Leona towards the north*).
Lose yourself in the maze of streets and you will come across
this small park, an absolute oasis of greenery in the midst of
asphalt and downtown diesel fumes. This place has a fine view of
the city and its surrounding peaks.

El Picacho (*summit of 2,300 m to the north of the city*). Take the
bus that goes regularly to El Hatillo. From there the road
becomes very rough and an all-terrain vehicle is needed to cover
the last three kilometres. You must walk or go in a private
vehicle. Some taxis occasionally take people there. The panoramic
view from the top will take your breath away and is a true feast
for the eyes.

Museo Histórico de la República (*$1.50; Mon-Sat; Calle Morelos,
two streets east of Parque Concordia*). Probably the most interesting museum in the city, with its many artefacts representing
the country's numerous historical periods. You'll learn a lot
about ethnology and anthropology.

PRACTICAL INFO

Transportation: All the bus lines leave from the Comayagüela area. Take Calle 6 and go south past the market.

To **San Pedro Sula:** The company El Rey (*$3; Av. 6 and Calle 9*) serves this destination each hour between 2:30am and 6:30pm. Count on five hours of travelling. There are other companies around with buses going in the same direction, which stop at midway points such as Comayagua and Siguatepe.

To **Tela** and **La Ceiba:** Traliasa (*$5; Av. 7 and Calle 8*) brings you to the coast in seven hours with departures at 6am and 9am.

To **Santa Rosa de Copán:** Sultana (*$3; Av. 8 and Calle 12*) buses go to the region of the famous Copán ruins at 6am and 10am (seven hours of travelling).

To **Trujillo:** Buses depart from the Cotraipbal terminal (*$6; Av. 7 between Calles 11 and 12*) at 5am, 9am and noon. The last departure passes through **La Unión** and takes nine hours.

To **Choluteca:** A trip with Mi Esperanza (*$2; Av. 6 and Calle 24*) lasts three hours. Departures start at 6am and continue every hour.

Nicaragua: Tica Bus serves this country (*$20; Calle 16 between Av. 5 and 6*). It's nine hours to Managua for $20. The deluxe bus is air-conditioned. The other option is to take a Mi Esperanza bus (see **Choluteca** above) to **San Marcos de Colón** for $2, at 6am and 7:30am, and from there take a taxi to the border. Tica buses also go to the capitals of **Costa Rica** ($30) and **Panama** ($40) in 24 and 48 hours respectively.

Guatemala: Take a bus to **San Pedro Sula**, and then a connecting bus from there.

Money: You might have to visit several banks before you can change your traveller's cheques. The banks and foreign exchange counters are situated around the Plaza Morazán. The Banco Ficensa on Morazán Boulevard is probably your best bet.

Tourist Information: Instituto Hondureño de Turismo is on the third floor of the Europa Building on Avenida Ramón Cruz near the Calle Rep. of Mexico above Lloyd's Bank. Here, you'll find maps and lists of hotels, as well as information on the city's cultural life.

Mail and Telephone: The post office is at Av. Cervantes and Calle Morelos, four streets from the park and has general delivery service. To use a phone, go to Hondutel, open 24 hours, at the corner of Avenida 4 and Calle 5.

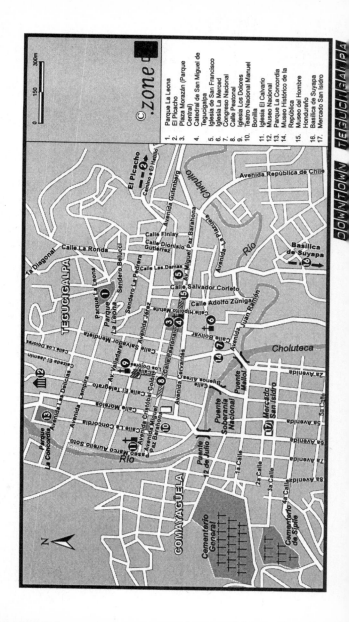

©zone

1. Parque La Leona
2. El Picacho
3. Plaza Morazán (Parque Central)
4. Catedral de San Miguel de Tegucigalpa
5. Iglesia de San Francisco
6. Iglesia La Merced
7. Congreso Nacional
8. Calle Peatonal
9. Iglesia Los Dolores
10. Teatro Nacional Manuel Bonilla
11. Iglesia El Calvario
12. Museo Nacional
13. Parque La Concordia
14. Museo Histórico de la República
15. Museo del Hombre Hondureño
16. Basílica de Suyapa
17. Mercado San Isidro

Mercado (*Av. 6, Comayagüela*) The commercial part of the city is spread out over several blocks and everything can be found here. If you have forgotten your sandals or want a large papaya, or even a key chain, this is the place. But don't go when it's dark unless you want to be pickpocketed.

Teguci-galpa

$

SWEET DREAMS

ⓩ **Hoteles Granada** (*$5-$10; Av. Gutemburg and Calle Finlay,* ☎372-318). ▶ They are called hotels, plural, because there are three of them, each one as comfortable as the rest and much appreciated by travellers on a tight budget. Their cleanliness is indisputable and only the noise from the buses and trucks may bother you somewhat (less disturbing in Granada 2 and 3). In any case, you can't escape noise in this city.

Hotel Marichal (*$8; Av. 5 and Calle 5,* ☎370-069). ▶ Some of the rooms are a little dark. Well situated and always clean.

Hotel Nan Kin (*$9; Av. Gutemburg opposite the San Miguel gas station,* ☎380-271). ▶ A friendly place that has its own Chinese restaurant. Very clean and safe. Laundry service.

Teguci-galpga

$

BON APPETIT

Longi Li (*Av. Gutemburg, northeast of Granada 1*). ▶ Affordable Chinese food and fresh vegetables.

Pizzería Tito (*Morazán and Colonel Palmira*). ▶ Serves cheap pizza and Italian food.

El Patio 2 (*Morazán*). ▶ Good quality Honduran and international cuisine. A pleasant atmosphere that can get very lively, and portions that are more than reasonable ($5 and up).

⏭ THE CARIBBEAN COAST ⏮

As you reach the coast, the mountains give way to the enormous ocean. You can climb the summits, though many take weeks to reach, and you may see only clouds once you get to the top. It rains a lot in the mountains and the paths are not always visible. As you get closer to the water, people's skin colour becomes increasingly darker. Many Garifunas, a mix between the descendants of slaves and the indigenous people of the Caribbean Islands, live here. There are numerous small Garifunas communities strung out between the larger cities of the region. The Garifunas live from fishing and are suffering a rural exodus as young people look for jobs elsewhere. Their culture is slowly disappearing, but there are still numerous elders in their eighties who are full of life. In fact, they're in as good shape as many to North Americans in their fifties.

Tela

Tela is a small city on the western Atlantic coast of Honduras. It is one of the country's main banana ports. The United Fruit Company had its headquarters here until a fire destroyed a part of the wharf, which prompted it to move closer to San Pedro Sula. Today, Tela is quieter, but it attracts the most tourists visiting Honduras because of its magnificent beaches. Still, it's not overrun by tourists and there is plenty of room on the beach. However, avoid walking along it alone or after sundown because there are always thieves lurking about, and cases of mugging and rape have been reported. The place is very relaxed and people come here to take life easy. A nature reserve to the east of the city is the perfect place to observe wildlife.

Beaches. The beaches around the city can be a bit grimy. So we recommend that you go a little further west, or even cross one of the bridges towards Nuevo Tela, across from the Telamar hotel.

Ⓩ **Garifuna villages.** The most beautiful, authentic native villages are situated around Tula. Several westbound buses pass through them, but another way to get there is to rent a bicycle at the Telemar hotel or from an individual. **San Juan, Tornabé** and **Miami** are the villages to visit. Miami is 12 kilometres from Tela, and all the houses here are typically "Garifuna." You can also see the far end of Punta Sal Park which is accessible only with an all-terrain vehicle or by boat. Trucks sometimes take people there. You can make a day of it and walk to all three towns, but it's less exhausting by bicycle or truck. The beaches are all incredible around here.

Ⓩ At the **Parque Nacional Punta Sal** (*22 km west of Tela*) you'll find life at its fullest and in every form. The park contains a great many ecosystems with its mangroves, coral reefs, swamps, rocky beaches and tropical forests. Monkeys and tropical birds are plentiful. Getting here is another story. The best way

PRACTICAL INFO

Transportation: The bus for **El Progreso** leaves every half hour all day long for $1. El Progreso is the transfer point for San Pedro. There is one bus a day for **Tegucigalpa** *(8 hours; $4.50)*, it leaves from the hotel Los Arcos. Finally, the trip to **La Ceiba** takes 2.5 hours and costs $3. Take the buses near the park. You can also take the train Friday and Saturday at 1pm via **Puerto Cortés** for $1. The return trip leaves at 7am and each way take five hours. Lastly, if you want to go the **Islas de la Bahia** from Tela, hop aboard a boat in the port that's headed there (no regular service).

Money: It's better not to come to Tula only with traveller's cheques because it can be a pain to change them into lempiras. The casa de cambio **La Teleña** *(Av. 4 and Calle 9)* might be the only place that will do it.

Tourist Information: Garifuna Tours *(southwest of the park, info at* ☎448-1069, *garifuna@hondutel.hn)* know the area like the backs of their hands. They organize all kinds of trips every day and also **rent bicycles** *($5/day)*.

Telephone, Mail and Fax: Av. 4 towards the northeast.

Internet: E-mail service is available at the Villas hotel next to the park.

by far is to find a truck leaving the Shell station at 7:30am that will take you to Miami. From there, you'll have to pay someone to ferry you by boat for the short stretch that remains. If you are equipped for camping, beautiful beaches await you. Trips *($15-$18)* organized by Garifuna Tours *(at the southwest of the park,* ☎488-1069*)* are also very good, especially the one by boat on the sea. Information is available at the Telamar hotel.

Refugio de Vida Silvestre Punta Izopo *(12 km east of Tela)*. To get there, take a bus from Tela to **Triunfo de la Cruz**, another Garifuna village. From here ask for directions to the park. Someone will take you across a pond of water, then after a few hours walk, you can rent kayaks and meander through the lagoons admiring wildlife and vegetation that is just as wonderful as it is in Punta Sal. The cushy alternative is to take the trip with Garifuna Tours (see "Punta Sal" above).

Jardín Botánico de Lancetilla *($4; 5 km west of Tela, on the highway)*. This garden was conceived in 1926 by The United Fruit Company to test plants' resistance to disease and to develop new species. Here you will find tropical plants not only from America but from around the world. Birds nest in the numerous fruit trees in the garden. The best way to get to the park is by bicycle.

Tela

$

SWEET DREAMS

Posada del Sol (*$5.50; Av. 3 and Calle 8, 448-2111*). ▶ A good price for a place that's always clean and welcoming with its little garden.

Hotel Mar Azul (*$9; Av. 5 and Calle 11, 448-2313*). ▶ Rudimentary, but in a beautiful setting with an owner who is right at your service.

Mi Casa es Su Casa (*$11 bkfst incl.; Av. 6 between Calles 10 and 11*). ▶ Yes, it's a little more expensive, but you'll be very warmly received. A family atmosphere in a private home. Only four rooms.

Tela

$

BON APPETIT

Generally, food in hotel restaurants is delicious and not too costly. It's also where you'll find fish and other seafood.

Luces del Norte (*one street north of the park*). ▶ All meals are served here and the fish is as fresh as it is delicious. There is also a selection of books for sale or for exchange. A good place to find out what's happening in town because it's a regular hangout for travellers.

Tía Carmen (*Av. Honduras and Calle 8*). ▶ Typical food at ridiculously low prices. The food disappears quickly, so arrive early.

⏭ WEST OF TELA ⏮

Guatemala is just a shot away, but it's impossible to get there by road. However, a new road now connects San Pedro Sula to **Puerto Cortés**, the country's main seaport where all bananas are shipped abroad. Other than that, there isn't much to see here. Certainly the neighbouring beaches are beautiful, but so are those on the eastern part of the coast. The old fort of San Fernando in **Omoa**, 15 kilometres west of Puerto Cortés, is worth

checking out because you won't see another one this big unless
you go all the way to Campeche in Mexico or Cartagena in Colombia. This fortress defended shipments of money coming from the
capital against attacks by English pirate ships. Omoa is the
departure point for boats going to **Livingston** in Guatemala. It's
also renowned for its beaches and its enormous mountains that you
can visit. You'll have no problem finding accommodations and food
in these two towns. Friday and Saturday morning, the train goes
to Tela at 7am (5 hours journey for $1).

La Ceiba

La Ceiba is the third most important city in the country. It's
too big to be a quiet coastal town, but too small to be consid-
ered a real metropolis. We're not being very nice to La Ceiba. It
was the main shipping port for the United Fruit Company for a
long time before losing its hold on this precious market to
Puerto Cortés and Puerto Castilla. The splendid scenery makes up
for this loss, though. The city is built against a backdrop of
immense mountains rising to almost 2,500 metres. To reach their
summits takes a week of walking in the jungle with a guide. The
mountains also block the clouds so the city gets plenty of sun.
Finally, you can only get to the underwater paradise of Islas de
la Bahía by boat from La Ceiba.

Playa Perú and Río María (*9 km east of La Ceiba*). You can get
there in two hours by following the beach from the village or
else take one of the buses marked **Sambo Creek** (a Garifuna
village) that leave every 45 minutes from the terminal. On the
road to Playa Perú, ask the driver to let you off at Río María
which you follow uphill for about half an hour before arriving at
superb natural pools formed by the river which then rushes down
in magnificent waterfalls. You can swim here, of course, but come
here during the week, or the place will be crowded. Playa Perú is
a glorious beach with white sand, numerous palm trees and clear
water.

Cuero y Salado Refugio (*$10; 40 km west of La Ceiba*). This park
is named after the two main rivers that run through it. Sea cows,
jaguars and monkeys are just some of the animals found here. Take
the bus towards Tela and get off at **Unión Porvenir**. From there it
will take you an hour to go 8 kilometres in a small, manually-
powered car on train tracks (*$8*). The park harbours both land and
water ecosystems which are connected by little waterways that
widen out into channels. There are also many migrating and swamp
birds. Don't forget to bring your lunch and your water, and even
your camping equipment in case you want to spend the night. For
information or a permit, go to FUCSA, one street north and three

PRACTICAL INFO

Transportation: There is only one bus station in La Ceiba, halfway between the airport and the city. You can get there by taxi or by bus from Parque Central. Buses leave every half hour for **Tela** ($1 for a 2-hour trip); every hour and a half for **Trujillo** ($3 and a 4-hour trip); every hour for **San Pedro Sula** ($2 and a 4-hour trip). For **Tegucigalpa** there is a bus at 6am and 3:30 pm, $6 and a minimum travelling time of 7 hours. Buses generally leave between 5am and 6pm.

Boat: The new quay is 6 km to the east of the city. The only way to get there is by taxi ($5). Boats going to the **Islas de la Bahía** depart from here. During the week, boats go to **Roatán** at 3:30pm (except Monday, at 5am); the trip takes 2 hours and costs $11. The boats leave at 11am on Saturday and at 7am on Sunday.

To Útila: The boat makes the hone-hour trip during the week at 10am from the same quay and costs $10. There are no trips to Útila on the weekend.

We suggest you arrive half an hour before the departure time to get a spot and not to miss the boat.

Money: Bancomer, on Parque Central, changes traveller's cheques and is even open on Saturday morning.

Tourist Information: There is a 24-hour information service for travellers at the hotel **Colonial** on Avenida 14 de Julio just south of Calle 6.

Mail and **Telephone:** For mail go to Avenida Morazán at the corner of Calle 13, southwest of the park. The Hondutel building is closer, on Avenida 1 at the corner of Calle 5.

Internet: The **Internet Café** (*hondusoft@gbm.hn*) is situated in the Centro Comercial Panoyotti. You can surf, use the e-mail and even chat. Open from 8am to 9pm, Monday through Saturday.

Spanish courses: The **Centro Internacional de Idiomas** gives week-long courses for $130, which includes staying with a local family. For information call ☎40-0574.

to the west of Parque Central in La Ceiba. You can reserve a shelter at the office for $2 per night.

Museo de mariposas y otros insectos (*$1; Colonia El Sauce, Segunda Etapa, Casa G-12*). The 5,000 species of butterflies from this country make up a good part of the museum's exhibition, and there are 1,000 other insects as well. Educational for anyone interested.

Ⓩ Pico Bonito (*the entrance to the park is 12 km west of La Ceiba*). This is the largest park in Honduras, created in 1987. The peaks of Pico Bonito and Santa Bárbara in the park are so high (2,435 m and 2,480 m respectively) that you can see them even when heading away from La Ceiba, particularly when you are on the quay or on a boat going to the islands. To get to the park, take the bus Ruta 1 de Mayo from Parque Manuel Bonilla and get off at **Armenia Bonito**, then walk five kilometres until you come to a little hut, which is the information office. You can camp here, as well. A few paths follow the Río Bonito where you can swim, and even have splendid views of the Caribbean Sea. If you want to climb Pico Bonito itself, you need a guide because there are no paths. Watch out for poisonous "spearhead" snakes. It takes 7 to 10 days to make the trip. An ex-Contra owns a house in the jungle and makes the rounds of the quay at Le Ceiba almost every day. He'll take you to see the spectacular waterfalls of Las Gemelas (200 m) or to the summit of Pico Bonito, for a fee. You'll recognize him by his tattoos and by his motorcycle which tows a small trailer.

La Ceiba

Ⓢ

SWEET DREAMS

Hotel Los Ángeles (*$2, Av. La República and Calle 6*). ▶ Old wooden buildings whose rooms are poorly ventilated. Not expensive, but extremely noisy with lumpy beds. Shared bathrooms. Recommended only as a last resort.

Ⓩ Hotel California (*$6; Calle 6, a little to the east of Avenida República, 442-0303*). ▶ Much better, with a small interior courtyard and well-ventilated rooms with private bathrooms. The owner is friendly.

Hotel Granada (*$9; Av. Atlántida, near Calle 6, 443-0181*). ▶ Conveniently located between the park and the quay, this hotel also has a little restaurant and a telephone in the entrance hall. Each of the 58 rooms has its own shower and fan.

La Ceiba

$

BON APPETIT

My Friend (*Zona Viva, runs alongside Calle 1 towards the east*). ▣ As its name indicates, this restaurant is a very friendly place, and the thatched roof makes it more welcoming. It's popular for its grilled fish.

El Canadiense (*Av 14 de Julio and Calle 1*). ▣ A little resto-bar opened by a Quebecker a few years ago. Try your French if you can speak it, and eat good food all day long. You can also play pool here.

Ⓩ **Pulpusería Universitaria** (*Calle 1 before Av. 14 de Julio*). ▣ Excellent Honduran food in a friendly place that's open in front.

Islas de la Bahía

This archipelago, a rich coral reef, is made up of three main islands: Útila, Roatán and Guanjo. They are situated about 35 kilometres from La Ceiba, but the atmosphere is totally different. Their heritage is more English than Spanish and a good number of the inhabitants speak only English. In fact, for a long time, these islands were controlled by the British who transferred their unmanageable slaves here from St. Vincent during the last century. This explains the Afro-Caribbean makeup of the population today. Many of the tourists who come to Honduras go exclusively to the islands. There are other places to see, but the islands' splendour can't be matched; a visit to Honduras would not be complete without a trip to some of them! Life is more laid back here than on the mainland, with fewer cars and a resolutely West Indian atmosphere.

Útila

Ⓩ We've only written about Útila because it's the least expensive of the islands. Anyone going to Roatán will have to pay more and probably won't be reading this book. Yes, Roatán does have a variety of places to scuba-dive and it's the only spot where you can swim with dolphins. But Útila is sure to please in all other respects. It's a real oasis of palm trees with a beach running around the whole island like the white of an egg surrounding the yolk. Útila's only drawback is that one day, you'll have to leave. Talk to all the people who came for a week and are still here three years later — there are more than you

PRACTICAL INFO

Transportation: The only place to go and come from Útila is **La Ceiba**. Generally, you take the ferry which leaves Monday to Friday at 11:30am for $10. Arrive at the quay at least 30 minutes before departure. You can also take a plane to go or come from the island. This alternative costs a little more ($17), but takes only 15 minutes instead of an hour. Several stands sell tickets, including the one a little to the right of Bancahsa.

Money: Bancahsa is opposite **Captain Morgan**, by the quay. You can cash traveller's cheques and get advances on Visa only.

Tourist Information: There is no real office, but the people at **Gunter's** will answer your questions. They also organize boat trips to the smaller islands west of Útila.

Mail: It's directly opposite the quay next to **Captain Morgan**. Open from 8am to 5pm and Saturday before noon.

Telephone: Hondutel is situated opposite **College of Diving** to the left when you leave the quay. The hours are the same as for the mail. You can also telephone from the counter at the entrance of **Reef Bar and Grill** (see "Bon Appetit").

would think. This is a scuba diving paradise and the cheapest place in the tropics to become certified. Take note that the beaches near town are not suitable for swimming and that the electricity is shut off at midnight every night. Don't walk around alone at night and avoid the quay near the bridge.

Scuba diving. You'll have to stay a while to discover all the great diving areas. As soon as you get off the ferry, representatives from the different schools will swarm around you advertising their discounts. Take your time; there's no hurry. The first thing you should look for when choosing a school is how it takes care of its equipment. Don't go to a school whose masks, flippers, regulators and wet suits are messily piled up. Next, choose an instructor you like and make sure you get along well with the person because you're going to spend three days together. Some schools have package deals that include accommodations; one of these is **Útila Watersports** whose personnel are very pleasant and professional. Schools with the best equipment are **Gunter's** (☎425-3350), **Captain Morgan** (☎425-3161) and **College of Diving** among others. Prices vary according to the season. In June 1998, the basic course (open water, including five dives) cost $125.

Excursions. Rent a boat at **Gunter's** for $10 a day and follow the coast west towards the **lagoon** after **Blue Bayou** point. You will soon be in the canal that connects the north and south of the island. Take your snorkelling gear so you can explore the reefs on the north shore if the sea is not too rough. You can also walk to **Pumpkin Hill** by following the road that starts at the quay and goes northeast for four kilometres. The view is not fantastic, but legend has it that pirates buried their treasure in the caves not far from here. We recommend renting a bicycle. Near the airport, at the eastern end of Útila, you can follow a path that runs along the east coast for two kilometres and ends at **Big Bight** Bay. Here you can admire the natural pools of water, but the coast is rocky so wear sandals.

Útila	## SWEET DREAMS
$	

Hotel Crosscreek (*$9; tv, to the right of the quay, behind the school of the same name,* ☎*425-3134*). ▶ Superb rooms on the water. Packages are available with the Crosscreek School.

Hotel Celena (*$7; 500 m east of the quay*). ▶ One of the only hotels to have a generator, which means there's electricity all night and, most importantly, a fan working all the time. Comfortable and clean with individual or shared bathrooms. This is the hotel included in the package deal with Útila Watersports: $130 for the course including three nights at the hotel.

Laguna del Mar (*$11; a little further than the Celena,* ☎*425-3103*). ▶ Very clean with fans and screens on the windows. A beautiful terrace but no electricity (no fans) after midnight. A man sells cinnamon rolls made by his wife from a stand next to the hotel. Get there early to enjoy one because the secret is now out!

Útila	## BON APPETIT
$	

Reef Bar and Grill (*on the south side to the east of the quay*). ▶ Enjoy large portions of grilled chicken served outside on a magnificent terrace.

Útila

$

BON APPETIT

Seven Seas (*a little further away from the Reef*). ▣ Typical food that might upset your stomach if you aren't used to it. If you think you can stomach it, try the *baleadas con ensalada y huevos*.

Ⓩ **Bundu Café** (*a little before the Reef*). ▣ Good for coffee and light snacks in the morning and at lunch. A friendly atmosphere and an interesting collection of books of all kinds.

Top Three Lies Told in Útila

1) I'm leaving tomorrow
2) I'm not drinking tonight
3) I love you

Trujillo

Trujillo was founded when Christopher Columbus arrived in 1502, on his fourth and final voyage. The city was the capital for a time before being subjected to pirate attacks that lasted for several centuries. In fact, it was abandoned a number of times by its inhabitants before the old fort with cannons was built to protect this strategic point of land at the far end of a marvellous bay. The city is perched on a cliff that you can easily descend to reach the sea, where you can swim and try to resist its hypnotic power. Trujillo is famous for being the last stand of William Walker. In his attempt to conquer the city, he was shot dead at point-blank range.

Fortaleza de Santa Bárbara (*$1; to the right of the central square*). This old fortress dates from 1599 and was built to repel attacks from pirate ships. Some of the foundations remain, along with about a dozen large cannons. It's nothing special, but the view of Trujillo Bay is wonderful.

Aguas Calientes (*$3; 7 km in the direction of Tocoa*). Take a bus and ask the driver to let you off at the hot springs. You'll arrive in front of four pools of sulphurous water with magical healing properties right near a luxury hotel.

PRACTICAL INFO

Transportation: All buses stop next to Parque Central before leaving. They go on the hour for **La Ceiba**, **Tela** and **San Pedro Sula**. Some leave beginning at 2pm and cost between $3 and $5. The bus for **Santa Fe** goes to the beach at 9:30am *(40¢)*.

Money: The banks are situated around Parque Central and you shouldn't have any problem changing traveller's cheques or getting advances on Visa or MasterCard.

Mail and Telephone: One street south of the church.

Spanish courses: the **Centro Internacional de Idiomas** (☎44-4777) and **Ixbalanque** (☎44-4461) have weekly courses with four hours of classes a day. You can stay with a family for $85 a week.

Parque Nacional Capiro y Calentura (*to the south towards the Villa Brinkley*) A path goes past this villa and continues up the mountain. The hike takes about five hours and for security reasons it's better not to go alone. A few monkeys will surely surprise you on your way up. On a fine day you can see the Islas de la Bahía in the distance.

Garifuna villages (*take the beach road to the west*). **Santa Fe, San Antonio** and **Guadalupe** are three small Garifuna villages a dozen kilometres from Trujillo. You can get there by walking on the beach or hopping a bus. The Garifunas are friendly people who are fun to hang out with and make the freshest fish in the country. The sparkling white beaches are never-ending.

Trujillo

SWEET DREAMS

Hôtel Mar de Plata (*$6; four blocks west of the park*, ☎434-4458). ▶ Not always clean and noisy at times. Get a room upstairs. The owners are friendly and fans are included.

Hotel Emperador (*$8; two streets west of the park*, ☎434-4446). ▶ Small rooms where you don't want to spend too much time. The usual conveniences in a pleasant setting. An interior courtyard.

Trujillo $	**SWEET DREAMS**

Hotel Trujillo (*$10; near the market* ☎434-4202).
▶ Well situated and sparkling clean. There's a shower, a toilet and a fan in each room.

Trujillo $	**BON APPETIT**

Restaurante Pantry (*two streets from the park*).
▶ Open all day long. A varied menu with something for everyone. Good pizza and a bar that makes all kinds of cocktails.

Restaurante Granada (*near the Emperador*). ▶ The personnel are very friendly and the food varies from fresh fish Garifuna style to a full breakfast. A good choice.

El Patio (*three streets from the park*). ▶ The food is good and the staff is amiable, but they often serve only one dish, which limits your choice. Inexpensive.

⏭ EAST OF TRUJILLO ⏮

The vast **Mosquitia** territory is sparsely populated and has a high rate of malaria, but is just bursting with nature. Expeditions are arranged to pristine beaches or to cross the thick jungle along one of the *ríos* that disappear into the once impenetrable vegetation. Flights from La Ceiba or the capital arrive in **Palacios** and **Puerto Lempira** almost every day. Accommodations are difficult to find and you can only pay for them in Honduran currency, which you must change beforehand. Excursions into the jungle are organized at the two villages mentioned above; however, renting boats, pirogues and other small craft is expensive. Your best bet is to hang around on the quays and find a freighter or another boat carrying goods that can take you along.

⏭ WESTERN AND SOUTHERN HONDURAS ⏮

Western Honduras boasts the country's largest archaeological site, Copán. Situated near the Guatemalan border, it was one of the most grandiose centres of the Mayan Empire. Looking at these ruins, you cannot help but be amazed. The region itself is hilly and there are several national parks, one containing the country's highest peak. There are also pretty little villages from the colonial era where traditional handicrafts are made. More to the north is the city of San Pedro Sula, an important industrial centre which might only be of interest to prospective business people.

Southern Honduras is a small strip of land squeezed between El Salvador and Nicaragua, with 124 kilometres of coastline on the Pacific Ocean. The beaches here are definitely less attractive than those on the Caribbean coast, but the small volcanic islands in the Golfo de Fonseca are interesting. Inland the heat is stifling.

San Pedro Sula

It's interesting to know that San Pedro is the fastest growing city in Central America because of its clothing industry and its strategic position right in the heart of banana-plantation country, but we'll skip this to tell you that this city of 650,000 inhabitants is a necessary transit point for anyone intending to travel through the whole county. Try to make your bus connection quickly so you don't have to stay here. Not that it's dangerous, it's just boring. Also, the heat in the city is much more suffocating than on the coast where there's always a breeze.

Museo de Antropología y Historia *(35¢; Av. 3 and Calle 4 north)*. Closed Monday. This museum has a special collection on the first inhabitants of the fertile Ulúa valley, where the city is situated. A good choice if you have time to kill in this city.

Parque Nacional Cusuco *($9; 20 km east of San Pedro)*. This park encompasses two summits of more than 2,200 metres which you can climb following paths that take between one hour and two days. The paths are easy to follow because they're old logging roads. You can get information at the **Fundación Hector Rodrigo Pastor Fasquelle** (Av. 7 and Calle 1 north, ☎521-014 or 596-598, ≈576-620). The park contains the highest elevation of pine forests in Central America, and you can walk through this forest from the coast all the way to Tegucigalpita.

PRACTICAL INFO

Transportation: To Tegucigalpa, Calle 6 between Avenida 6 and 7, buses leave about every hour from 5:45am and cost $4 for a six-hour trip.

To **La Ceiba:** Av. 2 Sur between Calles 5 and 6 South. The three-hour trip costs $2, buses leave every hour between 5am and 6:30pm.

To **Copán:** Calle 6 between Avenidas 6 and 7. Buses leave at 7am, 11am, 1pm, 2pm and 3pm (six hours of travelling for $3).

Money: The **Banco Atlántica**, on the Parque Central, has the best exchange rate for changing traveller's cheques.

Tourist Information: Sectur, Calle 4 between Avenidas 3 and 4 North. They sell maps of the region.

Mail and Telephone: Mail at Avenida 3 between Calles 9 and 10 South. Hondutel is situated at the corner of Avenida 4 and Calle 4 South.

San Pedro Sula

SWEET DREAMS

Hotel Brisas del Occidente (*$5; Av. 5 and Calle 7 South, ☎522-309*). ▶ Most of the rooms are spacious, but ask specifically for one with a window. Cleanliness is minimal but okay.

Hotel San José (*$8; Av. 5 and Calle 7 South, ☎571-208*). ▶ Really not expensive and very clean. Rooms are located in a new building where a TV and purified water are available in the entrance hall.

San Pedro Sula

BON APPETIT

Café Skandia (*on the north side of the park, the ground floor of the Gran Hotel Sula*). ▶ Open 24 hours. They serve good club sandwiches, waffles, salads and many other good things.

Comedores (*Av. 17 and Calle 10*). ▶ You'll find many stalls here where Honduran food is served.

Copán Ruinas

The small town of Copán is the closest urban area to the ruins, only one kilometre from the famous Mayan site. Because it is well-situated high up in the mountains, its climate is always comfortable. People in the town are friendly and seem less afraid of talking to you than elsewhere, probably because they're used to the hordes of tourists who come to visit the ruins. Cobblestone streets and houses of colonial architecture create a peaceful atmosphere. Other interesting, small colonial towns scattered in the verdant surroundings of Copán are **Santa Rita**, **Santa Rosa de Copán** and **Gracias**.

ⓩ **The Ruins** (*$10; a 10 min. walk from the centre of town*). The entrance fee includes a guide who will explain the historical and cultural importance of the site. An enormous museum has opened at the site which costs $5. A more modest museum in town costs $2. You should visit the new museum first because it'll put you in the mood for the ruins. More than 2,000 sculptures, steles and other objects are in the museum. We advise you to spend a whole day here because the site is enormous and you can walk around for hours. Several monuments are still buried in the surrounding jungle. Archaeologists believe the town was at its peak around AD 500 and had about 20,000 inhabitants.

Trucks leave near the soccer field and at the Paty hotel for **Aquas Calientes** (*$1.10; 20 km north of town*). You can bathe in these sulphurous waters, but stay clear of the zone where the water is boiling!

PRACTICAL INFO

Transportation: Trucks leave all day long for the **Guatemalan** border and charge $2.50. Bargain them down if they charge more. Buses for **San Pedro Sula** leave the hotel Patty at 4am, 5am, 6am, 7am and 3pm (six-hour trip for $3). To return to **Tegucigalpa** you must pass through here.

Money: The **Banco de Occidente** on Plaza Central changes US money and traveller's cheques.

Mail: Near the old museum, open during the week and Saturday morning.

Telephone: **Hondutel** is situated in the same place as the post office, and is open every day from 8am to 9pm. There is also a fax service but only during the week.

Internet: At the Gemelos hotel.

Spanish courses: Ixbalanque (☎983-432, ⊷576-215) gives private lessons for four hours a day. You stay with families where your food is provided. The total cost is $125 a week.

Copán Ruinas

$

SWEET DREAMS

Hotel Los Gemelos (*$5; slightly to the south of the bridge that leads to the ruins*). ▣ Plain, clean and friendly. Wake-up and laundry service. The coffee is good, free and to be enjoyed in the beautiful garden!

Hotel California (*$8; opposite the Gemelos*, ☎651-4077). ▣ A little more expensive, but very comfortable and safe. The evening meal is delicious and the decor of the place is original. Recommended for backpackers.

Copán Ruinas

$

BON APPETIT

Llama del Bosque (*two streets from the park, after the old museum*). ▣ Spaghetti, chicken, hamburgers and other dishes in big portions. Very popular with tourists.

(Z) **Tunkul Bar** (*opposite the Llama del Bosque*). ▣ Soups, salads and chicken or beef burritos. It has a superb terrace where you can stargaze, dance to reggae music or simply relax while you eat breakfast.

Golfo de Fonseca

Most people fly right by this region to get to El Salvador, Tegucigalpa or Nicaragua. Sure, the cotton fields and producers don't merit too much attention, but the area is interesting in a number of respects. You'll appreciate the Golfo de Fonseca, especially once you leave the excessive heat of the inland cities where everyone moves so very slowly because it's the only way to stay cool. Choluteca, the main city in this region, has its charm, but it's too far from the coast for a breeze or for the magnificent sunsets.

Isla del Tigre

If there's one place to visit in southern Honduras, this is
definitely it. The many abandoned buildings give the place an
eerie feel. The main town on the island, Ampala, was once a
thriving seaport, but it lost this title to San Lorenzo on the
mainland. Sir Francis Drake landed here several centuries ago,
and legend has it that pirates hid their treasures here. The
island has beautiful beaches where you can swim and camp, but
they're nothing like those on the Caribbean coast.

Excursions. The island has an extinct volcano that is about
750 metres high. The hike up is along a road that goes right to
the summit where there is a US army base. The view of the gulf
and the islands is impressive. Bring a lunch. The tour of the
island can be made in half a day.

Beaches. Playa Grande and Playa Negra are situated 1.5 kilometres
and 3 kilometres from Amapala, respectively. The sand is of the
dark volcanic type, the water is very warm and the waves gentle.

Fishing. Fishermen will take you on board with them for a fee.
Walk around and look for them on the beach. Better yet, approach
them when they return at the end of the day and set up a time and
a place for the next morning.

PRACTICAL DETAILS

Transportation: To get to
Isla del Tigre and Ampala,
take a bus (Avenida 6 and
Calle 24, from Tegucigalpa,
at 6am, 10am, 2pm and 6pm)
for **Choluteca** and get off at
San Lorenzo. From San
Lorenzo, buses leave regularly for **Coyolito** where you
take a boat to the island.
The boat leaves when it's
full (10 people) and costs
40¢. It takes at least half a
day to get there from Tegucigalpa.

Money: Banco El Ahorro
Hondureño.

Isla del
Tigre

SWEET DREAMS

Pensión Internacional (*$3; near the quay*).
▶ Dilapidated but colourful. Try to get a room
on the ground floor because the natural ventilation makes all the difference.

Isla del Tigre	**SWEET DREAMS**
$	**Hotel Al Mar** (*$3; Playa Grande*). ▶ Situated in magnificent surroundings near the beach and the mountain, with fans in each room. The **naval base** on the Playa Negra road has clean, air-conditioned rooms for up to 12 people. It's $12 for two, but the rooms are extremely comfortable and the place is charming.

Isla del Tigre	**BON APPETIT**
$	**Comedores** (*Nuevo Mercado Municipal*). ▶ Clean restaurants that serve traditional dishes such as beans, rice and chicken. **Miramar** (*near the port and the quay*). ▶ This restaurant and others nearby serve good meals including fresh and yummy seafood.

||||| There's always something going on in Nicaragua. When it's not an earthquake, it's political tensions. The 1931 and 1972 quakes marked the country as much as the bombings ordered by a dictator desperately clinging to power.

||||| The largest country in Central America, Nicaragua has many impressive sights, with its dramatic landscape of volcanic mountains interspersed with tropical jungles and abundant plant life. There are even volcanoes right in the middle of Lake Nicaragua, the larger of the country's two vast interior lakes (52 and 148 km long). The mountains in the western part of the country slowly give way to the mosquito-infested flatlands on the Atlantic coast.

||||| An unusual country where peace is hard to come by, Nicaragua suffered under the Somoza dictatorship (father and son) from the 1930s to 1979, when the Frente Sandinista de Liberacion Nacional (FSLN, established in 1961) came to power following the civil war which had raged for several years. But even this didn't guarantee peace, since Nicaraguans now had to contend with Western opposition to their regime.

||||| Because Nicaragua was seen as a communist enclave in the Americas, the United States imposed economic sanctions on the country in the 1980s. In fact, they spared no effort in trying to oust the regime, and used money garnered on the black market through an unsuccessful sale of arms to Iran to finance a group of contras trained in Honduras. Jungle combat lasted several years, and did not make things any easier for the Sandinista government which had just come into power.

||||| The Sandinistas were not re-elected in 1990, nor in 1996. Rather, the party of Violeta Chamorro, the widow of a journalist murdered during the civil war, has been president ever since. The economy is idling and the country wants to build a 377-kilometre-long railroad from coast to coast to attract some of the traffic — and profit — that currently sails down the Panama Canal.

||||| Despite its extreme poverty, the country is an interesting place to visit, and you'll see many careworn faces of people who have suffered great hardships. In fact, with all the turmoil in the country's past, one wonders how it managed to survive at all. One thing is for sure; it is undergoing reconstruction, and there's a lot of work to be done.

holidays and festivals

Maundy Thursday and Good Friday of the Semana Santa (2000: April 20 and 21; 2001: April 12 and 13).

May 1: Labour Day.
July 19: Anniversary of the 1979 Sandinista Revolution.
September 14: Anniversary of the Battle of San Jacinto.
September 15: Anniversary of the Independence of Central America.
November 1: All Saints Day.
November 2: All Souls Day (The Day of the Dead).
December 7 and 8: Commemoration of the Immaculate Conception.

Most businesses are closed during the Semana Santa, and from
December 24 to January 2.

▶▶ MANAGUA ◀◀

With its population of over a million people spread over 600 very
diversified neighbourhoods, none of which are all that reputable,
Nicaragua's sprawling capital is home to one quarter of the
country's population. If it takes a long time to find downtown,
it's for good reason: within a period of only fifty years, it was
devastated by two earthquakes and one civil war. In any case,
even if there were a downtown, it would be difficult to find your
way there, since most of the streets are not signed out.
¡Bienvenido a Managua!

The business sectors are scattered through the city haphazardly,
with nary a thought to urban planning. Given that Somoza diverted
most of the international aid sent to rebuild the capital core
after the 1972 earthquake for his personal use, and then bombed
the city centre after backed into a corner by the Sandinistas in
1979, the downtown mainly consists of ruins and vacant lots,
interspersed with a few modern buildings that survived: a truly
surrealistic landscape.

The country incurred an astronomical debt because of the economic
sanctions imposed by the Americans, so few reconstruction
projects have been undertaken, and even those that were completed
did little to improve the area.

This city has come of age the hard way: it has seen dictators,
wars, earthquakes, and was the only socialist enclave on the
continent. During the eighties, culture came to life in certain
sectors where intellectual circles gathered to discuss the state
of the world over countless cups of coffee. Painters, sculptors,
musicians, political refugees and international aid workers all
converged here, creating a highly stimulating atmosphere in
Managua over the past decade. This movement has dwindled, but
pockets of it still exist here and there.

Lago de Managua

N

MANAGUA – CENTRO HISTÓRICO

1. Monument to the Heros of the Revolution
2. Plaza de la República
3. Palacio Nacional
4. Catedral de Santiago
5. Teatro Nacional Rubén Darío
6. Malecón
7. Casa Julio Cortázar
8. Museo Nacional de Managua
9. Huellas de Acahualinca

©.zone

Airport

AV. Julio Buitrago Urroz

LOS ANGELES

BUENOS AIRES

SANTO DOMINGO

Parque Luis Alfonso Velásquez

Asamblea Nacional

Centro de Convenciones Olof Palme

Avenida Bolívar

Barrio Martha Quezada

SAN SEBASTIÁN

SAN ANTONIO

Telcor

Dupla Norte

Dupla Sur

Pista Juan Pablo II

JULIO BUITRAGO

Carretera del Sur

Calle 27 de Mayo

Diagonal de los Martires

Calle 15 de Septiembre

SANTA ANA

JAVIER GUARA

Calle El Triunfo

Cemetery

1. Restaurante
   Antojitos
2. Hotel
   Intercontinental
3. Mural
4. Catedral
   Metropolitana
   de la Purísima
   Concepción

©zone

Map labels:

Radial Santo Domingo

BUENOS AIRES

Avenida Simón Bolívar

Calle José Martí

JORGE DIMITROV

Paseo Tiscapa

Catedral Metropolitana

Avenida Rubén Darío

Laguna de Tiscapa

Avenida Universitaria

Avenida Bolívar

Cine Cabora

TricaLBus

Femel

Cine Dorado

MARTHA QUEZADA

Calle 27 de Mayo

Paseo Tiscapa

Politécnica Nicaragüense

JONATHAN GONZÁLEZ

Avenida Monumental

LAS PALMAS

EL CARMEN

BOLOÑIA

BOSQUES DE BOLOÑIA

Plaza de España

RENE CISNEROS

Pista de la Municipalidad

Benjamín Zeledón

ALTAGRACIA

EL RECREO

Avenida Mariano Fiallos

PISTA EL Recreo

Managua is located on the south shore of the lake of the same name. From the shore, you can see the mountaintops across the lake, the most impressive being Momotoma, which rises 1,360 metres. Unfortunately you can't swim in the lake, at least not around the capital, because the water is very polluted.

The Martha Quezada *barrio* (neighbourhood) is probably the best place to stay if you want to be close to downtown (only 15-odd city blocks away) without driving yourself crazy. The friendly residential area has good budget hotels and pleasant little restaurants, and you're sure to meet up with other travellers who are as out of their element in this city as you are.

The silence that pervades the streets of this city that lies half in ruins can be deceptive. It almost seems to be hiding something, and you get the feeling that this city, which has seen so many hardships in its time, is waiting to see whether the future will bring a reprieve from violence and poverty, or still more suffering.

The **Hotel Intercontinental** (*Av. Bolívar and Laguna de Tiscapa*). This hotel is a good place to start from because from here you can walk down the Avenida Bolívar to Lake Managua (2 km), passing through the old city. We do not necessarily recommend that you eat at the Restaurante Antojitos along the way (it's expensive!), but take a peek at the photos in the dining room to get an idea of what the city looked like before the earthquakes, bombing, and other catastrophes. No need to order anything; a simple smile should be enough to let the waiters know you only want to see the pictures. The Intercontinental can be easily recognized from afar because of its weird pyramid shape.

Plaza de la Revolución (or "de la República," depending on the prevailing mood and political ideology) (*Bolívar and Revolución*). Near the lake, there's a profusion of historical buildings and ruins that serve as stark reminders of the nation's troubled past. The Plaza de la Revolúcion is the heart of the country, and is the place from which Somoza went into exile on July 19, 1979 (he was assassinated soon afterwards in Paraguay). Since then, a massive demonstration is held here every year to mark the anniversary. The rest of the time, the place looks like the immense parking lot of a bankrupt shopping centre.

Catedral de Santiago (*east side of the square*). It withstood the first earthquake in 1931, but not the second in 1972. Though it was partially restored in 1995, there is still some work to be done. You can't visit the cathedral during certain times that are set aside for reconstruction work. And whatever you do, do not visit the cathedral alone, since this is a prime area for theft. Your chances of being robbed are even greater on the upper floors, so if you want to get closer to Jesus, stick to a safer means of worship. The tomb of Fonseca, the founder of Frente Sandinista Liberacion Nacional, is located on the east side of the square.

Palacio Nacional (*south side of the square*). Portraits of Sandino and Fonseca were taken down after the Sandinistas lost their majority. This was the spot where the Sandinistas took the entire National Assembly hostage a year before toppling Somoza. The Assembly has since moved, and the building now houses the Department of Finance.

Teatro Nacional Rubén Darío (*north of the square*). Because it was of relatively new construction (built between 1966-1999), it managed to withstand the 1972 earthquake. Plays, concerts and conferences are held in this building which is named after the country's most famous poet. It is elaborately fitted with marble and other luxurious fixings throughout.

Centro Cultural de Managua (*south of the square*). This structure was built in the ruins of the former Gran Hotel, and was fully restored by 1994. Various events are held here, including exhibits, theatre and dance performances. There is always a lot of activity going on around the many stores and workshops on both levels. Check the *Guía Facil* for special events.

Casa Julio Cortázar (*across from the Telcor*). This museum of fine arts was named after the Argentinean author, who wrote about Nicaragua during the Sandinista years. Supposedly open Wednesday to Sunday in the afternoon, but call ahead (✆222-7272) since this is not always the case.

Malecón (*at the far north end of Avenida Bolivar*). The seawall is the perfect place to end up after you've wandered through the streets and seen the buildings and ruins still left standing in the historic centre. Here, you can sit by the lake and enjoy the view of the Momotombo volcano on the other side. Vendors sell drinks and snacks here. A reminder: the lake water is not clean enough for swimming, let alone drinking.

Managua	
	ⓩ Barrio Martha Quezada (*west of the Hotel Intercontinental*). ▸ Peaceful area near the historical sites, with plenty of budget hotels. Ideal for meeting people and rehashing your Managua adventures.

ayer,
the
t

...aje Santos ($3; on the road to the Intercon-
...l, ☎02-23713). ▶ The most popular of the
budget hotels, but not the cleanest. It has shared
washrooms and a courtyard complete with hammocks
and rocking chairs. It serves local food.

Hospedaje Meza ($6; a couple of blocks east of
Santos, ☎02-22046). ▶ Its rooms are smaller and
sometimes even dirtier than Santos', but very,
very cheap. Indifferent staff. Curfew at 11pm.

Hospedaje Norma ($8; one block south and a half-
block east of the Cine Dorado, ☎02-23498). ▶ Lots
of foreign travellers stay here, but there is no
common room where you can swap stories. Nice
owners and affordable prices. Midnight curfew.

Managua

BON APPETIT

S

Kiosque Tica-Bus (across from the Tica Bus terminal). ▶ You eat standing up, but the food is
served quickly and at rock-bottom prices.

Comedor La Victoria (two blocks south of the Ciné
Cabrera). ▶ Good local food (rice, beans, meat).
Clean and friendly. If it's too hot, you can
sometimes sit in the shade of the palm trees.

Vecadi (one block north of the Intercontinental,
five blocks west and then a half-block north).
▶ A very popular place. Best to arrive early if
you go for supper. The portions are as big as the
crowds that come here!

Sara's (seven blocks west and one block south of
the Intercontinental). ▶ A popular meeting place
during the Sandinista years. Still affordable, and
you can meet up with plenty of gringos from all
over the world.

Managua

BON APPETIT

Mirna's Pancakes (*one block south and one block east of the Ciné Dorado*). ▣ At breakfast and lunch time, you get a large meal for your money. Friendly atmosphere where the owner will often sit and chat with clients.

Casa del Café (*Altamira de Lacmiel, one block up and one block south*). ▣ If you've had instant coffee for so long that you can't even remember what a good cappuccino tastes like, remind yourself by coming here. The meals and pastries are also delicious, but this café is more expensive.

the good life

Buena Nota (*Km 3.5, Carretera del Sur, ☎66-9797*). A bit out of the way and expensive. The decor is reminiscent of 1950s America, but the music is mainly Nicaraguan.

Cinemateca Nacional (*Centro Cultural*). Shows foreign and recent films.

Cinemas 1 y 2 (*Centro Comercial, Camino del Oriente, ☎267-0964*). Shows first-run American films dubbed in Spanish.

Día de la Revolución. Every July 19, the Revolution is commemorated with an immense gathering at the Plaza de la Revolución. Speeches are given and dances are held.

El Cipitio (*one block north, four blocks west and 1.5 blocks south of the Intercontinental*). The perfect place to hang out and drink cerveza at a small table, or have friendly discussions with other patrons. They also have good and inexpensive food.

El Repliegue. A long procession that begins at the Huembres market in Masaya to commemorate the defence of the population by the Sandinistas when the Gardia Nacional tried to stage a coup to remove the grass-roots social movements. This event is held the last Saturday in June.

Festival de Santo Domingo. The city's patron saint is celebrated every year from August 1 to 10. If you stop to consider this country's tragic history and the state of the capital, however, you might well wonder whether Santo Domingo appreciates — or even deserves — such a gathering. Maybe he just wants to be left alone? Thieves thrive in the carnival atmosphere, taking advantage of those who have had too much to drink. So stay alert and do not stray from your group.

La Cavanga (*next to Centro Cultural*, ☎228-1098). The most popular place with Managuans, it has elaborate cocktails, jazz bands and a lively atmosphere. A small kitchen serves food — the *ceviche* is especially good.

La Pinata (*next to the UCA*, ☎267-8216). If you like to boogie, you shouldn't miss this terrific open-air club where different music is played at deafening volumes on the various dance floors, which are all very close to each other. People from all walks of life come here to let loose.

La Ruta Maya (*near Montoya*, ☎222-5038). Young and cool. All styles of music are played. The concert sometimes gets off to a rather late start. There's a pleasant terrace and good food, but you'll have to pay a cover charge.

Lobo Jack (*Camino de Oriente*). You would have to travel hundreds of kilometres before coming across another discotheque as gigantic as this one.

Mansión Reggae (*Km 6, Carretera del Norte*, ☎289-4804). A warm, delightful tropical ambience. Reggae, salsa, merengue: the country's Caribbean side is celebrated here where people of all ages come to soak in the atmosphere.

Rancho Bambi (*Km 3.5, Carretera del Norte*). Same atmosphere as the Mansion Reggae, but slightly less expensive.

Teatro Nacional Rubén Darío (*Parque Central*, ☎222-3632). Classical music, dance or ballet. Phone them or consult the *Guía Facil* for information.

Videoteca (*one block northeast of Estatua Montaya*, ☎222-7092). Foreign films in English or with English subtitles, shown on a large television screen.

shopping

Mercado Oriental (*southeast of downtown, take the MR3 bus north from the Barrio Martha Quezada*). You will find everything here, including the camera stolen on the Léon bus. Local crafts galore.

Mercado Huembes (*take the MR4 north of the Barrio Martha Quezada*). Not quite as huge as the Mercado Oriental, and not quite as smelly. It has a good selection of handicrafts.

Musical (*across from the craft section of the Mercado Huembes*). A great place to pick up local music not available in North America.

Centro Cultural de Managua (*near the Palacio National*) A wide array of handicrafts. Especially interesting the first Saturday of every month, when artists and craftspeople come from all over the country to sell their wares in the courtyard.

Liberia Amatl (*two blocks south of the Intercontinental*, ☎66-2485) Sells mainly Spanish literature.

Hotel Intercontinental (*Bolivar and Laguna de Tiscapa*) Good selection of books with a fair number in English.

▶▶ AROUND MANAGUA ◀◀

Huellas de Acahualinca (*Barrio de Acahualinca*, ☎266-5774; bus 06, 112, 123, 159 or 202). A small museum that preserves the footprints of human beings and animals who walked across the mud over 6,000 years ago.

Laguna de Tiscapa (*to the left of the Intercontinental*). This small park has a beautiful view of the city directly below and the statute of Sandino to the north.

Catedral Metropolitana de la Purísima Concepción (*Plaza de España*). Built in 1993, its style contrasts with the older churches found downtown. Central America is the only place where churches are still being built; it's worth the trip for this reason alone.

Murale (*Plaza de España and Parque de las Madres*). One of the only visible examples of this revolutionary art still remaining, since this form of expression was quite literally wiped out by the governments succeeding the Sandinista regimes. Bright colours and dramatic scenes dominate. The mural is not far off from the Catedral Metropolitana.

▶▶ THE SOUTHWEST
AND LAGO NICARAGUA ◀◀

The strip of land stretching south of Managua, between the Pacific coast and the huge Lake Nicaragua (148 km long and 50 km wide), is the most heavily populated area in the country. The history of Nicaragua is closely linked to its great lake, the tenth largest body of fresh water in the world. It is believed that some of the indigenous Olmèque people from Mexico migrated to the lake, via the Río San Juan, and settled on its peaceful islands long before Spain used it as a strategic transit point for precious goods. Artifacts dating from the ninth century attest to this. It is believed that Lago Nicaragua was linked to the Pacific Ocean long ago, before being closed off by a volcanic eruption. That the lake is home to the world's only species of freshwater shark lends credence to the argument.

Conquistadors and colonizers soon swarmed to this false peninsula lured by its rich volcanic soil that is favourable to agriculture. The volcanic chain runs the whole length of the southern Pacific coast of Nicaragua, with a few perfect cones looming up like islands in the middle of the lake.

In terms of the environment, this corner of Nicaragua boasts not only mountains, but also glorious, quiet beaches from which fishermen make a living. The summits to climb are also among the attractions that will lure passing sports buffs. More sedentary types, however, will be glad to learn that handicrafts here are as ubiquitous as volcanoes. What is more, old cities like Granada have interesting examples of colonial architecture — even more than in Managua, since earthquakes have been less devastating here.

Though the fertile soil made this a choice destination for the pioneers of South American colonization, the region cannot be said to be thriving today, even though 80 percent of the nation's economic activity is concentrated on the Pacific coast. Like most Latin American countries, Nicaragua is a poor nation that must comply with adjustment and economic-recovery measures dictated by the likes of the World Bank and the International Monetary Fund, that make up an economic-development plan for the country that has yet to prove itself useful.

Masaya

The capital of the smallest and most densely populated department in the country, Masaya is a city of 100,000 inhabitants with a rich indigenous past. Small wonder then, that myriad native handicrafts are to be found here, which are more and more commercially marketed (a far cry from ancestral traditions, which are nothing like modern-day capitalism). Masaya has the highest native population in the country. Ever since the conquest, they have fought more fiercely than other peoples to preserve their culture, and they continue the struggle even today. True to its

PRACTICAL INFO

Bus station *(near the market)*: buses leave for Managua *(45-minute trip for 40¢)* and Granada *(1-hour trip for 30¢)* every 20 minutes. Service to Jinotepe, via Niquinohomo, Masatepe, San Marcos and Diriamba is also provided every 20 minutes throughout the day. The train has been out of commission since 1994.

Money *(also near the market)*: Banks and money changers.

Tourist Info *(on the highway, between the two main streets that run into the city)*: useful if you speak Spanish, though the staff can sometimes get by in English.

Mail and Telephone: office on one side of the park.

rebellious tradition, the city was a Sandinista bastion during the 1979 revolution against Somoza.

Anyone passing through the region from late September to early October can whoop it up at a week-long festival honouring the town's patron saint, San Jerónimo. Other than that, there is an active volcano (Volcán Masaya) nearby, a fabulous body of water (Laguna de Apoyo) perfect for a dip, and an old fortress with ghosts, among other things.

Parque (Central) 17 de Octobre *(central square, in the heart of the city)* is the perfect starting point for going on a tour of the town. October 17 commemorates the day in 1977 when the Sandinistas stormed several of Somoza's outposts. Built in the 19th century, the Victorian-looking **Catedral Asunción**, with its richly adorned interior, is sure to attract your attention.

Laguna de Masaya *(six blocks west of the southwest corner of the park)*. After a few minutes' walk, you'll arrive at a promenade that offers a view over this lagoon, which seems calm from above. This is not the case, however, and swimming in it is dangerous. The place also offers a good view of Volcán Masaya, on the other side of the lagoon.

Centro de Artesanía Nacional *(by the lagoon)*. This school teaches traditional regional artistic techniques to budding local artisans and sells a few wares.

Barrio Monimbo *(five blocks south of the park, Calle San Sebastián)*. This district is home to the descendants of the native *Dariana* people. Several walls are painted with frescoes depicting conflicts with their enemies, from the Spanish to

Somoza's troops. On a lighter note, Monimbo is just the place to pick up local handicrafts (pottery, hammocks, wood carvings, etc.).

Mercado de Artesanía *(five blocks east of the southeast corner of Parque Central)*. With its reputation for being the largest native crafts market in the country, this huge jumble of merchandise measures up to the most colourful marketplaces in Latin America. Leather accessories, hammocks, native paintings and decorated pottery are its star attractions.

Cailagua *(20 minutes' walk, east of Monimbo)*, which, appropriately enough, means "where the water falls," is a 100-metre waterfall that cascades into the Masaya lagoon. The cliff is chock-full of petroglyphs. Day trippers also have access to a cave (Cueva de las Duendes), but must ask the locals how to get there.

Fortaleza de Coyotepe *(on the Managua-bound road, turn right 2 km past the Escuala Coyotepe sign)*. You must climb a hill to reach these Spanish ruins. Here, the United States stuck its nose into Nicaraguan affairs as early as the last century when a U.S.-backed Conservative dictator defeated a Nicaraguan Liberal who demanded the departure of the U.S. Marines. More recently, the abandoned fortress was a stronghold of Somozists who tortured their prisoners here and launched rockets on Masaya, below. It is said that the victims' ghosts haunt the place, so arm yourselves with flashlights and keep your eyes peeled...

Niquinohomo *(15 km south of Masaya; take the Rivas-bound bus that goes by every hour and ask the driver when to get off)*. Only hard-core history buffs will come here to see the birthplace of the one and only General Sandino, who inspired the Sandinista movement and the 1979 revolution. The former museum no longer receives subsidies since the downfall of the Sandinista government in 1990 — *quelle surprise!* It has become a library, with nary a commemorative plaque.

Parque Nacional Volcán Masaya *($2.50; Tue to Sun; entrance at Km 23 of the road linking Granada and Managua, ☎522-5415)*, which became Nicaragua's first national park in 1975, is just the place to observe a volcano in action. Those who forego driving here must climb a five-kilometre hill to reach the summit of the Santiago crater. Halfway up there is a little stopping place at the Centro de Interpretación Ambiental for those who wish to learn more about the place — or catch their breath. It is, in fact, a small museum (well-kept, with bathrooms) on the geological and cultural history of the park. The park itself offers several excursions for a pittance: the steepest one costs a whopping 25¢. There is but one restaurant, which seems to cater to *gringos* with lots of money. Thus, it is better to bring your own food and drink for the day, and put off buying pottery and other handicrafts until in Masaya. Camping is permitted here, but get the go-ahead from the museum first. Several volcanoes are still active. What is more, the sulphuric gas emanating from the Santiago crater is poisonous. Despite this, a colony of green parrots has somehow managed to build its nests nearby, without taking the slightest notice of the danger sign. To see the width of the crater, which is one of the major atmospheric contaminators on the planet, you have to climb to the top. Also at the top is a cross erected in 1529 by the Spanish, who believed that planting it there would stop the eruptions from the "mouth of hell"! If you leave at the crack of dawn, a single day will be enough to appreciate the splendour of the park. Getting an early start is also a wise idea because the sun beats down mercilessly.

Catarina y Laguna de Apoyo *(take the Rivas-bound bus and ask the driver to drop you off here)*. This country *pueblito* would be nothing without its famous *mirador* (lookout), which will inspire you or perhaps make you feel spiritually uplifted. From here you can see a lot: Granada's rooftops; the Apoyo Lagoon, the largest volcanic crater lake in the country; the great Lago Nicaragua and, on a clear day, the 1,363-metre Volcán Mombacho. Another bonus: you can swim in the lagoon's tranquil waters. Better yet: if you firmly believe in the legend, these waters will cure all your ills.

Masaya 	### SWEET DREAMS
	Masayita *($6; two blocks east of the park).* ▣ Cheaper, clean and well kept. Basic comfort.
	Hotel Regis *($10; four blocks north of the cathedral, on the main street).* ▣ A family-run hotel with shared bathrooms, firm mattresses (oh joy!) and breakfast on request. Just peachy.
	Hospedaje Rex *($8; half a block south of the Iglesia San Jerónimo).* ▣ They'll deny it, but the name of the place comes from the fact that it must have originally been a refuge for dogs. Atrocious, filthy, stinky and noisy. An ultimate last — we repeat, last — resort.

Masaya

$

BON APPETIT

Alegría *(one block north of the park)*. ▣ Nice and cheap. Grilled chicken, typical fare and lip-smacking pizzas are featured on the menu.

Jarochita *(one block north of the park)*. ▣ A friendly eatery chock-full of plants and colourful furniture. The place dishes out good Mexican grub.

Comedores *(at the market, five blocks east of the park)*. ▣ The name of the umpteen food stands in the market where typical *comidas corrientes* are served at $2 a pop.

Granada

Granada, the third most important city in the country, was founded in 1524 during the first Spanish expedition to the territory that is now Nicaragua. It quickly gained prominence because of its geopolitical position on the economic chessboard of the time. To place this in context: during the first two or three centuries, or until all the wealth was gone, the Spaniards robbed and pillaged the Amerindian civilizations in the area and dispatched the booty back to Spain. The preferred mode of transport in the colonies was by boat. Granada, situated on the northwest corner of Lake Nicaragua and easily accessible from the Atlantic by way of Río San Juan, became the ideal commercial port. It is said that the goods often came from as far away as Guatemala. All this was before the construction of the Panama Canal.

Granada became very rich and prosperous thanks to the good business sense of those who controlled the port and its opera-tions. Things remained pretty much the same until independence in 1820 marked the beginning of a rivalry with the conservative city of Léon. The more liberal Granada usually managed to keep the upper hand until the American hero William Walker (who tried to conquer Trujillo, Honduras, in 1860) arrived on the scene in his epic quest for total control of Central America, and managed to take control of the city for two years (1856-1858). He proclaimed himself President of the Republic (what a guy, that Bill!). When he finally found himself surrounded, he set fire to the city before escaping. Granada was seriously damaged and despite efforts at reconstruction, the city never regained its former glory. Moral of the story: It's always the Americans' fault!

PRACTICAL INFO

Bus Station *(eight blocks west and three blocks north of Parque Central).* Buses leave here for **Masaya** and **Managua** every 20 minutes from 4am to 4pm. Fare $1.

Two blocks west and four blocks south of the well-known Parque Central, is the departure point of buses going to **Rivas**. Buses run from 6am to 6pm for $1 and take two hours to get there.

Money *(one block west of the park).* Banco de América Central and Banco Centro are located in this area. Traveller's cheques can be cashed here, but for a better exchange rate, go to the money changers on the street. It is impossible to get cash advances on credit cards in Granada.

Tourist Information *(Hotel Alhambra, Parque Central).* There is no longer a tourist bureau in Granada, but the personnel in this hotel are helpful and will be able to answer your questions. They will also organize tours if you have the time and the money (does anyone ever have both?)

Mail and Telephone *(to the left of the cathedral, Parque Central).* Open until 10pm.

Despite these bizarre historic events, Granada remains interesting for its colonial atmosphere and its Catalan heritage, not to mention the marvellous Volcán Mombacho, which Walker did not succeed in destroying during his flight.

The **Parque Central** is almost always the best place to begin a tour of a city. This one has a **Catedral** (how typical!) dating from the sixteenth century, which was destroyed by Walker in 1857. It took half a century to rebuild it in the neoclassical style. Colonial architecture is best represented here by the municipal and cultural buildings around the park. And if you are interested in churches, there are three others to the west on Avenida Caimito, one on every two or three blocks.

Casa de los tres Mundes *(one street north of the park)* is probably the best example of restoration work in the city. Wars and Walker considerably damaged this building, but finally a foundation took charge of rebuilding it, paying particular attention to details evoking its colonial past. The result is absolutely beautiful. Today, the building is a fine arts school with a library and rooms for occasional exhibits. For 50¢, a map of the city and a brochure explaining the history of the building are available. The red house slightly to the right across the street was once Walker's home. Its red colour represents the blood that he spilt. If you like, you can spit on it. Heading one block north and one block east will bring you to the blue and white exterior of the **Iglesia y Antigua Convento de San Francisco** that Walker used as his general headquarters. This building was also burned and reconstructed (as usual). Try to go up the tower for an interesting view of the city.

The walk to Lago de Nicaragua *(Calle la Calzada, from the Parque Central)*. If you don't want to walk the kilometre from the Parque Central, a carriage drawn by pitiful horses can be hired to take you there for a paltry sum. On the way you will pass **Iglesia Guadalupe,** yet another neoclassical witness to the past. Along the riverbank to the right is the **Complejo Turistico,** a pleasant park with paths, picnic tables and benches, and a number of restaurants and bars.

Volcán Mombacho *(30 km south of Granada)*. This volcano lost its perfect cone some time before the arrival of the Spaniards and was thus reduced from 1,800 to 1,363 meters. No clearly marked path leads the way up, but it is possible to hire a guide. Information is available at the Hotel Alhambra beside the Parque Central.

Las Isletas *(on Lake Nicaragua)*. Some 300 small, emerald-green islets near Granada were created by the explosion of the cone of Volcán Mombacho several hundred years ago. Excursions by boat are available. The islands will thrill birders as well as anyone who just wants to take a pleasant outing on the lake. Don't miss the magnificent sight of Mombacho erupting and witness the ongoing evolution of the islands. A low-budget option is to plan an excursion for a Sunday afternoon, when a boat tours the islands starting at 2pm, for $3.30. The boat leaves from the restaurant at the end of the road, past the Complejo Turistico. Further south, **Puerto Asese,** a small village accessible by the morning bus, offers all sorts of excursions and package deals around the islands. This option is slightly more expensive *($12/hour)*.

Granada	**SWEET DREAMS**
	Hospedaje Vargas *($8; three blocks east of Parque Central, Calle Calzada)*. ▶ Rooms and bathrooms that are always clean. Kitchen access and no curfew.

Granada

$

SWEET DREAMS

Hospedaje Central *($6; Calle Calzada)*. ▣ Clean with a warm welcome. There is also a restaurant with good food and a garden to relax in.

Hospedaje La Calzada *($7; Calle Calzada, next to Iglesia Guadalupe)*. ▣ Standard rooms and ventilation. Super breakfasts and friendly atmosphere.

Granada

$

BON APPETIT

Comedor *(Calle Calzada, near the Hospedaje Cabrera)*. ▣ This no-name outdoor barbeque serves delicious grilled chicken at a great price.

Mercado *(two blocks south of Parque Central)*. ▣ The market is perfect for morning and noon meals. There's a good choice at modest prices. Forget about cleanliness, so only eat here if your stomach can handle it.

Oriente Lejano *(Av. Central, one block west of Parque Central)*. ▣ Inexpensive Chinese food. Open evenings only. The nearby **Rostícería Del Monte** will draw those who haven't had their fill of grilled chicken.

Rivas

This town is ideally located for globetrotters, since it is the last stop before Costa Rica. It is not only the closest port to the large islands in Lake Nicaragua, but also on the way to the beautiful Pacific coast beaches and San Juan del Sur.

Of course, the city was important long before tourism existed. The road to San Juan de Sur served as the starting point of the land passage to the Pacific Ocean, 30 kilometres to the southwest. This completed the continental voyage of passengers and merchandise that came from the Atlantic via the Río San Juan and Lake Nicaragua. Starting in 1849, Rivas was a mandatory stop for North Americans heading for the gold fields of California. Its history would not be complete without the appearance of William Walker, whose folly led him to Rivas in 1855.

Parque Central. Once again, the churches around the park are typical of the city's heritage. The exterior of **San Pedro** may need serious work, but the frescoes inside are worth seeing. They depict a Catholic boat defeating armies of Communists and Protestants: what symbolism!

San Jorge. This town, a half-hour from Rivas, is the port of entry for the Isla de Omotepe in Lake Nicaragua. Boats, either yachts or ferries, make the trip five times per day from Monday to Saturday, and twice on Sunday. The trip costs between $1 and $2.50 depending on what kind of boat you take (see "Practical Information" p 150).

Rivas

$

SWEET DREAMS

Hotel El Coco *($7; on the highway, near the place where buses leave for the border)*. ▶ A low-budget option, but somewhat noisy (bring earplugs). The rooms are small, but there is a garden and a good restaurant.

Hospedaje Lidia *($8; a half-block behind the Texaco on the highway)*. ▶ Cleaner than the above, but by this little family-run hotel is just as noisy as El Coco.

Hotel Nicaragua *($18; two blocks west of Parque Central)*. ▶ More expensive than the others, but much better. Quieter, with more comfortable beds and a fan.

Rivas

$

BON APPETIT

Rinconcito Salvadoreno *(Parque Central)*. ▶ Typical local fare. Really cheap.

Restaurante El Ranchito *(Near the Coco hotel)*. ▶ Chicken and friendly service are the norm here.

San Juan del Sur

Of all the beach towns that line the Pacific Coast, this is probably the most terrific. This sleepy *pueblo* is crowded with sun worshippers on weekends. To enjoy life at a slower pace, more in tune with the rhythm of the sea, it is best to come during the week. The village is in a lovely bay surrounded by beaches whose laid-back atmosphere is perfect for backpackers. We suggest you head for the beaches away from the port; they are less crowded and the water is cleaner. They are also great for surfing. (This

PRACTICAL INFO

Bus Station *(two blocks west and three blocks north of the park)*: Buses depart from here for **Managua** *(from 4am to 5pm; $1.40, travel time: 2.5 hours)*; for **Granada** *(take the Managua bus and transfer at Nandaime)*; for the border with **Costa Rica** *(from 6:30am to 2pm; $1, travel time: one hour)*; for **San Juan del Sur** *(all day; 60¢, 50 minutes)*.

Another bus station *(at the market)* is the departure point of the bus to *San Jorge* (where you take the boat that goes to **Onotepe**) on sunny days *(60¢; 45 min. by minibus)*.

Money: Banco Nacional de Desarrollo will sometimes cash traveller's cheques. It is better to bring enough cash with you for your stay here.

Mail and Telephone: northeast corner of the central square.

is becoming repetitive but, in 1857, William Walker came here and set up a military base).

On one side of the bay there is an Amerindian head carved out of stone by the best artist of them all: nature. At sunrise, a few indomitable souls can be seen practising the age-old occupation of fishing. And as for the famous sunset – we're still searching for fresh adjectives to describe the spectacular display! If you want to camp must contact the government office in town. This office can also provide a schedule of high and low tides: valuable information for surfers. One last warning: the sand fleas are voracious and so tiny that it is hard to see them. Stay cool, and arm yourself with the usual arsenal: mosquito netting, insecticide coils and insect repellent.

Playa Marsella *(7 km north of the village; 2 hours by foot or hitchhiking)* is the easiest of the beaches to get to away from San Juan. Take the road along the beach that goes by the Lago Azul hotel. Between two bridges, you will see a sign on the left that indicates the trail to Playa Marsella. It is a gorgeous beach with few people on it, and the nearby hills are fun to explore. Bring a picnic lunch.

ⓩ **The beaches south of San Juan** *(hitchhike or take the bus)*. **Playa del Coco** and **Playa Tamarindo**, two magnificent beaches, are the closest to San Juan del Sur. However, since they are still 15 kilometres away, so it is best to drive there. The bus

---

PRACTICAL INFO

Bus Station *(in the centre of the village)*. Buses depart for **Rivas** throughout the day *($1; travel time: one hour)*.

Money: Banco Nacional de Desarrollo will only exchange currency.

Mail and Telephone: two blocks south of Hotel Estrella.

---

that goes from Rivas to San Juan continues on to Ostional, after stopping at these two beaches. There aren't any hotels in Ostional, but you will have the beaches practically to yourself.

San Juan del Sur

SWEET DREAMS

Hospedaje Casa 28 *($8; near the beach and the minibus stop for Rivas)*. ▣ This is a good spot where the staff is friendly and know how to keep the place clean. Bring insecticide coils.

Hotel Estrella *($13; on the beach)*. ▣ Only rooms five and six have balconies. The walls do not touch the ceiling, so the rooms are naturally ventilated, but it is sometimes noisy. Popular with sixties' hippies, now in their fifties.

Buengusto *($8; across from the Estrella)*. ▣ More basic than the above. Friendly personnel and a good restaurant. The main advantage of staying here is that it's close to the beach.

San Juan del Sur

BON APPETIT

ⓩ **Casa Internacional Joxi** *(just east of the Estrella)*. ▣ Elaborate breakfast with crepes and fruit juice. The other meals are served to guests at Estrella only.

The restaurants on the beach are numerous and differ in quality. Ask the other tourists. Fish is available here for slightly more *($6-$8)*. Local dishes at the market cost about $3.

San Juan del Sur

$

BON APPETIT

Restaurant La Soya (*in front of the Cabanita*). ▶ Serves chicken, fish or beef, depending on the day, and is inexpensive. This restaurant is special in that it is run by an organization that helps women start their own businesses. The same organization offers workshops and has a library that is open to the public. There is a room for rent and laundry service is available.

Isla de Omotepe

Just an hour away from San Jorge by boat, not far from Rivas, Omotepe is truly enchanting. It has two volcanoes, 1,610 metres and 1,394 metres high, linked by a narrow isthmus. As the boat slowly approaches the island, the impact of its natural beauty will leave you speechless. Nature has retained its dominion over the land here, as opposed to its mass exploitation in the rest of the country. To the friendly residents, political issues also seem far away and not worth mentioning.

Omotepe, 35 kilometres long and about 12 kilometres wide, is the biggest island in the lake and has a population of 20,000. The two largest towns are ideal for pedestrians, and climbing the volcanoes is not only possible, it is recommended. This is a great way to get to know the island's flourishing plant and animal life, including brilliantly coloured birds, monkeys and all sorts of vegetation.

The two "large" towns, **Moyogalpa** and **Altagracia**, are on opposite sides of the higher volcano. These are the only places on the island where you can eat and sleep. Roads follow the shoreline around the two round segments of the island that has the overall shape of a lopsided figure-of-eight.

Oasis de Paz (*Moyogalpa*). This wooden model with a fountain in the middle celebrates the island's nickname, "oasis of peace." The work is a smaller-scale reproduction of the island, and can be used by new arrivals to get their bearings.

Petroglyphs (*Altagracia*). Pre-Columbian remains are on display in the central plaza in Altagracia. There are many more to be seen, near Balgue, on the same part of the island as Volcán Madera, and at the *finca* (farm) in the village of Magdalena. Ask for precise directions when you get there, because the petroglyphs aren't easy to find.

PRACTICAL INFO

Transportation: people come here by boat.

Granada-Altagracia: the trip takes at least four hours. There are departures on Mondays and Thursdays at 1pm. **Atagracia-Granada:** Wednesday at 3pm and 4pm, Sunday, 10am *($1.40)*. **San Jorge-Moyogalpa:** the trip takes only one hour and costs $1. Departures *(Mon to Sat)* at 11am, 12pm, 3pm and 5pm. Sunday, 12pm and 5pm only. Departures for the return trip are at 6am, 6:30am, 7am and 1:30pm. There are faster and more expensive boats.

Money: Get some cash in Rivas or Granada before coming.

Bicycle Rentals: Hotelito Mary (cheaper) and Hotel y Marina Cari rent bicycles. The latter also rents **horses** for $10 per hour. Both are in Moyogalpa.

Tourist Information: *The* best source is Señor Castillo, owner of the hotel of the same name in Altagracia. Also, Ecotur, a non-profit organization, has published a small magazine *($1.25)* with useful information about the island. Their offices are one block to the right and two blocks up from the wharf in Moyogalpa, and in the southwest corner of the Parque Central in Altagracia.

Mail and Telephone: in Moyogalpa, the Telcor office is three streets up from the wharf and one block to the right, just in front of Ecotur. In Altagracia, their office is one block south of the southwest corner of Parque Central. Open from Monday to Saturday from 8am to 6pm, with a siesta from noon to 2pm.

Santo Domingo *(about 10 km south of Altagracia; several buses daily)*. Despite the rapid growth of the ecotourism industry, this beach is still charming. It's ideal for long walks on the volcanic-sand shoreline.

Punta Jesús María *(5 km south of Moyogalpa)*. An easy half-hour trip by bicycle, this beach extends far out into the lake. The trees gradually disappear as the route progresses.

Ⓩ **Volcán Maderas** *(take the bus from Altagraia at 5:30am, 9:30am or 2:30pm; the return buses depart one hour later)*. Mosquitoes and perspiration await you on this approximately five-hour hike. On the way, you will come across more pre-Columbian petroglyphs, tropical birds, monkeys and giant insects. But before that, there are banana plantations and other crops to cross. A superb lagoon, just before the final ascent, is a great place to rest and wash off the sweat. The trail varies from easy to quite steep, and is not always well indicated. But the spectacle of nature in all her glory makes all this effort worthwhile! Guide service is available at Hospedaje Castillo or in the village of Magdalena. Bring your own food and water.

Vocán Concepción *(from Altagracia)*. A trail leading out of the village going towards *pueblito* Pull crosses several *fincas* before arriving at the foot of the 1,610-metre-high volcano. The climb itself is an approximately five-hour adventure. The trail is more difficult than at Maderas, and the summit is some 200 metres higher. Make sure you are in good condition before undertaking this hike. Also, be sure to hire a guide, so you won't waste time trying to find the trail. Note that Volcán Concepción is on the more developed part of the island, and the scenery is less breathtaking than at Maderas. It is also possible to make the climb starting from Moyogalpa. Ask for directions in the village.

Laguna Charco Verde *(southern extremity of Concepción, 12 km from Moyogalpa)*. This little body of water is said to have magic powers and is nestled in a completely natural setting. Whichever myth you choose to believe, the lagoon will grant you either wealth or success in love. To get there, take the bus that goes south from Moyogalpa. Ask the driver where to get off.

Moyogalpa

$

SWEET DREAMS

Pensión Jade *($5; three blocks up from the wharf)*. ▶ Good value for the money. Basic services and rooms that are sometimes dark. Breakfast served.

Hotel Bahía *($8; next to the Shell station)*. ▶ Recently renovated, so it should be better. The hotel was already flawless, but the noise from the bar-restaurant downstairs was a bit too much. But then again, it is so convenient to have good food right nearby. You can exchange money and cash cheques here.

Hotelio Aly *($9; half a block east of the Shell station)*. ▶ A favourite spot of backpackers because of the laid-back atmosphere. It can be noisy when full. The rooms are clean and the restaurant serves meals all day. Some claim it's the best food in town. Bicycle rentals cost $1 per hour.

Altagracia

SWEET DREAMS

Hospedaje Astagalpa *($6; two blocks east of Parque Central)*. ▶ Simple pleasant rooms that are cooler at night thanks to the concrete foundation walls. Breakfast is served here.

 Hospedaje Castillo *($6; one block south and half a block east of Parque Central)*. ▶ Unbeatable, thanks to Señor Castillo, if he is still alive (he was at least 80 the last time we saw him). He is an inexhaustible source for tourist info and the history of the island, and rents horses and can find you a guide for mountain trails. As for the rooms; they are very comfortable. The staff is friendly and the food is inexpensive.

Hotel Centra *($10; two blocks south of Parque Central)*. ▶ A handsome and tastefully decorated colonial building. If you have the extra money, rent one of the little cabins in the rear garden. They are prettier and more exotic. The owner also has cabins on the beach at Santo Domingo.

Moyogalpa

BON APPETIT

Most of the hotels serve good food.

Bar-Soda El Chele *(on the main street)*. ▶ The owner, a foreigner, serves local cuisine at modest prices. Beer, sandwiches and light meals are on the menu at this open-air restaurant.

Altagracia

BON APPETIT

 We recommend the food at **Hotel Central, Castillo and Hospedaje Astagalpa**. They serve typical local cuisine in settings that range from cozy to busy, but always very friendly.

⏭ THE NORTH AND
THE ATLANTIC COAST ⏮

Northern Nicaragua near the Pacific Ocean is mostly dry. Volcanoes litter the landscape that leads to superb ocean beaches. The closer you get to the Caribbean coast, the thicker the jungle becomes, and more omnipresent are the coffee plantations in the highlands. As in all Central American countries, the Caribbean coast is a world completely in and of itself.

In Nicaragua, the Atlantic region makes up more than half of the country's landmass, but is home to only ten percent of the population. Its inhabitants are of African descent, with slave trading having been practised here until the end of the 19th century. Half of the population, however, identifies more closely with the Caribbean islands (Jamaica, in particular) than with Nicaragua itself. The mix of natives and black Caribbean slaves gave birth to a distinct cultural group known as "Garifunas," who live in small towns scattered along the coast and who use fishing as their major means of support. The region was under British rule until the 1890s, which explains why the language spoken here is English, with smatterings of Spanish and Creole.

At the end of the 1970s and during the 1980s, the province, stretched along the Honduran border, was used as an arms passage for *Contras* from American bases stationed in neighbouring Honduras. This section of the country sustained considerable damage during this period, while the powerless people were subjected to the conflicts of others. The inhabitants are generally far enough removed from Managua and national politics, indeed underlining the paradox of "foreign" conflicts being waged on their territory. The region was given its autonomous status approximately twelve years ago, and is now rather peaceful, with an atmosphere similar to that found in the islands.

For the adventurous traveller, the region provides an interesting challenge, since it is unmistakably and literally off the beaten paths. Paths, in fact, often do not even exist, so you should consider travelling around by boat and plane. Jungle and swamp are king of the Nicaraguan Atlantic coast. Another word to the wise: come with American cash or Cordobas, since travellers' cheques will be as useful to you here as your cross-country skis!

León

Capital of Nicaragua until 1857, León was completely destroyed in 1610 after the eruption of Momotombo, then reconstructed some 25 kilometres west. Unlike the country's other large cities, León

PRACTICAL INFO

Bus Station: Called *Posada del Sol*, located at the new market. Service for **Managua** every half hour for $1.30. For **Matagalpa**, one bus daily at 2pm for $2.80. A less expensive and more flexible option would be to take one of the buses for **San Isidro** leaving every half hour, and once there, take the bus coming from **Estelí**, which goes to **Matagalpa** for 80¢. This method can also be used to reach **Estelí**, since the León bus leaves only at 3pm. This Tica bus, which goes to El Salvador and then Honduras, stops at approximately 6:30am at the Shell station on route to Managua.

Money: Many currency exchange offices can be found behind the cathedral. Banks, located close to the park, will change your travellers' cheques.

Tourist Information: One and a half blocks from the San Juan church is the city's tourist office. Staff speaks many languages. Numerous brochures and maps of the area are also available.

Mail and Telephone: The Telcor site is in the park across from the cathedral. Open all week from 7am.

succeeded in keeping its main cathedral intact despite numerous conflicts with Granada conservatives in the 19th century, and the later 1979 bombings of the fallen dictator. The problem, however, is that little else remains of León except a few monuments from its rich past as capital. What's more, the city was once a Sandinista stronghold, but they have not been in power since 1990, which has resulted in unemployment and bitter hostility in this potentially glorious city.

Iglesias *(Parque Central)*. Located in the park is the *catedral*, which has stood the test of time. Spain provided financial support for the cathedral's restoration in 1992, commemorating the 500-year anniversary of Columbus's discovery of the Americas. The cathedral is well worth the visit, not just because it is the largest in Central America, but also for its incontestable elegance. Two and a half blocks north is La Recolección church with its Baroque façade. Three blocks east of the cathedral is El Calvario, with its crucifixion theme, amongst others. During your walk around the park, note the many colonial buildings with stunning architecture. La Merced church is situated one street north of the park.

Ruines Penelas y Sirena *(in front of the north side of the cathedral)*. The ruins of this old shop, destroyed during the revolution of 1979, have been ingeniously restored. Stunningly beautiful frescos chronicle the tumultuous history of a country that never seemed to rest in between intense periods. This is a fascinating way to learn a little of the area's history. Not far from here, an evocative statue of Sandino stands over Somoza and Uncle Sam at the entrance of a firehall. Those who would like to adventure further can go to the Galería de los Heroes y Martires, one block west of the park, where thorough explanations are provided on important historical figures. Located three blocks west of the park is a superb museum dedicated to the famous poet Rubén Darío.

Subtavia *(10 blocks west of Parque Central)*. This neighbourhood is ideal for a stroll into the area's native past. Somewhat like old León, natives were already living here when the city was relocated in 1610. A market is situated close by, and the neighbourhood is home to the oldest church in the city, San Juan de Batista de Subtiava, built in 1530.

El Fortin *(2 km south of the city)*. For a beautiful view of the city and volcanoes in surrounding areas, the walk is well worth it. This hilltop fort was used for battles in the 19th and 20th centuries.

Poneyola *(24 km west of León)*. Buses depart from the station every hour all day long, and cost only 60¢ for a one-hour trip. This will bring you to a fantastic beach (best avoided on the weekend when packed with visitors). Lining the sandy beaches are coconut trees and restaurants with refreshment stands. Caution is advised, since waves can be phenomenally, even dangerously, powerful.

León Viejo *(30 km southeast of León)*. The original site of the city, destroyed by the eruption of 1610. Take a bus to La Paz Centro *(departures every hour on the hour between 7am and 5pm for 50¢)*. From there, you can take a group taxi or truck. Although the ruins are not particularly impressive, it makes for a pleasant walk through enchanting nature, and a view of the volcanoes as well as Lago Managua.

Ⓩ **Volcán Momotombo** *(Puerto Momotombo, 10 km after La Paz)*. Although paths are more or less well kept, the climb is impossible without a guide. It takes about four hours to complete the 1,630-metre climb, but the reward is a breathtaking 360-degree view of the north of the country. In theory, you should be carrying a special INE pass, available in Managua *(☎266-8756)*.

León

SWEET DREAMS

Hotel Telica *($6; four blocks north of the train station)*. ▣ Only if you are on a strict budget, since you will be dealing with horrible bathrooms, cockroaches, and a staff who is helpful only on a good day.

ⓩ **Hotel Avenida** *($8; five blocks north and four blocks east of the cathedral)*. ▣ A little piece of heaven — very clean and quiet! Bonus: you can even do your laundry here!

Hotel Europa *($15; two blocks south and one block east of the train station)*. ▣ Many different types of rooms, all great. Friendly and professional service. Lush garden. Fantastic breakfasts, and great coffee.

León

BON APPETIT

Comedores *(at the market, behind the Cathedral)*. ▣ Local food that is easy on your wallet.

La Cueva del León *(two blocks north of Parque Central)*. ▣ A little more expensive. Good selection of Chinese dishes. Building has interesting architecture.

ⓩ **El Rincón Azul** *(two blocks west of the park)*. ▣ Highly recommended for its relaxed ambiance, this is favourite student hangout in León. A great stop for a coffee and a bite to eat. Sometimes converted into an art gallery. Service is friendly.

Matagalpa

After the stifling heat of the Pacific Coast, escape to the fresh altitudes of the mountains surrounding the city of Matagalpa, especially if you are planning to go into the equally stifling Puerto Cabezas on the Atlantic Coast.

History is heavy here. Two of the most important Sandinista leaders were born here, and the city saw many violent conflicts during the later part of the 1978-79 revolution. At 700 metres above sea level, the climate is comfortable, and a

PRACTICAL INFO

Bus Station: Terminal Sur *(Mercado del Oeste)* leaving for **Managua** at half past every hour — $1.40 for three hours travel. **Jinotega**, every 45 minutes — $1 for two hours travel. **Esteli**, every half-hour — $1 for a two-hour ride.

Also, the **Terminal Norte** *(Mercado del Norte)* serves mostly León. A bus leaves only once daily at 6am for $3.

Money: Banco Nacional de Desarollo and foreign currency exchange offices near the cathedral. Exchange rates tend to be good.

Mail and Telephone: Enitel, one block est of Parque Central in a tall building, is open from 7am until 9pm every day.

magnificent mountain backdrop surrounds the city. A climb to some of these summits is highly recommended.

Parque Central. Home to another interesting cathedral and a monument dedicated to the soldiers of the revolution.

Museo Casa Cuna Carlos Fonseca *(one block east of Parque Dario)*. This museum is dedicated to the founder of the Sandinista national liberation movement. A recommended stop for whoever would like to know more about this topic. Open every day.

El Calbario *(south of the city, on the highway)*. After a bridge, take the route to the right that leads to a hill. From there it's about a forty-minute walk uphill. Once you reach the top, you can admire the beauty of the vast horizon. Looking towards Honduras, you can see Jinotega, a small, quiet village in the mountains.

Matagalpa	SWEET DREAMS
$	**Hospedaje San Martin** *($6; Parque Dario)*. ▶ Friendly staff, but cleanliness is not always first priority. Shared bathrooms.

Hotel Bermúdez *($8; two blocks east of the north-east corner of Parque Dario)*. ▶ Reasonably clean. Meals served all day. |

Matagalpa	SWEET DREAMS
	Hotel Plaza *($8; Parque Darío)*. ▶ Your typical basic hotel. Rooms are small but well-lit, clean and quiet.

Matagalpa	BON APPETIT
	Vicky's Cafetín *(a half block south of Parque Central, Avenida de los Bancos)*. ▶ Nice place with a good selection of delicious sandwiches, pastries, and breakfasts complete with delectable coffee. **Pizza Don Diego** *(one block south of Parque Central, on Avenida José Benito Escobar)*. ▶ Budget- and appetite-friendly specialties include the chicken and pizza. **Comedor San Martin** *(a bit north of Parque Central, also on Escobar)*. ▶ A city hot spot. Serves local cuisine all day long in a typically Nicaraguan atmosphere.

Bluefields

The main port of the Atlantic region, Bluefields is the area's most central city, but also the most isolated from the rest of the country. Basically, this means that getting to the city takes several hours (see "Practical Info" below), and once there, the many idyllic beaches, camouflaged lagoons, paradisiac islands, and native jungle tribes are accessible only by boat. Historically, the city was under British rule until 1894, when one of the country's dictators decided he had had enough.

The United States later attacked the city and overthrew the same dictator. More recently, during the 1980s, the Contras attacked Bluefields and, some years later, a hurricane nearly completely destroyed the city.

El Bluff *(other side of the bay)*. Friendly and aesthetically pleasing, this small village also has a pretty little beach, perfect for a nice walk. To get there, you can ask the boat captains on the dock *($1.50)*. They regularly make the 20-minute trip between Bluefields and El Bluff.

PRACTICAL INFO

Transportation: There are two ways to reach Bluefields: by seabus or plane. For plane schedules, refer to **Corn Islands** below. From **Managua**, buses make the trip to **Rama** *(280 km)* in eight hours. Since there is absolutely nothing to do in Rama, take the night bus there, which leaves the Terminal Atlántico at 10:30pm Mondays, Wednesdays, and Fridays. This way, you can take the boat leaving Rama for Bluefields at 10:30am on Tuesdays, Thursdays and Saturdays. Everything should cost about $15. Add another 6 hours for the boat trip.

Money: The Banco de Desarrollo is located in front of the Moravian church, open Monday to Saturday, and will convert cash and traveller's cheques.

Mail and telephone: There is postal service in the morning, but phones can be used all day. The Telcor building is situated a half block north and two and a half blocks west of the Moravian church.

Laguna de Perlas *(80 km north)*. This enormous, 50-kilometre-wide lagoon is surrounded by many native and Garifuna villages. No roads or vehicles around.

Corn Islands *(100 km east)*. Two small, charming islands in the Caribbean Sea. You can walk around the larger of the two in four hours. A wonderful place to lay in the sand, swim in the crystal-turquoise waters, or relax in the shade of a palm tree. You can take the boat from Bluefields on Wednesdays at 8am for $5. Flying there is more expensive at $40, but is much faster than the six-hour boat ride. Flights leave daily at 8am and 3pm, or one and a half hours earlier from Managua for an extra $20.

Bluefields $

SWEET DREAMS

Hotel Hollywood *($9; four blocks south of the pier)*. ▶ Best value for the money in Bluefields. Clean, pretty veranda. Restaurant serves good breakfasts.

Hospedaje Pearl Lagoon *($6; one block from the market)*. ▶ Cheap but good. Try to get a room at the back so as not to be disturbed by noise.

Laguna de Perlas

SWEET DREAMS

You will have peace and quiet, but be prepared to stand out. The only place to stay *($6)* is **Hospedaje Ingrid**, a pleasant well-known inn. Just ask any of the locals how to get there. Boats leave Bluefields every morning at 6am for the lagoon *($5; less than a three-hour ride)*.

Corn Island

SWEET DREAMS

Prices are still affordable, although somewhat more expensive. There are at least three hotels for about $15 a night: **Hospedaje Playa Coco**, **Brisas del Mar**, and **Casa Blanca** (try this one if possible).

Bluefields

BON APPETIT

Salon Siú *(a half block north, one block west, and a half block south of the Moravian church).* ▶ Sandwiches, pastries, simple meals and delicious milkshakes.

China Nica *(a half block west of the Moravian church).* ▶ China meets Nicaragua to a reggae tune! Spicy Chinese dishes. Food and ambiance to savour.

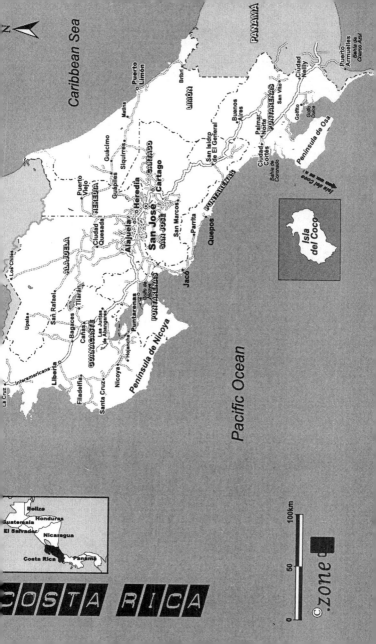

||||| Costa Rica is Central America at its best, with beaches galore, scads of volcanoes, hundreds of thousands of hectares of protected tropical forests, political stability comparable to that of Switzerland, a friendly population, extraordinary biodiversity that is something out of the ordinary... all in all, this is the stereotypical paradise of the New World on which Columbus landed 500 years ago — except that the indigenous population has been almost completely wiped out by the diseases brought over by the Europeans. Hollywood even came here to shoot the set of the movie *1492* using the few remaining natives. As the saying goes: first God created life. But then he needed a marketing scheme. So he put life in Costa Rica.

||||| But the *Gringos* from the North soon got wind of this paradise and flooded the country. The leaders, seeking to turn a profit from this "manna from heaven," exclaimed: *"We could turn this country into the world's #1 ecotourism destination!"* The Council agreed and tried to get permission from God, who had dozed off for a few thousand years. The country's reputation soon travelled round the globe. People starting pouring in but were puzzled and asked: "Is this really Central America? Where are the guerillas? Where are the soldiers? Why do so many people speak English? Why do the national parks look as good as North American ones?" What we are trying to say is that Costa Rica is made for tourists and many pleasant surprises await you in the country's varied natural landscapes.

||||| Costa Rica has a lot to offer travellers. The scenery is absolutely amazing, and the amount of diversity it offers on such a small territory is incredible. It has to be seen to be believed. Costa Rica's commitment to protecting its exceptional biological richness and diversity is reflected in its extensive network of protected areas (some 25% of the country) into which tourists can venture... and live to tell the tale. You can even hike along the well-marked trails without a guide. And thanks to the political stability, which is sadly lacking in several of its neighbouring countries, you won't have any reason to cancel your trip here. There are no two ways about it: travelling to Costa Rica is a delight!

►► SAN JOSÉ AND THE CENTRAL VALLEY ◄◄

Right smack in the geographical heart of the country, between the mountains of the central cordillera, lies the metropolis of San José. Like all the capitals in the region, it is the commercial centre and starting point for many interesting trips in the vicinity. The city and its surrounding area boast approximately a third of the country's total population.

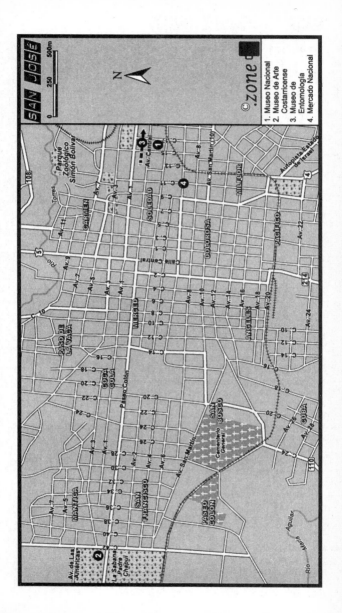

The panoramas are extraordinary, and a bus ride into the various districts of the valley is like a trip to paradise. The departmental capitals of Alajuela, Heredia and Cartago are located very close to the nation's capital, San José. Though the capital boasts all the services, it is better used as a base for expeditions to the surrounding area. The Central Valley is the economic centre of the country, a region with a perfect climate — neither too hot nor too cold — and many interesting natural attractions. Spending the day at the Volcán Poás and returning to the metropolis the same afternoon is like going from one world to another.

It's hard to get lost in San José's perfect city grid. The colonial buildings and several old churches are huddled around the heart of the city, which is pleasant to roam on foot, particularly the pedestrian stretch of Avenida Central. The incredible number and variety of shops from street to street in the boundless city centre is astonishing. This urban jungle is safe provided you stay in the downtown core. Green spaces are seriously lacking in San José, and the traffic noise and pollution just make things worse. Yet another paradox for the capital of a country that likes to think of itself as environmental...

Museums. The **Museo Nacional** *($1.40; Calle 17 between Ave. Central and Ave. 2)* chronicles the nation's history, from the pre-Colombian era to the present day. The **Museo de Arte Costarricense** *($2; La Sabana, at the beginning of Paseo Colón)* has a collection of the best works of both national and international painters and sculptors. The **Museo de Entomología** *(University of Costa Rica, San Pedro)* has a wonderful insect display thanks to its spectacular collection of butterflies. The city also boasts a slew of other museums. Information on site.

Handicrafts. The best place to find bargain souvenirs is the **Meríacado Nacional de Artesanía** *(at Calle 11 and Ave. 6)*. **Sarchí** is renowned for its typical Costa Rican oxcarts, while the best leather goods come from the **Moravia** region.

The **Butterfly Farm** *(La Guácima, southwest of the airport, ☎438-0400)* is by far the biggest butterfly breeding farm in the country. Many kinds of butterflies and very knowledgeable staff.

(Z) **Volcán Poás** *($8 for the bus and entrance fees; 40 km north; take the bus leaving from the corner of Calle 12 and Ave. 4 at 8:30am)*. Easily reached, this volcano has one of the largest craters on earth. Light steam emanates from the turquoise lake in the centre, and clouds almost always cover it. Though it is over 2,500 metres high, reaching the top is easy. Watching the clouds hover over the crater and the surrounding summits is one of the most amazing sights to be seen. A few small trails allow visitors to discover the impressive flora and fauna.

(Z) **Parque Nacional Braulio Carillo** and **Volcán Barva** *($6; 20 km north of San José)*. Daily departures every 30 minutes *(Calle 1 between Avenidas 7 and 9)* from 5:30am to 9:45pm. Ask the driver to drop you off at the Quebrada González station. For the return trip, you'll have to wait for the bus near the road. A region of plateaus and high mountains, the park is a vast, wild expanse near the city. This region is in fact a conservation area that protects the environment bordered by the Pacific-bound highway of the same name built some twenty years ago. With seven ecological life zones, ranging from the wet tropical rainforest to the premontane rainforest, the park boasts countless plant and animal species. The park's lowest region is at an elevation of 36 metres, while the highest, the summit of the Barva volcano, reaches 2,906 metres. At the reception centre, the wardens will tell you all about the various trails over a nice hot cup of coffee or tea. The volcano has denser vegetation, and more adventurous types can go for a two- to three-day hike. Another **Butterfly Farm** is located on the Atlantic-bound side of the highway (see further above).

(Z) **Volcán Irazú** *($6; 8am to 4pm; ☎232-5324, ≈290-1927)* is a very popular volcano due to its proximity to San José (53 km) and Cartago (31 km) and because of the paved road that goes right up to the top of the volcano. Though the volcano has neither an interpretive centre nor real walking trails, the beauty of the place, the altitude and spectacular craters alone are worth the visit. Take note that the volcano is higher than that of Poás, so dress warmly. Three of its craters can be easily reached and, in good weather, you can see both the Atlantic and Pacific Oceans from the top.

(Z) **Bosque Nuboso Los Angeles** *(between San Ramón and La Tigra)*. A private 800-hectare nature reserve usually covered by clouds, this forest is the alternative to Monteverde. It belongs to a former president of Costa Rica, who takes good care of it. There are several trails from which you can observe jungle life. Easily covered in one day.

The **Bosque de Paz** *(60 km northwest of San José, between Zarcero and Bajos del Toro, ☎234-6676)* is a private cloud-forest reserve located between the Poás and Juan Castro Blanco national parks, thus serving as something of a natural biological corridor between the two. It is becoming a very prized nature centre and is being favourably compared to La Selva in Monteverde. Depending on your interests and physical condition, 10 different interpretive trails are available. You must reserve in advance to visit this place.

PRACTICAL INFO

Transport to **Alajuela** and the **airport:** Departures every 10 minutes from 5am to 10pm *(Ave. 2 between Calles 10 and 12)*; 17-kilometre trip (30 minutes). The bus to the **Poás** volcano leaves from the same spot every morning at 8:30am and returns from the volcano at 2:30pm.

Cartago: Departures every 10 minutes *(Calle 5 between Avenidas 18 and 20)* throughout the day; 20-kilometre trip (45 minutes). The driver can also drop you off at the **Lankester Gardens**.

Volcán Irazú: Departures Saturdays and Sundays *(Ave. 2 between Calles 1 and 3)* at 8am. Return at 1pm.

Heredia: Calle 1 between Avenidas 7 and 9. Every 10 minutes, all day.

Jacó: Departures are at 7:30am, 10:30am and 3:30pm *(Calle 16 between Avenidas 1 and 3)*; 3-hour trip (20 minutes). Return at 5am, 11am and 3pm. Fare: $3.

Limón: Departures on the hour between 5am and 7pm *(Ave. 3 between Calles 19 and 21)*. Travel time: 2 hours, 30 minutes; fare: $3.

Tapantí Wildlife Refuge: You must first take the San José-Cartago bus, then the Cartago-Orosi Valley bus, which runs to Rio Macho (just past Orosi), 9 kilometres

from the park entrance. From there, you can take a taxi (about $6) to the park.

Monteverde: Departures at 6:30am and 2:30pm on Calle 14 between Avenidas 9 and 11. Return at the same times; 4-hour trip; fare: $5.30.

Puntarenas: Every 30 minutes from 6:30am to 9pm on Calle 16 between Avenidas 10 and 12; 2-hour trip; fare: $3.

Quepos Manuel Antonio: The bus leaves for this beach, 145 kilometres away, at 6am, noon and 3pm in both directions, from Calle 16 between Avenidas 1 and 3; 4-hour trip; fare: $4 to $5.

San Isidro: The bus leaves from the same station as for Quepos every hour from 5:30am to 5pm.

Turrialba: Throughout the day, on Calle 12 between Avenidas 3 and 5.

Money: The banks are located between Avenida Central, Calle 2, Avenida 3 and Calle 3. **Scotiabank**, on Avenida 2, has good rates and fast service.

Tourist Info: Calle 5, between Avenidas Central and 2, ☎222-1090. Expensive souvenirs, but you get a free map of the country and of the city. You can also pick up bus schedules here.

Mail: At Avenida 1 and Calle 2. Open seven days a week.

Phone: Long-distance calls can be made from any phone booth, especially if you have a direct-access number to your country.

Internet: Radiográfica Costarricense rents terminals for $3 per hour and is located at Calle 1 and Avenida 5, right across from a café.

Sarchí Norte, Grecia and **Zarcero** *(take a Zarcero-bound bus)*. These small villages are much quieter, cleaner and more rural than the capitals. Handicrafts, sugarcane and coffee are produced here.

Cartago *(22 km east)*. Formerly the nation's capital, Cartago is now the capital city of the department of the same name. The place still bears the scars of earthquakes, visible in the ruins of a church whose construction was never completed. On August 2 of every year, a pilgrimage from San José to Cartago takes place to honour the national (female) patron saint who appeared to a young peasant woman in 1635. Also near the city are the **Lankester Gardens**, which were created by the English botanist of the same name. Here you can see an impressive variety of flowers, such as orchids and bromeliads.

Tapantí Wildlife Refuge *($6; 6am to 7pm; ☎771-3155)*. In a wild and well-protected area 50 kilometres from San José (past Cartago), in the upper reaches of the superb Orosi Valley, this quiet park is teeming with hundreds of species of birds. It is best to get here by car because the bus stops in Río Macho (just past Orosi), nine kilometres from the park entrance. And because camping is no longer permitted in the park, getting here (bus and taxi, or walking) takes so long that it leaves you little time to appreciate the sights, especially since you have to walk quite a distance to reach them. Going in a group and renting a car (preferably a four-wheel drive) is the best way to enjoy the many attractions and spectacular views along the often-muddy narrow trails. End your day at the **Agua Thermales de Orosi** *($1.50)*, located right next to the Los Patios restaurant. Here you can swim in one of two pools fed by warm and soothing volcanic hot springs (41°C and 51°C).

Guayabo National Monument *($6; 8am to 4pm)*. The biggest archaeological site in Costa Rica is a fabulous place to take a walk and to relax. It is located 19 kilometres northeast of Turrialba and more than 80 kilometres from San José (about 2 hours away). There is a bus service between Turrialba and Guayabo. Besides the reception centre, there are camp sites, washrooms and drinking water on site. Since the place is in the mountains (960 to 1,300 metres in altitude), the climate is warm but downright humid, with annual precipitation exceeding 3.5 metres! Only one-tenth of the site has been uncovered, but these excavations have determined that people lived here from 1,000 BC to the 15th century. Cobblestone roads, hillocks, bridges, house foundations, retaining walls, aqueducts, water reservoirs, tombs and petroglyphs have been uncovered here. The various structures were composed of round as well as large, flat stones. The site is well set up: a short 1.2-kilometre trail, lined with explanatory signs, runs through the park and provides visitors with valuable insights. Other trails, though less "archaeological," are also worth exploring.

Kayaking and **rafting** are practised on several rivers in the region. If you have some $85 to spare, the experience promises to be truly memorable. Here are the addresses of the main agencies: Costa Rica Expeditions (white water) ☎257-0766; Aventuras Naturales ☎225-3939; Ríos Tropicales ☎255-4354; Pioneer Raft ☎253-4687 and Aguas Bravas ☎229-4837. The second one also offers mountain-bike rentals and organizes expeditions to the volcanoes.

San José

$

SWEET DREAMS

We have only listed San José hotels because they are cheaper and located in the heart of the region. This does not mean that you can't find good accommodations deeper in the country where the air is as refreshing as your sleep.

Gran Hotel Imperial *($8; Calle 8 between Avenidas Central and 1, ☎222-7899)*. ▣ A favourite haunt of budget travellers, the place has a great restaurant with a balcony overlooking city life. The rooms are more like prison cells, the only difference being you are given the keys. Sometimes noisy. Clean, shared bathrooms.

Hotel Generaleño *($8; Ave. 2 between Calles 8 and 10, ☎233-7877)*. ▣ Clean and roomy, with private bathrooms but cold water only.

Pensión Otoya *($8; at Ave. 5 and Calle 1)*. ▣ Friendly and offering hot water more often than elsewhere, this establishment is also spick n' span.

Reserva Forestal Grecia

SWEET DREAMS

You can camp at the picturesque **Bosque del Niño de la Reserva Forestal Grecia** *(Zarcero-bound bus)* and take in all its natural beauty. Entrance fees are next to nothing; the site is closed on Mondays.

Parque Nacional Braulio Carillo

SWEET DREAMS

The **campsites** ($1.25/person/day) and the small shelter ($4.20/person/night) that can put up four people are located next to the reception centre. For reservations, call ☎283-5906.

San José

BON APPETIT

Niny's *(Ave. 3 between Calles 2 and 4)*. ▶ Standard, dirt-cheap fare.

Mercado Central *(at Ave. 1 and Calle 8)*. ▶ This huge market boasts all kinds of grub at rock-bottom prices, mainly typical Costa Rican dishes.

Vishnu *(Ave. 1 between Calles 1 and 3)*. ▶ Primo vegetarian food served to a motley clientele, each more alternative than the last. A popular spot.

the good life

El Cuartel de la Boca del Monte *(Ave. 1 between Calles 21 and 23)*. There's no better place than this nightclub to party with the country's younger set. As deafening as any other bar, a lot of dancing and a small cover charge.

Las Risas *(at Ave. Central and Calle 1)*. A huge three-floor nightclub right downtown that draws a large upbeat crowd.

⏭ GUANACASTE ⏮

Having gained its independence long ago, the Guanacaste region joined Costa Rica (after having belonged first to Costa Rica, and then to Nicaragua) in the mid-19th century. It has thus retained a unique cultural heritage. Though it boasts the largest amount of pasture land in the country, and its livestock is exported to such consumers as McDonald's, this province also encompasses the greatest number of national parks. As the Guanacaste region is vast, there are also a slew of beaches where you can relax or practise your favourite water sports. In addition to this, the region draws more and more tourists thanks to its dry climate that contrasts sharply with the stifling heat of Jacó and Quepos further south on the Pacific Coast.

Liberia *(300 km northwest of San José)*. A provincial capital with a population of 40,000, the friendly little city of Liberia is a great starting point from which to explore the bevy of parks and beaches around it. The city boasts all the necessary services for travellers and one of the most beautiful *Parque Central*s in the country, with great big trees and a lively crowd both day and night.

Parque Nacional Palo Verde *($6; 8am to 4pm; ☎659-9039 or 284-6116, ⇒659-9039)*. Teeming with animals, including 300 species of birds and 12 natural habitats, this park contains part of the country's always-astounding nature. The **OTS** *(Organization of Tropical Studies, ☎240-6696)* offers guided tours *($17, lunch included)* that focus on the natural history of the place and provides accommodation in a B&B for those who wish to stick around for a few days.

The park boasts the greatest concentration of aquatic birds and waders in Central America, as well as a small network of walking trails (6 km in total) and several forest roads. Keep in mind, though, that the heat can be stifling during the dry season. There are more animals during the dry season, whereas there are more birds during the rainy season. Remember above all to bring plenty of fresh water. The **Las Calizas** (300 m), **El Manigordo** (1.5 km), **El Mapache** (2 km) and **La Venada** (2 km) trails are short, but cover the different natural habitats that make up this region. Along these trails you'll see such views as seasonally flooded plains and magnificent neighbouring hills. However, before venturing onto the trails or pitching your tent for a few nights, find out the latest news about the very aggressive **African bees** that have taken up residence in the park.

PRACTICAL INFO

Transport (from Liberia) to **San José**: Departures at 4:30am, 6am, 7:30am, noon, 2pm, 4pm, 6pm and 8pm (4-hour trip for $3). The station is at the corner of Avenida 14 and Calle 3.

Buses to other destinations leave from Calle 12 between Avenidas 7 and 9. Several buses a day go to **Santa Cruz**, **Nicoya**, **Puntarenas**, **Nicaragua** and **Playa del Coco**.

To reach **Brasilito**, you must go to **Belén** on a Nicoya- or Santa Cruz-bound bus and from there take one of two daily buses, at noon or 4pm.

Lastly, you must transfer in **Nicoya** if heading to **Sámara**. Buses leave at 8am, 3pm and 4pm, returning every morning at 5:30am and 6:30am.

Money: The banks are located around the Parque Central in Liberia.

Mail: At Ave. 3 and Calle 8 in Liberia.

Tourist Info: Head south down Avenida Central for five blocks from the Parque Central in Liberia and you're there. The staff is always well up on the bus schedules and can help you find your way around. Free maps available, and a **telephone**.

With an area of 2,279 hectares, the **Lomas Barbudal** biological reserve lies just northwest of the Palo Verde national park. Besides the scores of African bees, the reserve is home to 60 species of butterflies and over 200 bird species, including a few scarlet macaws and jabirus. Of the mammals more likely to be seen here are howler and white-faced capuchin monkeys, coatis, racoons and coyotes. Like at Palo Verde, camping is permitted here.

Ⓩ Parque Nacional Santa Rosa *($6; 8am to 4:30pm; ☎695-5598 or 695-5577)*. To get here, you must take a bus from Liberia. It's rare to find a park that has everything: the sea, a beach, plains, mountains, tourist facilities and a well-maintained historic site. The park is also exceptional in that the area of protected territory is always expanding, with the purchase of many neighbouring plots of land. A good example to follow.

The park is easily reached via a paved road and therefore receives a lot of visitors. Another draw is its major historic site, **La Casona** *(free admission)*, the main house of one of the biggest ranches in Costa Rica, the Santa Rosa hacienda, which marked the nation's history back in the 18th century. A symbol of

Costa Rican independence and national pride, La Casona was the scene of three major decisive battles (including the first against the illustrious William Walker) whose outcome helped preserve democracy in the country.

With an extensive territory and different natural environments (sea, beaches, mangrove swamps, plains, mountains, etc.), it harbours fauna that is as diverse as it is amazing. To date, 155 species of mammals, 250 bird species, 100 species of amphibians and reptiles and over 30,000 species of insects have been counted! You might be lucky enough to spot white-faced capuchin and howler monkeys, white-tailed deer, coatis and big iguanas. Rarely sighted are the puma, coyote and boa constrictor. Thousands of turtles flock (well, crawl) to the beach from July to November.

Numerous walking trails lead to the beach, where there are even more campsites. Mountain biking can also be done on these trails.

The **Refugio Nacional Bahía Junquillal** *($1.50; 8am to 5pm; ☎695-5598 or 695-5577)* is located about 20 kilometres south of the small city of La Cruz (via Puerto Soley), the last major town before the Nicaraguan border. This small reserve, a little over 500 hectares, is also part of the Area de Conservación Guanacaste (ACG). The place boasts a superb two-kilometre stretch of beach, which occasionally welcomes olive Ridley, leatherback and Pacific green sea turtles that come to lay their eggs. Besides lolling on the beach and observing the raft of aquatic bird species, you can swim and scuba-dive here. There is also a short 600-metre trail named **El Carao** that winds through the dry and coastal forests where you can witness the miracle of regeneration.

Parque Nacional Guanacaste *($6; 8am to 5pm; ☎695-5598 or 695-5577)*. To get here, you must take a bus from Liberia. With a surface area of 32,512 hectares, this national park is an extension of that of Santa Rosa on the east side of the Interamericana, forming a natural corridor essential to the survival of the umpteen animal species inhabiting the region. Three stations have been built to support research in this fabulous biological reserve. The Maritza station is located at the foot of the Orosi volcano (1,487 m), while that of Cacao is at 1,100 metres in altitude, near the volcano of the same name (1,659 m). The third station, Pitilla, is located on the Atlantic slope of the Orosi volcano, where the natural habitats are different from those on the Pacific side, with more precipitation and humidity. On the Atlantic side, the rivers run (eastward) to the Caribbean Sea, a little less than 200 kilometres away.

The trails are many and relatively short, so you can easily get from one station to the other and even climb the few summits around. You can also rent mountain bikes and roam the few trails laid out for that purpose. Go to the park entrance for more information.

Parque Nacional Rincón de la Vieja *($6; 7am to 5pm; ☎695-5598 or 695-5577)* is a well-kept secret and thus less frequented than other parks, so get out there and enjoy its trails while you can. The park boasts magnificent scenery, breathtaking views, a distinctive volcano, calm rivers, spectacular waterfalls, relaxing hot springs, places to swim, picnic areas, campsites, well-marked trails as well as very detailed travel literature (brochures and maps), something of a rarity in the country. With an area of 14,084 hectares, the park lies about 25 kilometres northeast of Liberia. It is named after the loftiest mountain in the area, which is 1,895 metres high. Several trails make for hikes of varying degrees of difficulty. You must tackle a 16-kilometre trail to scale the mountain, which means setting out at the crack of dawn. The Liberia youth hostel offers a return transport service to Rincón at 7am. There may be up to three departures during peak season.

The park has two sectors, **Las Pailas** and **Santa María**. The latter has longer trails. Camping is permitted near the entrances of both sectors, and the same conditions apply as those of the other parks.

Playas del Coco *(35 km from Liberia)* are two beaches separated by a small stream. Though they are very close to each other, they are reached by two different roads. The Coco beaches are very popular, though the one to the south is more residential. People use all sorts of boats, which they moor near the shore, to get around the little bay where the beach is located. The Playas del Coco are a typical Costa Rican resort, with their pier jutting out into the sea and a small central park by the beach, the whole setup surrounded by low-priced bars and restaurants. A fair share of these places have been around for over 20 years now. Newer hotels have and continue to set up shop as you move away from the heart of town. The whole is rather densely developed and has a distinctly Costa Rican flavour. Playa del Coco is also a very popular fishing port. The greyish-brown sand beach is fairly wide at low tide, but almost disappears at high tide. **Playa Hermosa**, a little farther north, will lure casual surfers.

Playa Ocotal *(a few km south of Playas del Coco)*. If you're looking for peace and quiet but don't wish to stray too far from town, you might want to head to this magnificent little beach, which is tucked away in a cove between steep slopes. For safety's sake, it is wiser to swim from the middle part of the beach. Just spend the day here, because hotels here will cost you an arm and a leg.

The number to dial to make reservations in all **Costa Rican parks** is ☎257-2239. Very useful.

Playa Brasilito *(farther south; go through Belén)* is the exact opposite of Playa Flamingo, its famous and pricy neighbour. A little village made up mainly of middle-class homes (permanent and vacation), it doesn't have much to recommend it to foreign tourists and is still relatively underdeveloped. All this means you can spend the night here for little money.

ⓩ **Parque Nacional Marino Las Baulas** *($6; guided tour included; open at all times; ☎/⌐680-0779)*. If you're looking for a fascinating, moving and enriching experience, witness **leatherback turtles** laying their eggs on **Playa Grande**. This event takes place almost every night between the months of October and March, especially in December and January.

El Mundo de la Tortuga *($5; from 4pm between Oct 1 and Mar 15; right before the park entrance, ☎653-0471)* is a must for anyone who wants to learn more about sea turtles. Moreover, if you plan on visiting the Las Baulas National Marine Park to watch the leatherback turtle egg-laying ceremony, the small outdoor café of the museum is the perfect place to wait (sometimes several hours) for the tide to go down.

Playa Tamarindo *(70 km southwest of Liberia)* is a surfer's paradise, with its long stretch of white sand. Swimmers should watch out though: the waves here can be quite strong and there are lots of rocks jutting out of the water near the shore. Avoid swimming near the estuaries or you might find yourself being carried out to sea by the currents like a sack of potatoes.

ⓩ **Playa Junquillal** *(25 km west of Santa Cruz)* is bordered by tall grass, so it's not your run-of-the-mill beach. Indeed, it feels like you're at the ends of the world here, save for the eight small hotels scattered about the forest and on the one-kilometre stretch of clean, dark sand. The water is not very deep but the waves are rather powerful. Furthermore, the beach is off the tourist-beaten path, away from the camera-toting masses.

Parque Nacional Barra Honda *($6; 7am to 4pm; ☎659-9039 or 659-9194)* lies 23 kilometres northeast of the charming little town of Nicoya, a good starting point for the park. It was created on August 20, 1974, after members of the Costa Rican Speleology Association discovered a network of forty-odd caves, some of which are very deep, several years earlier. Barra Honda is also the name of the large 423-metre-high mountain that dominates the plain. Three caves are open to the public, but can only be visited with a local guide *(about $25/person, and much less for a group, maximum of 8 people at a time; reservations required;* ☎685-5580 or 685-5667*)*.

The park comprises a lovely hiking trail, **Los Laureles**, which forms a 9.3-kilometre-loop. It takes between three and five hours to hike, and passes the park's most interesting sights. The trail is easy to cover since 70 percent of it is flat, except for the section that goes to the summit of **Cerro Barra Honda** (423 metres). The view from the top is phenomenal; it encompasses the Gulf of Nicoya, Isla Chira and a vast plain covered with forests and small villages.

The **Ostional National Wildlife Refuge** *($6;* ☎659-9039 or 659-9194*)* is located about 50 kilometres southwest of Nicoya, on the beaches of Nosara and Ostional. It is 8 kilometres long, but only a few hundred metres wide, covering a total area of 162 hectares of land and 587 hectares of water. This reserve was created to protect this exceptional spot where thousands of olive ridley sea turtles (which weigh 40 kg on average) come to lay their eggs every year between July and November. The giant leatherback turtles (which can weigh as much as 500kg) lay their eggs here less often, but when they do, it is an equally fascinating sight.

Sheltered by coral reefs, **Playa Sámara** *(35 km from Nicoya)* is a pretty beach with calm waters ideal for swimming. The village of Sámara, located alongside the beach, is has a fairly developed tourist infrastructure for the region; there are even a few bars and nightclubs worth checking out. There are other beaches farther south, including the magnificent **Playa Carrillo**, five kilometres away.

Refugio
Nacional
Bahía
Junquillal

SWEET DREAMS

Camping is permitted on site *($1.25/person/day)*, and 25 sites are provided for that purpose. There are picnic tables, cooking grills, drinking water, bathrooms and showers.

Parque Nacional Santa Rosa

SWEET DREAMS

The Santa Rosa national park has the best accommodation setup with eight rooms (provided there are vacancies) for $14.50/person/night for tourists and a little less *($10)* if you stay at the Nancite biological station, near the beach of the same name. The well-equipped (drinking water, bathrooms, showers, picnic tables, trash cans) campsites *($1.25/person/day)* are located between the administrative offices and La Casona. Two other campsites lie north and south of Naranjo Beach (bring your own food and drinking water), a dozen kilometres from the administrative offices. A cafeteria serves high quality meals *(breakfast: $3.50; lunch: $5; dinner: $4.25)*, and if you are camping near the administration and want to eat there, let them know at least three hours in advance.

Playas del Coco

SWEET DREAMS

The **Cabinas Sol y Mar** *($20; 150 m north of the Astilleros Club, on the Playas del Coco-bound road, ☎670-0368 or 551-3706)* are brand-new.

Hotel Anexo Luna Tica *($20; ☎670-0127, ⚏670-0459)* is a small *Tico*-style hotel. The rooms are rather drably furnished but relatively clean and ideal for casual surfers who can tackle the waves at **Playa Hermosa**, a little farther north.

Playa Brasilito

SWEET DREAMS

The **Ojos Azulejos** *($20; on the main road of Playa Brasilito, ☎654-4346)* and **El Caracol** hotels and **Cabinas Nany** *($20; 200 m south and 75 m east of the soccer field, Brasilito, ☎654-4320)* are three good choices.

Parque Nacional Guanacaste

SWEET DREAMS

When the three biological stations are not all occupied by researchers, visitors are welcome to stay in them. The accommodations are rustic and dormitory-style with shared bathrooms and cold water. Each station can house 20 to 30 people, for $10 to $15/person/night. Reservations are required and visitors must bring their own food. Though there are no actual campsites, you can pitch your tent near the stations *($1.25/person/day)*, provided you obtain permission first.

Playa Tamarindo

SWEET DREAMS

Here are two affordable havens to rest your weary bones: **Cabinas Coral Reef** *($10; ☎653-0291)* and **Cabinas Dolly** (a little more expensive, but a younger clientele). Both are located on the beach and are very welcoming.

Playa Junquillal

SWEET DREAMS

You can pitch your tent at **Camping Los Malinches** *($5; ☎653-0429)*. The owner is affable and the site, covered in trees and facing the beach, enchanting. Otherwise, the **Junquillal** hotel, popular with budget travellers, will do just fine *($11; ☎653-0432)*.

Parque Nacional Palo Verde

SWEET DREAMS

Camping *($1.25/person/day; bathrooms, showers and drinking water)* is permitted next to the park wardens' residence.

Playa Sámara

$

SWEET DREAMS

If you have a tent or hammock, get your beauty sleep at **Camping El Coco**, in the heart of the village: very affordable, clean and the owners are friendly.

If not, the **Hospedaje y Abastecedor Yuri** *($10; northern section of the beach, ☎680-0022)* offers amazingly clean and decent rooms. The decor is rather minimalist, but the beds are comfy. Ugly exterior, but friendly owner.

Parque Nacional Barra Honda

$

SWEET DREAMS

In the southwestern part of the park are the reception and administration buildings as well as picnic and camping areas *($1.25/person/day)*. If you don't have food or a camping stove to prepare your meals (campfires are forbidden due to risk of forest fires), you can eat on site by reserving your meal a day ahead.

Liberia

$

SWEET DREAMS

Hospedaje Lodge La Casona *($10; 300 m south of the central park, ☎/≈666-2971)* is a pleasant place with the comforts of a youth hostel, much like the **Posada Del Tope** *($10; 150 m south of the central park, ☎385-2383 or 666-3876)*.

Hotel Liberia *($12; 75 m south of the public garden on Calle 1, ☎/≈666-0161)*. Clean, with minimalist furnishings. Welcoming staff and decor. Laundry facilities and breakfast available.

Hotel Guanacaste *($15; discounts for Hostelling International cardholders; 25 m west and 100 m south of the Pulmitán bus station, ☎666-0085, ≈666-2287, htlguana@sol.racsa.co.cr)*. A youth hostel with very simply decorated rooms. Friendly welcome, restaurant and laundry service. Camping available.

Liberia

BON APPETIT

Las Tinajas *(on the north side of the central park)*. ▶ Good little snack bar serving North American and other fast food. A fairly popular spot.

Jardín de Azúcar *(one block north of the public garden)*. ▶ Cheap and eclectic little menu.

Pan y Miel *(at Calle 2 and Ave. 3)*. ▶ A bakery and pastry shop where you can sit down to eat. The place makes yummy little cakes and *enchiladas*, among other things.

Rancho El Dulce *(at Calle Central and Ave. Central)*. ▶ A small fast-food stand that also sells a whole gamut of little candies and chocolates. Watch your sweet tooth!

⏭ NORTHERN COSTA RICA ⏮

Longtime a "no man's land," northern Costa Rica is becoming increasingly popular with travellers. And not lazy-type travellers, since the number-one attraction is Lake Arenal, a huge artificial lake in the shadow of the volcano of the same name, from which Aeolus (the wind god) constantly blows, making the place a windsurfing mecca.

Beside Lake Arenal, the magnificently green Monteverde park breaks the patchwork quilt pattern of the many pastures and fields under cultivation.

Ciudad Quesada or **San Carlos** *(100 km north of San José)*. San Carlos and its population of 35,000 is not only located in the middle of the country's northern territories but also in the heart of the most productive agricultural region of Costa Rica. Perched an altitude of 600 metres, it is neither too hot nor too cold. Once again, it is just the place to stay in a cheap hotel while having access to all the services of a mid-sized city. Moreover, this centrally located town is a good starting point for side trips to the surrounding area, depending on your interests.

Puerto Viejo de Sarapiquí *(60 km east of San Carlos)* doesn't have much in the way of budget accommodations, but is worth a stop for its sights.

PRACTICAL INFO

Transport: The trip from **San José** to **Ciudad Quesada (San Carlos)** takes three hours; the bus leaves from Calle 12 between Avenidas 7 and 9. Many departures throughout the day.

It takes an hour to get to **La Fortuna** from Ciudad Quesada (San Carlos); there are many departures throughout the day, though much more frequently in the morning.

To reach **Monteverde** from Ciudad Quesada? (departures at 6am and 3pm, return at 7am and 3pm), you must go through **Tilarán**. From Tilarán, a bus heads to Monteverde at 1pm and returns at 7am. Monteverde can also be reached from San José (Calle 14 between Avenidas 9 and 11) at 6:30am and 2:30pm; return at the same times.

Puerto Viejo de Sarapiquí: Buses heading in this direction are marked "Río Frío"; they leave San José six times a day (Ave. 11 between Calles Central and 1). The 6:30am, noon and 3pm buses take the scenic Heredia route (4-hour trip), while the 10am, 1pm, 3:30pm and 4pm buses follow the Guapiles-bound highway through Braulio Carrillo national park, then head back up north, passing through Las Horquetas and La Selva before reaching Puerto Viejo.

Los Chiles: Several buses a day link San Carlos to this town.

Caño Negro Wildlife Refuge: Daily departures from San José (Calle 12 and Ave. 9) at 5:30am and 3:30pm. The trip from San José to Los Chiles takes about 2.5 hours *($2.20; Autotransportes, ☎460-5032)*.

A few kilometres southwest of Puerto Viejo is **MUSA** *($5; El Tigre, on the road to Horquetas)*, a local women's co-operative farm where herbs are grown for medicinal, cosmetic and other commercial purposes. Very interesting for budding herbalists who can learn more about herbs and their healing properties. Certain products are available for purchase.

There are also three waterfalls in the region. In La Cinchona, a small community about halfway between San José and Puerto Viejo, there are the spectacular **San Rafael falls**, while the **La Paz falls** are located on the road from Poás to Puerto Viejo de Sarapiquí. By crossing the bridge over the river here, you will spot a second waterfall above the first. At night, the lighting effects are spectacular. The **San Fernando falls**, located a little farther north along this road, are also worth a look. These can be admired from a private home, **El Parador**, which is open to the public. The owners also feed a bevy of hummingbirds that are interesting to watch, especially when they drink the energy-giving sugar water (necessary for their survival) from the feeders outside the house.

Rara Avis *(☎/ ≈253-0844)* is a private nature reserve founded by American biologist Amos Bien, who first came to Costa Rica in 1977. Fascinated by the rich ecosystems in this corner of the world, he soon realized that they were threatened by clear-cutting and the excessive conversion of land into pastures with damaging effects on the environment, as seen in Guanacaste and along the Sarapiquí river. This led him to create the Rara Avis reserve in 1983 right next to that of La Selva and the Braulio Carrillo national park. The goal of the 1,300-hectare reserve is to prove that the preservation of natural habitats is just as, if not more, beneficial to society than their conversion into agricultural areas. As a nature-conservation and research centre, this reserve, somewhat off the tourist-beaten path, is more for adventurous types or real nature lovers. We say this for two reasons: first, getting there, via a rather dreadful road, is an adventure in itself and therefore requires a lot of patience and endurance. Second, it rains nonstop. However, if you decide to make the trip, you will be rewarded with a fascinating variety of animals and plants. There is also a magnificent 55-metre-high waterfall in the reserve's jungle. The trails can be explored alone or with a guide.

La Selva Biological Station *(3 km south of Puerto Viejo de Sarapiquí, ☎740-1515, ≈740-1414 or through the OTS ☎240-6696, ≈240-6783)* is essentially a research centre that attracts numerous ecology specialists and students from the world over, with facilities that have been set up for them to do fieldwork on site. It is nevertheless possible to visit La Selva and even stay there by reserving in advance. There are many (400) bird species and a lot of rain, but the trails are pleasant and the guides friendly. Reserve hikes in advance.

La Fortuna *(35 km northwest of San Carlos)*. Closer to sea level (and therefore hotter), La Fortuna was long a quiet little agricultural village until the volcano awakened from its slumber in the late sixties, causing a boom in tourism. Besides being near the volcano, La Fortuna lies only a few kilometres from the largest lake in the country, a windsurfer's paradise thanks to its constant 20-knot-plus winds. There are also good places to swim, hot springs, caves and more — all in all, a region with a lot to offer.

Catarata La Fortuna *(from town, take the first street west of the church, which crosses the Río Burío)*. Pay attention to the road, as it can be rough-going in places (especially during the rainy season) and the way to the falls is not clearly marked. But the waterfall is very beautiful, cascading down the rock face in tiers. It can be seen from the parking lot, but you can get closer to it by taking a steep path to the foot of the falls. You can also swim here, but watch out for the sometimes very strong current.

Tabacón Resort *($14/day, $20 with admission to the restaurant; 10am to 10pm; 13 km west of La Fortuna via the road to the Arenal volcano, ☎222-1072 or 233-0780, ≈221-3075).* A first-class complex featuring some ten landscaped hot-springs pools fed by the Tabacón River, with water temperatures ranging from 23°C to 40°C; waterfalls; two restaurants and a couple of bars. All this in a luxurious setting surrounded by a lush forest and with a great view of the volcano. A little too movie-star-sleek, but lots of fun. Taking a dip in the hot springs come nightfall, when everything is dark and sometimes hazy, is even better. It is less crowded during the week. A first-class hotel is slated to be built soon — *quelle surprise!*

Across the road from the Tabacón Resort, there is a less expensive way to enjoy the hot springs, though the facilities are the bare minimum *($5; bathrooms, changing room and small snack bar; 9:30am to 10pm).*

Ⓩ **Parque Nacional Volcán Arenal** *($6; 8am to 10pm; ☎460-1412 or 695-5908).* Costa Rica's signature volcano is only 1,633 metres high, but it is one of the most active volcanoes in the world, drawing people from everywhere to see it, particularly at night, when glowing lava flows can be admired from afar. Most hotels offer $7 packages that include a nighttime visit to the volcano. The mountain, with its perfect conical shape, is an impressive sight, made all the more majestic since no other mountains surround it blocking the show.

The park was recently opened, which means that the facilities are not as established as in the country's other parks. Still, a good number of trails are accessible, and you'll be warned about the dangers of going all the way to the top, where a few fatal accidents have occurred in the past. The most popular place at the park is the **Mirador**, located 1.3 kilometres from the entrance. It can be reached on foot via a small trail, or by car. This lookout point at the foot of the volcano is an excellent spot from which to see, hear and feel all the volcano's mighty activity. Here you can see the slew of lava flows that forced their way to the base of the mountain, consuming everything in their wake. Depending on the day, you may see showers of dust and ashes spewing out of the cone. And don't be startled if you feel the earth shaking and hear a loud rumbling, as though the Arenal wanted to demonstrate its power and destructive force. At the edge of the park is the **Arenal Observatory Lodge** *($1.50; bar-restaurant; ☎257-9489, ⌐257-4220, past the park, follow the signs)*, where you'll be treated to another breathtaking view of the volcano.

Cavernas de Venado *($15; one hour along a road that starts a few km east of Nuevo Arenal)* is a 2-kilometre-long cave where you'll find the typical geological formations (stalactites and stalagmites), and bats! Guided tours.

The **Arenal Botanical Garden** *($4; 9am to 5pm; on the road between La Fortuna and Nuevo Arenal, 5 km east of Nuevo Arenal and 25 km west of the Lake Arenal dike; ☎694-4273, ⌐694-4086)* is a lovely little reserve with over 1,200 plants from all over the world which can be admired along the trails running through here. Of course, several species of birds and butterflies frequent the place. There is even a little butterfly farm. Self-guided tour.

Nuevo Arenal *(halfway between La Fortuna and Tilarán)*. This region would have been nothing were it not for the reconstruction of this city after the original was submerged underwater as part of a hydroelectric project. Because of the constant wind, it can get very cool at night, but this makes the town beach a windsurfer's paradise. For seasoned pros only!

Ⓩ Monteverde *(150 km north of San José)*. Unarguably the most popular attraction in the country, the Monteverde area is composed of vast forests that cover wide valleys and lush mountains that are between 800 and 1,800 metres high. Though the region is swarming with tourists, it is a must. It feels like a whole different world here, probably because you are in Quaker land. Eleven families of Quakers came here from the United States in the early 1950s to escape imprisonment in their native Alabama for refusing to fight in the Korean war. These pacifists chose to live in Costa Rica because the country has no standing army and is politically stable. To secure their freedom and live out their convictions, they bought land in the Monteverde region, which, at that time, was accessible only by horse and buggy. A veritable ornithological and botanical paradise, the Monteverde region is stunning, especially on the way into the village, which seems to pop out of nowhere.

Monteverde is not built like a typical village with a grid-like pattern of streets and a central square. Instead, its houses, hotels, restaurants and stores line the five-kilometre stretch of unpaved road that runs from the village of Santa Elena to the Monteverde reserve. The church, post office, bank, medical clinic, grocery store, public phones and most of the low-cost hotels and rooms for rent in the region are found in **Santa Elena**. A visit to **Chunches** *(☎645-5147)*, a café that sells new and used books and has laundry facilities, might prove useful. The friendly owners, Wendy and Jim, will give you the lowdown on the region's activities, hotels and restaurants.

The Quaker days are gone, except at *La Lechería* *(7:30am to 4pm, Sun until 12:30pm; ☎645-5136)*, a cheese factory founded in 1953 and located halfway between Santa Elena and the Monteverde reserve. Here you can see the manufacturing process for many different kinds of cheeses (edam, gouda, emmenthal, cheddar, etc.), including the very popular *monterico*. The factory's output, which started at 10 kilograms per day in the 1950s, has grown to 1,000 kilograms per day. The cheese is distributed to all parts of the country, and more than 100 people are employed by the factory.

The **Butterfly Garden** *($6, guided tour included; 9:30am to 4pm; ☎645-5512)* is *the* place to admire the beauty and variety of the tropical forest's butterflies. The very affable guides will first introduce you to the complex and captivating process of the various stages of the butterfly life cycle. Inside the study centre, you'll see a large collection of butterflies and learn more about the role of the shapes and colours they sport. While some of them have "eyes" on their wings in order to frighten predators, others are camouflaged like leaves so that their enemies will overlook them. In one of the display units, you can even see caterpillars weaving themselves into chrysalides, and you might be lucky enough witness one emerge from its cocoon as a beautiful butterfly and take its first flight. Also worth visiting is the **Finca Ecológica** *($5; 7am to 5pm; ☎645-5222)*, a 17-hectare private reserve with umpteen trails from which you can easily spot many bird and butterfly species, as well as several wild animals such as coatis, agoutis, sloths and white-faced capuchin monkeys.

Serpentario *($3; 9am to 5pm; on the outskirts of Santa Elena, right near the Finca Valverde hotel, ☎645-5238)*. The aim of this serpentarium is not to frighten, but to teach visitors how to recognize the deadliest species, such as vipers and especially the dreaded fer-de-lance. So next time you set out on a trail, you will know what to do should you encounter one of these reptilian critters.

Several women from the Monteverde region have joined forces to create a local handicrafts co-op called **CASEM** *(8am to 5pm; ☎645-5190 or 645-5262)*. The co-op creates handmade clothing and other artifacts with plant and animal prints. The profits from the sale of these products go towards the artisans and the Monteverde community.

Easier to access, **Bajo del Tigre** *($5; 8am to 4:30pm; near CASEM)* is a network of short trails (3.3 km) that wind through forest that is less dense than that of other parks in the Monteverde region, but just as teeming with plant and animal life. This region, which is part of the Pacific Divide of the Tilarán Cordillera, affords lovely views of the Gulf of Nicoya. The tour begins at the small field station where you can find out what there is to see and do in the area. The place is renowned for ornithology, as more than 200 bird species have been counted here. Before setting off to explore the trails, which lead all the way to the Río Máquina canyon, you'll be given an excellent little booklet to guide you through the 22 interpretative stations about the site's flora and fauna.

(Z) **Reserva de Santa Elena** *($6; 7am to 4pm; ☎645-5390, ☞645-5014)*. This 310-hectare reserve is located 6.5 kilometres north of the village of Santa Elena, at an altitude of 1,670 metres — and receives a lot of rain. It would be a good idea to dress accordingly (rain boots can be rented on site). The reserve's terrain is more or less identical to that of Monteverde, with the slight (but crucial!) difference that it is less crowded, allowing you to be alone with nature. To get to the reserve, go north on Santa Elena's main road to the Colegio Santa Elena, and from there follow the signs. Transport service to the reserve *(departure at 7am; $1.70)* is now offered from the Santa Elena information office. A visitor and info centre, a snack bar, a souvenir shop, documentation about the reserve, and bathrooms are all on site.

The reserve has four hiking trails, covering a total distance of 12 kilometres. Each trail forms a loop that takes 45 minutes to 4 hours to cover and has some scenic views of the tropical cloud forest and the famous Arenal volcano. But don't expect to see much, as the lookouts are usually shrouded in clouds and mist. However, according to Eduardo Venegas, the reserve's friendly administrator and owner of Pensión La Flor de Monteverde, on a clear day you can make out not only the lake and the Arenal volcano, but the Tenorio (1,916 m), Miravalles (2,028 m) and Rincón de la Vieja (1,895 m) volcanoes to the northwest, as well as the Gulf of Nicoya to the south!

(Z) The **Monteverde Cloud Forest Reserve** *($8; 7am to 4pm; visitor centre, restaurant, souvenir shop, guides, documentation, rainboot rentals; ☎645-5122, ☞645-5034, montever@sol.racsa.co.cr)* is run by a nonprofit organization involved in scientific research and environmental education. Its mission is also to increase visitors' awareness of the need to preserve these tropical rainforests that are among the country's greatest natural resources. Indeed, the cloud forest, besides protecting the flora and fauna that are as abundant in the reserve as they

are rare in the country, also supplies water to the many surrounding valleys.

The Continental Divide runs through the reserve: rivers on its
western flank flow toward the Pacific Ocean, and those on the
eastern flank empty into the Caribbean Sea. And because this
split is located only two kilometres away from the reception
centre, there is a great geographical and climatic diversity in
the different parts of the park, to which visitors do not have to
roam very far. The different climates mean different weather
conditions (rain, sun, wind, more rain, a lot of humidity, etc.),
so be prepared for this when wandering the trails of the reserve
by bringing extra clothing, boots and rain wear, in addition to
a camera, insect repellent and of course binoculars. And since
the reserve is in the mountains, (the visitor centre is at
1,530 m in altitude), mornings can be quite cool and damp. The
landscapes also change according to the altitude. The lowest area
(600 m) is near the Río Peñas Blancas, while the highest is at
the summit of the Cerro Tres Amigos (1,842 m) in the northwestern
part of the reserve. Between these two extremes, the vegetation
consists of lush forests with sometimes gigantic trees covered in
mosses, lianas and thousands of epiphytic plants, preventing the
sun from shining through to the ground. Among the 2,500-odd
species of plants there are no less than 420 different varieties
of orchids. The reserve is made up of six different life zones,
and the biodiversity of each is so complex that new scientific
discoveries are constantly being made here.

The reserve is also home to about a hundred different kinds of
mammals, including the jaguar, the ocelot and Baird's tapir,
which are hard to spot but whose tracks are sometimes visible. On
the other hand, you won't have any trouble spotting – or at least
hearing! – noisy howler monkeys and capuchins. The reserve also
boasts 120 kinds of amphibians and reptiles and over 400 bird
species, making this an ornithological paradise. If you want to
get a glimpse of the "resplendent" quetzal, visit the reserve
between the months of March and May, during mating season when
this bird lays its eggs in its nest a dozen metres above the
ground. This bird is harder to spot during the rest of the year,
but an experienced guide can show you the most frequented areas.
The quetzal is a member of the trogon family and is remarkably
large. It is an average of 35 centimetres tall, and its formida-
ble emerald-green train, or extension of the tail, can be up to
60 centimetres long! The quetzal makes its home in the highlands
of the tropical rainforest at altitudes of 1,200 to 3,000 metres
from southern Mexico to Panama.

The Monteverde reserve has seven hiking trails, covering a total
distance of 12.4 kilometres (not including the trails where
access is limited). Only 120 visitors are allowed on the trails

at one time. It is therefore best to reserve your entrance ticket the day before (most hotels can do this and hire a guide for you), so you can arrive at the crack of dawn, which is prime birdwatching time. The other option is to spend the night in one of the three shelters located along the trails or the one near the entrance to the reserve (researchers and groups have priority, though). Very well marked and maintained, the hiking trails make it easy to penetrate the reserve's cloud forest (a small map of the trails will be given to you at the entrance). The most visited trails form a triangle (*El Triangulo*) to the east. The **Río** trail leads to the Cuecha river and its little waterfall. The **Chomogo** trail climbs to an altitude of 1,680 metres and leads to the **Roble** trail. Finally, the **Bosque Nuboso** interpretive trail (booklet available at the visitor centre) consists of 28 interpretive points that explain the reserve's flora and fauna. This trail ends at the **La Ventana**, a scenic lookout that affords a 360° view of the surroundings.

The 9,969-hectare **Caño Negro National Wildlife Refuge** (*$6; 8am to 4pm; ☎460-1412, ↪460-0644*) is located in the northernmost part of the country near the Nicaraguan border and is very popular for its 800-hectare lake, Lago Caño Negro, which expands during the rainy season, swelling the Río Frío considerably. During the dry season, namely from January to April, the lake, which has a maximum depth of 3 metres, gradually dries up, and sometimes disappears completely!

Though the reserve is mostly frequented by ornithologists, biologists and other naturalists, more and more organized groups are catching on to it and coming here to spend the day observing the exceptionally large number of animals in the reserve. The fact that there are less people here increases your chances of observing animal life. Many visitors take the boat excursion.

La Fortuna	**SWEET DREAMS**
$	Both **Hotel La Central** (*☎479-9004*) and **Cabinas Villa Fortuna** (*☎479-9139*) are suitable for travellers on a tight budget because of their decent quality for the price.

Santa Elena

$

SWEET DREAMS

The village of Santa Elena is full of inexpensive little inns and *pensións*. Check out the following places, all located on the only street in the village: **Hospedaje El Banco**, **Cabinas Martín** and **Pensión Colibrí**.

Monteverde Reserve

$

SWEET DREAMS

If you want to spend the night here, you can stay in one of the reserve's three shelters *($3.50/person/night; reservations required)* after undertaking a two- to six-hour walk, depending on which one you want. Each shelter can accommodate up to 10 hikers and is equipped with electricity, a stove, kitchen utensils, drinking water and a shower. Reservations are a must.

Ciudad Quesada

$

SWEET DREAMS

Hotel del Valle *($10; at Calle 3 and Ave. 0, ☎460-0718)*. ▶ A typical small-town hotel that is just the place for travellers on a shoestring budget who wish to spend a night in Ciudad Quesada.

Balneario Carlos *($14)*. ▶ Clean and spacious private cabins. Pool on site.

La Central *($12; on the west side of the central park, ☎460-0766 or 460-0301, ☎460-0391)*. ▶ Probably one of the best places to stay in Ciudad Quesada. With 48 clean rooms, it has the feel of a big hotel. It also has a casino.

Ciudad Quesada

BON APPETIT

Pizzería y Pollo Frito Pin Pollo *(at Ave. 1 and Calle 0, ☎460-1801)*. ▶ Pizza and fried chicken at reasonable prices.

Ciudad Quesada

$

BON APPETIT

La Jarra *(on the south side of the cathedral,*
☎460-0985). ▣ Serves local fare and fast food. It
is clean and one of the few restaurants in the
centre of town that isn't a hole in the wall.

Ciudad Quesada also has a whole series of small
restaurants that are more like *sodas* than real
restaurants, particularly around the central park.
El Parque *(at Ave. 0 and Calle 0)* is one of these.

⏭ THE ATLANTIC COAST ⏮

Like in its neighbouring countries, Costa Rica's Atlantic coast
is completely different from the rest of the country. This region
is characterized by flat, humid marshlands where a dry season is
unheard of, and a Garifuna population whose mother tongue is
English or Creole – not Spanish. Unfortunately, this part of the
country is seen as dangerous by *Joséphinos*. Because of these
prejudices, this region is less visited and is therefore less
expensive than the rest of the country, to the great pleasure of
budget travellers. Even though it is five times smaller than the
Pacific coast, the Atlantic coast also has many white- and black-
sand beaches which are surfer meccas. In terms of nature, there
are five national protected parks or reserves where you can
observe giant turtles as well as many bird species. If you're
still not convinced, the region has magnificent beds of coral.

Puerto Limón *(200 km east of San José)*. Capital of the province
of the same name and main port on the Atlantic Coast, Puerto
Limón lost its allure after the United Fruit Company withdrew
from Costa Rica in the 1940s and the earthquake of 1991 devastated the town. These events only served to further marginalise
this already struggling region. However, if you want to get to
the coast, you have to pass through Limón. And if you want to go
to the northern part of the country, you have to take a boat from
here. There is also a coastal road heading south. Every year, a
carnival is held on October 12 to commemorate Christopher
Columbus's arrival in the New World.

The popular **Mercado Central** *(Av. 2 between Calles 3 and 4)* is
surrounded by sodas, restaurants and inexpensive hotels, and is
the busiest place in town. You'll meet people with a mixed
Spanish, Chinese and West Indian ancestry. And where there's a
market, there are pickpockets and other undesirables, so be on

PRACTICAL INFO

Transportation from **San José** to **Limón**: departures every 30 minutes from the Parque Nacional *(Av. 3 between Calles 19 and 21)* from 5am to 7pm. The 162-km trip takes about 2 hours and 30 minutes. Coopelimón *($2.20 regular, $2.70 express; ☎223-7811)* and Transportes Caribeños *($2.56 regular, $3.20 express; ☎257-0895)* go there. The return trips *(Limón Calle 2 between Av. 1 and 2)* are at the same time.

San José - Cahuita - Sixaola: daily departures *(Av. 11 between Calles Central and 1)* at 6am, 1:30pm, 3:30pm for the regular service, and 10am and 4pm for the express service. The trip takes about three hours *($4.60)* to Cahuita and four hours *($6.25)* to Sixaola with Transportes Mepe *(☎257-8129)*.

San José - Puerto Viejo - Manzanillo: daily departures *(Av. 11 between Calles Central and 1)* at 10am and 4pm. The trip takes about 4 hours and 30 minutes *($6)* to Manzanillo with Transportes Mepe *(☎257-8129)*.

Limón - Cahuita - Puerto Viejo: from Limón *(Av. 4 and Calle 3)*, departures at 5am, 10am, 1pm and 4pm. It takes about an hour to get to Cahuita *($1)* and 1 hour and 30 minutes to Puerto Viejo *($1.25)* with Transportes Mepe *(☎758-1572 or 258-3522)*.

By Boat: to get to **Tortuguero**, you have to catch a boat from **Moín**. Note that this type of transportation is not regulated, and you will have to arrange the terms and conditions of your ride. At the Moín quay, ask which boats go to Tortuguero, when they leave (varies according to the water level in the canal) and how much it costs. It takes anywhere between 2.5 and 4 hours for the trip, depending on the speed of the boat and how many stops are made to admire the vegetation along the canals. Prices are negotiable, especially for groups.

Money: There is a **Banco Nacional** in Puerto Limón, near Parque Vargas.

Mail: Calle 5 and Av. 1 in Puerto Limón.

Phone: Calle 5 and Av. 2 in Puerto Limón.

your guard at all times. At the **Museo Etno-Histórico** *(Tue-Sat 9am to 5pm; Calle 4 and Av. 2, ☎758-3903)* near the Mercado Central, you can learn more about the history and culture of the people of the Atlantic Coast. At the edge of town by the beach is the pretty **Parque Vargas** *(Calle 1 between Avenidas 1 and 20)*. It is pleasant to stroll through its large palm trees and lush greenery. **Playa Bonita** *(4 km north of town)* is the closest swimming beach to Puerto Limón. It is also a great beach for surfing.

The **Hitoy Cerere Biological Reserve** *($6; 60 km south of Puerto Limón, ☎283-8004 or 758-3996)* was created in April 1978 and is the least visited park on the Atlantic coast, probably because of its very rudimentary tourist facilities. However, nature-lovers will enjoy its wild countryside, with its abundant rivers, flora and fauna, including 115 species of birds. The reserve encompasses mountains, with the highest peak at Mount Bitarkara (1,025 m) in the western part of the park. Hiking is without a doubt the most popular activity in the reserve. The trails are poorly signed and therefore confusing, so it is better to go with a guide. The 1991 earthquake also left its mark, felling numerous trees. Most of the trails run along the rivers. To get to the reserve, go through the Valle de la Estrella via Penshurst (20 km).

Ⓩ **Cahuita** *(43 km south of Limón)*. With its several sand-covered streets, its small hotels and friendly restaurants, and the Caribbean sea as a backdrop, this village is picture-perfect. The atmosphere is relaxed, and tourists wander around and socialize with each other at some of the more popular bars and restaurants. And staying in Cahuita is less expensive than in the rest of the country. For more information on the area and its hotels, restaurants and native reserves, contact **Cahuita Tours** *(7am to 8pm; north of the main road, ☎755-0232, ☞755-0082)*. There are a currency exchange counter and taxi, telephone and fax services. They also sell bus tickets for San José, rent snorkelling equipment and bicycles, and organize all kinds of guided tours of the region.

Parque Nacional Cahuita *(free admission or $6 depending on the sector; camping; ☎755-0060)*. This park protects the magnificent coral reef surrounding Punta Cahuita. With a total surface area of 1,067 hectares of land and more than 600 hectares of ocean, the park encompasses a superb tropical rainforest as well as two magnificent white-sand beaches. The coral reef is one of the largest and most fully grown in the country. However, this unique habitat is threatened with extinction by the deforestation of the surrounding areas and the waste being dumped into the rivers as they flow through the region's banana plantations. The coral reef was severely damaged by the 1991 earthquake, which raised the shoreline by as much as a metre in certain places, exposing and destroying much of the reef. You can go scuba diving here with Cahuita Tours (see above).

Puerto Viejo *(18 km from Cahuita)* is a small, lively village where tourists, mostly young North Americans and Europeans, stay — and stay — to make the most of its marvellous white sand beaches, small inexpensive hotels and restaurants, and especially the "cool" reggae-music-playing atmosphere similar to that of Cahuita. On either side of the town there are white or black sand beaches that are easy to get to. You can even walk 18 kilometres along the beach all the way to Cahuita, but this is very tiring.

At the centre of the village, in front of the Tarmara *soda*, the Asociación Talamanqueña de Ecoturismo y Conservación, or **ATEC** *(7am to 7pm; on the main street, ☎750-0188, atecmail@sol.racsa.co.cr, www.greenarrow.com/x/atec.htm)* is a good place to go for information about environmental protection and regional culture. Their guides will take you anywhere on the Atlantic Coast. Another agency worth checking out for its guided tours is **Terras Aventuras** *(next to the Comisariato Manuel León, at the end of the beach, ☎750-0004)*. They also sell local crafts.

The **Refugio Nacional de Vida Silvestre Gandoca-Manzanillo** was created in October 1985 to protect one of the most beautiful areas of Costa Rica from harmful tourist development. The park encompasses 5,013 hectares of land and 4,436 hectares of sea, and runs south of Puerto Viejo de Talamanca up to the Río Sixaola near the border of Panamá. Rarely visited by tourists, probably due to the lack of facilities, the park is still an exceptional site that protects threatened flora and fauna. It is home to vast coral reefs (at Punta Uva, Manzanillo and Punta Mona), an oyster bed, a mangrove swamp, fields, a rich tropical rainforest and breathtakingly beautiful white sand beaches lined with coconut trees. There are some 369 species of birds, including pelicans, toucans, parakeets and eagles, as well as howler monkeys, capuchins, sloths, tapirs, caimans and crocodiles. The park also has four species of turtles including the impressive leatherback, the largest turtle in the world, which lays its eggs between March and July. Camping in the park is free, but you have to register first at the information office in Manzanillo. The park has a 5.5-kilometre trail that runs along several beaches where you can snorkel out to an incredibly beautiful coral reef.

Tortuguero *(80 km north of Limón)*. This region is one of the most spectacular in the country. If you're a real nature lover, you'll appreciate the abundant flora and fauna found here. With five metres of rain a year, it's easy to understand why Tortuguero has exceptional natural surroundings. Thankfully, the region is pretty hard to reach (by plane and boat only), so it really feels like another world in another time where nature controls the inhabitants' way of life. To pack in the canals, the village, the beach, the turtle museum and lay back in a hammock and admire the vegetation, you will need at least three days. The canals between Puerto Limón and Tortuguero are impressive, even though they were seriously damaged by the 1991 earthquake which raised the shoreline by one metre.

The **Caribbean Conservation Corporation**, or **CCC** *(donations accepted; Mon-Sat 10am to 5:30pm, Sun 2pm to 5pm; ☎224-9215)*, north of the village, near the Río Tortuguero, has a natural history museum focussing on sea turtles. The CCC has been involved in sea-turtle conservation projects since 1959. Four species are found in the region (green, leatherback, Hawksbill and loggerhead). The museum opened in 1994 and presents information on the various specials of turtles and educates visitors on how to protect their natural habitats. An 18-minute video also explores the region's flora and fauna. A small onsite souvenir shop sells books, videos, T-shirts and other items to finance the museum.

A black-sand beach starts at the village and stretches five kilometres north along the lagoon, all the way to the mouth of the Tortuguero River. Strolling next to its lush forest is very pleasant. Along the way, at the end of the lagoon, you will see fisherman in water up to their knees, trying to catch enormous fish. On the other side of the lagoon is Cerro Tortuguero, the highest peak on the Atlantic coast.

The **Parque Nacional Tortuguero** *($6; camping; ☎719-2929 or 710-7673, the Cuatro Esquinas entrance is south of the village of Tortuguero, the Jalova entrance is south of the canal near Parismina)* is one of the most visited parks in the country, but it is also one of the biggest, so it isn't overcrowded. The quality and quantity of the plant and animal life here is incredible, and the sloths hanging from branches, howler and capuchin monkeys, freshwater turtles, iguanas, lizards, venomous frogs and even camouflaged caimans can be safely observed from the narrow canal. The mission of the park is to protect the turtles who come to lay their eggs here, which have been overhunted in the last century. To see the turtles lay their eggs on the beach, you will have to go with a park guide.

Limón	SWEET DREAMS
	Limón isn't the best place to stay. Cahuita and Puerto Viejo are much more pleasant and not far away.

Limón

SWEET DREAMS

Hotel Cariari *($8; Av. 3 and Calle 2, ☎758-1395)* is one of the cheaper establishments in town, but the bathrooms are shared and there are no fans in the rooms.

Hotel Oriental *(8; Calle 4 between Av. 3 and 4, ☎758-0117)* is another cheap hotel and is pretty clean.

Cahuita

SWEET DREAMS

Cahuita is a dream, literally. It is beautiful and the cheapest place to stay on the coast. You can stay at an array of friendly little hotels such as **Cabinas Jenny, Nan Nan Spencer Seaside** and **Colibri Paradise**.

There are **campgrounds** *($1.25/person/day)* south of town in the Parque Nacional Cahuita.

Cabinas Surf Side *($10; ☎755-0246)* are directly across the street from the school. There are 23 clean rooms with bathrooms and fans.

Cabinas Smith *($20; ☎755-0068)* have six little rooms with showers and fans.

Puerto Viejo

SWEET DREAMS

Hotel Kiskadee *($10)* and **Cashew Hill** *($18)* are just a few minutes' walk from the soccer field and are like youth hostels, with dormitory-style rooms, kitchen access and a friendly atmosphere.

Cabinas Salsa Brava *($15)* are among the only affordable *cabinas* with private bathrooms and ocean views. There is also a café, open all day.

**Tortu-
guero**

SWEET DREAMS

Caninas Aracari Lodge (☎798-3059) are located behind the soccer field, and rooms with private bathrooms cost less than $10.

Limón

BON APPETIT

Three of the most popular *sodas* with travellers and residents alike are **La Estrella** *(Calle 5 and Av. 3)*, where the atmosphere, service, food and prices are excellent; the lovely **Soda Mares** *(Av. 2 between Calles 3 and 4)*, which serves various dishes at reasonable prices in the lively ambiance of the nearby *mercado*; and **Soda Yans** *(Av. 2 between Calles 5 and 6)*, a local dive.

the good life

The most popular spot in **Cahuita**, especially on a Saturday night, is the **Vaz**, where you can listen to reggae music as well as salsa and meringue.

Jimmy *(northwest of the village, Playa Negra)* is very popular with pool sharks. You can also play chess or checkers while listening to rock and blues. If you're hungry, try the "Power Soup," composed of beef, bones, manioc and yams.

The other "in" place in town is the **Sarafina**, which plays international music and serves reasonably priced food, including pizza, until 1am.

Bambú *(as you leave the village towards Manzanillo)* is a reggae bar.

The locals go to **Standford's** *(as you leave the village, near the sea)*, a nightclub mixing reggae, calypso and salsa.

But the most popular nightclub with tourists is **Jonny's Place** *(near the police station)*, which plays world beat music and gets packed after 10pm.

⏭ THE CENTRAL PACIFIC COAST ⏮

This area is a favourite with both tourists and locals because it is only a few hours from the capital. Vast beaches stretch out along the coast whose beauty is marred in places by uninviting and intrusive hotel complexes. Haphazardly interspersed between the hotels are large undeveloped tracts of land; one of these is the superb Manuel Antonio national park. Take note that considerably less visitors frequent the park during the rainy season from May to December. You can take advantage of this, as long as the two hours of torrential rain don't put a damper on your enthusiasm.

Puntarenas *(80 km west of San José)*. The region's major city, Puntarenas has lost much of its splendour since the last century. Formerly the country's busiest seaport and the gateway to rich European markets, it has now become the obligatory transit point for tourists visiting the southern Nicoya Peninsula and its many beaches. Puntarenas is built on a long point of land surrounded by water, but its beaches are not particularly attractive so you must go a little farther away. In the centre of greater Puntarenas is the **Casa de la Cultura** *(Avenida 1 and Calle 1, ☎661-1394)* where exhibitions, concerts and plays are presented. The **Museo Histórico Marino** *($1; Tue-Sun, 9am to 5pm; Avenida Central between Calles 3 and 5)* shows a multi-media exhibition on the history of the city, and the **Iglesia de Puntarenas**, located on Avenida Central, west of Museo Marino, is probably the most beautiful building in this city.

Ⓩ The **Curú National Wildlife Reserve** *($5; reservations necessary, ☎661-2392, ☎641-0060)* is situated seven kilometres south of Paquera where the boat from Puntarenas docks. Since 1983, this private reserve has encompassed part of the old hacienda in order to protect the coastal area's fragile marine life. The reserve contains a dry tropical forest, a wet tropical forest, mangroves, pastures and fruit tree orchards. There are enough trails to spend a day exploring, and the beach is right there, so you can go scuba diving. And of course, the fauna and flora are incredibly rich.

The reserve has truly exceptional fauna and flora. There are 500 species of plants, a dozen of which are indigenous to the region. There are also 232 species of birds, 78 species of mammals, 87 species of reptiles and 26 species of amphibians. Depending on the day, you can observe sea turtles, iguanas, crocodiles, boa constrictors, peccaries, armadillos, agoutis, pumas, monkeys, and more. The refuge shelters three kinds of monkeys: the howler monkey, the white-faced capuchin monkey and

PRACTICAL INFO

Transportation: (Puntarenas and all of the central Pacific region). **The Puntarenas - Paquera Car Ferry:** there are five crossings from Puntarenas to Paquera and back each day between 4:15am and 9:15pm. It costs $1.25 for an adult. Each way takes about one hour and 30 minutes *(Naviera Tambor, ☎661-2084)*. There is also a passenger ferry *($1.25; three departures a day between 6am and 5pm; ☎661-2830)*.

Puntarenas - Playa Naranjo Ferry: this car ferry is the best way to reach Carmona and Nicoya. There are five departures daily between 3:15am and 7pm. The crossing takes one hour and the fare is approximately the same as the Puntarenas-Paquera ferry *(Ferry Conatramar, ☎661-1069)*.

San José - Puntarenas: daily departures every 30 minutes between 6am and 9pm. The trip takes 2 hours *($2.30; Calle 16 between Avenida 10 and 12; Empressarios Unidos; ☎221-5749)*.

Paquera - Montezuma: a bus runs from Paquera to Cóbano and Montezuma, where the ferry arrives from Puntarenas. The bus returns from Montezuma at 5:30am, 10am and 2pm.

Quepos - Puntarenas: buses leave at 4:30am, 10:30am and 3pm and return at 5am, 11am and 2pm via **Playa Jacó**, which is 1.5 hours from Quepos.

Playa Jacó: Buses leave San José *($2; Coca Cola terminal, ☎223-1109 or 643-3135; the trip takes 3.5 h)*. Departures are at 7:30am, 10:30am and 3:30pm, and the return is at 5am, 11am or 3pm. Arrive at the bus stop well before departure times on the weekends.

A bus linking Quepos and Puntarenas also stops at Jacó around 6am, noon and 4:30pm. As well, all buses going to Quepos and Manuel Antonio make a stop at Jacó *($3 to $5)*; get off at the El Bosque restaurant, two streets from the southern tip of the beach. From there, you can take a taxi to the beach.

Quepos: daily departures from San José *($3; Coca Cola terminal, ☎223-5567 or 777-0263; 4-h trip)* leave at 7am, 10am, 2pm and 4pm and the return trip leaves at 5am, 8am, 2pm and 4pm. These buses are slow because they make many stops. Beware of pickpockets at the Coca Cola terminal.

Manuel Antonio: There is a bus going from San José to Manuel Antonio *($5; Coca Cola terminal, a direct trip at 6 am, noon and 6pm and returns at 6am and noon)*

Money: The banks are situated on Avenida 3 in the north-eastern part of the penin-sula.	Maps and up-to-date timeta-bles.
Tourist Information: In the centre of town near the park.	**Telephone:** You can make long-distance calls from the tour-ist information counter.

the spider monkey. Most of the hotels in the area and even the tourist office in Montezuma offer guided tours of the reserve. A few minutes from here is **Tambor**, a small village with reasonably priced places to stay (**Cabinas y Restaurante Christina**) and small, inexpensive restaurants.

The village of **Cóbano** is just 11 kilometres from Tambor and has many services such as a bank, a post office, a medical clinic, public telephones, grocery stores, shops and little *comedores*. From Cóbano, take another small road (to the left in the centre of town) south to **Montezuma**.

Montezuma *(7 km from Cóbano)* is a beautiful beach with affordable and pleasant facilities. Montezuma is a must for many globe-trotters. A little haven that is slightly too popular but beautiful all the same, Montezuma is the realm of hippies, freaks, granolas and other free-spirited youth who come here for a few weeks to vacation cheaply. A visit to the tourist office in Montezuma *(8am to noon and from 4pm to 8pm)*, in the heart of town opposite the municipal park, will arm you with information on all the activities and natural attractions this region has to offer. From among the most popular tours, we recommend the superb **Cabo Blanco reserve** (see further below) and the spellbinding **Isla Tortuga**. The trip to Isla Tortuga *($30)* lasts all day *(9am to 4pm)* and includes transportation by high-speed boat, lunch and snorkelling gear as well as various other activities. You will spend an unforgettable day on a paradisiacal island of white sand surrounded by turquoise water.

If you spend the day on the beach and want something to read, go to the **Topsy** bookstore where they buy and sell second-hand books. On Wednesday evenings, the **El Sano Banano** restaurant shows popular films for your entertainment or you can make conversation with someone while sipping one of their fabulous milkshakes.

The **Río Montezuma waterfalls** make for a great outing that is both pleasant and refreshing. To get there, take the road to Cabuya for about 700 metres, until you reach the La Cascada hotel, which

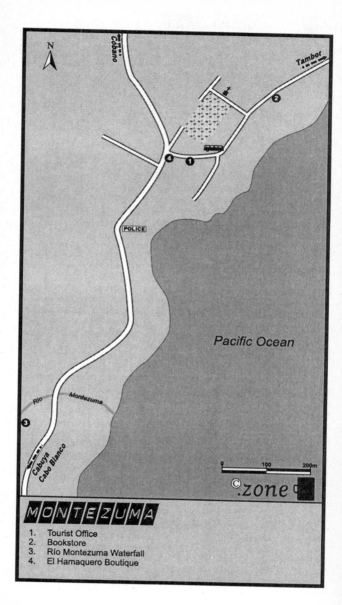

N

Cóbano

Tambor

2

4 **1**

POLICE

Pacific Ocean

Río Montezuma

3

Cabuya
Cabo Blanco

0   100   200m

©.zone

MONTEZUMA

1. Tourist Office
2. Bookstore
3. Río Montezuma Waterfall
4. El Hamaquero Boutique

is situated on the river. Cross the small bridge and a sign will indicate the path that climbs through the forest to the falls. After about 15 minutes of walking you will arrive at the falls and their basin which is great for swimming or just relaxing and basking in the sun.

The **Cabo Blanco Nature Reserve** *($6; Wed-Sun, 8am to 4pm, ☎642-0093)* is a haven of nature only 11 kilometres from Montezuma. Since 1980, two hiking trails have been opened and visitors are very welcome to use them. However, a large part of the reserve is off limits, and you must stay on the marked paths. It takes a day to hike the two trails. This park was established in 1955 by **Nils Olof Wessberg**, the father of Costa Rica's parks. He tried to create a park in Costa Rica's "other" peninsula, the Osa Peninsula, but he was assassinated there because of his conservation efforts. You can pay your respects to him at the small commemorative plaque at the entrance to the park.

The **Malpaís** and **Santa Teresa** region is situated northwest of Cabo Blanco and is the best-kept secret of the southern Nicoya Peninsula. First discovered by surfing enthusiasts who come here for the excellent waves, this region has gorgeous and almost deserted beaches (depending on the season), as well as a good choice of hotels and restaurants that will suit any budget. Here, there is no central square because the houses, hotels and restaurants are spread along the six-kilometre coastal road. If you are looking for a quiet, calm place and are not sure if Montezuma fits the bill, come to this area — you will not be disappointed! You can tour it on mountain bicycles or on horseback, take introductory surfing courses, sunbathe on the beach or swim in the sea all day long. And the sunsets are simply incredible, especially from a hammock!

Bahía Gigante is a pleasant bay in the south of the Golfo de Nicoya where you can discover **Isla Gitana** and its native burial ground. Formerly called "Isla de los Muertos" (Island of the Dead), the island now welcomes visitors for a day or more as it has accommodations, campsites, a restaurant and a bar. Hiking trails, an attractive beach and several water sports are available, as well as boat transportation to the island *(☎661-2994, ➛661-2833)*.

The **Carara Biological Reserve** *($6; 7am to 5pm; ☎416-6576, ➛416-7402)*, situated only 17 kilometres from Jacó, is one of the most visited parks in Costa Rica. The reserve protects some 4,700 hectares of forest essential to the great many animals who live there. Two kinds of forests are preserved here: the wet tropical forest originating in the southwest of the country; and the dry tropical forest found in the northwest of Costa Rica, mainly in the province of Guanacaste. The variations in altitude go from a few metres to a little more than 1,000 metres where numerous trees reaching 50 metres in height can be seen. The animals most often observed are monkeys (white-faced capuchins, howlers and spiders), sloths, agoutis, coatis and white-tailed deer. Birds are numerous and are a joy to ornithologists.

The Carara Biological Reserve also includes 15 archaeological sites dating back to the area's two main eras of settlement: the Pavas era (300 BC to AD 500) and the Cartago era (from the 9th to the 16th century AD). These sites are mostly visited by archaeology students, but you can go there if you are accompanied by a guide. The reserve has two official hiking trails. The **Las Aráceas** trail (one km) forms a loop that takes less than an hour. It goes into the primary forest and crosses four different life zones where many plant and bird species can be seen. The **Laguna Meándrica** (4 km each way) is near the Río Tárcoles and leads through a secondary forest. Monkeys and brown coatis, called *pizotes* in Costa Rica, are often encountered along this trail. Count on three hours to make the round trip (8 km), which will give you plenty of time to observe the reserve's flora and fauna.

You can take a road two kilometres south of Carara which climbs and climbs and climbs up the hills to get to the **Catarata Manantial Agua Viva,** apparently the highest waterfall in the country.

Playo Jacó *(15 km south of Carara)*. This sandy beach with great waves is large enough for both surfers and tourists in search of the sun. Jacó is a little too "chic-cool," so it can eventually get on your nerves. The parade of singles is interesting to see, but can turn off anyone not interested in appearances. Jacó is the ideal place to see and be seen. The place attracts some very "trendy" surfers, which has led to the proliferation of fashionable shops around here. Jacó is very popular and lively, particularly because it is easily accessible for Costa Ricans who come here for the weekend or even for the day. Jacó even has a **zoo** *($6; just south of Jacó on the Jacó-Quepos highway)*.

Parque Nacional Manuel Antonio *($6; Tue-Sun, 7am to 5pm; ☎777-0644, ☎777-0654)*. The Quepos region has quickly become one of Costa Rica's most highly developed tourist destinations. Within the last several years, hotels have sprouted up like mushrooms, considerably reducing the amount of lush vegetation found in the area. Fortunately, part of the territory has been protected by this park's creation on November 15, 1972. Manuel Antonio is the country's smallest park, but it has the second most visitors. It contains habitats with everything from jungle to beach. Walking on the park's trails you are almost sure of seeing — or at least hearing capuchin monkeys. You will notice that a good part of the forest was damaged by Hurricane Gertrude in 1993.

At the end of one of the beaches is a unique geomorphological formation called the **Tombolo de la Pointe Catedral**. The tombolo is a layer of earth that has slowly formed over thousands of years, connecting what was once the Catedral island to the mainland. Take the time to explore the place: the giant trees and the vast expanse of the Pacific are awe-inspiring. Not far off is the Manuel Antonio beach, a superb expanse of white sand embracing crystal-clear water where you can swim and even snorkel.

Punta-renas

$

SWEET DREAMS

Pensión Cabezas *($7.50; Avenida 1 between Calles 2 and 4, ☎661-1045)*. ▶ Friendly, clean and really cheap. The rooms are quite small and stuffy so ask for a fan if there isn't already one.

Chorotega *($20; ☎661-0998)*. ▶ Spiffy clean, making it one of the best choices for budget travellers in terms of value for their money. It is near the bus station in the centre of town.

Ayi Con *($12; Calle 2 between Avenida 1 and 3, ☎661-0164 or 661-1477)*. ▶ Clean, but a little dark.

Montezuma

$

SWEET DREAMS

The following places are recommended for budget travellers: **Pensión Jenny**, **Pensión Lucy** and **Cabinas Tucán**.

Bahía Gigante

$

SWEET DREAMS

Numerous camp sites are available on the island facing the bay.

Jacó

$

SWEET DREAMS

If you want to sleep here, the following places are inexpensive: **Cabinas Antonio**, **Cabinas Clarita** or the Québec-run **La Cometa**.

Punta-renas

$

BON APPETIT

The town of Puntarenas has many small *comedores*.

You will find good, reasonably priced seafood at the **Casa De Mariscos** and at the **Bar-Restaurante Cevichito**.

Kahite Blanco *(Avenida 1 between Calles 15 and 17, ☎661-2093)* is very popular with *Ticos* for its hearty portions of seafood and *bocas*.

⏩ SOUTHERN COSTA RICA ⏪

The southern part of the country has it all in terms of the biodiversity that has earned Costa Rica its international reputation. Featured are the nation's highest peak and most humid jungles as well as a handful of beaches that will make surfers feel as if they've died and gone to heaven. Although the Interamericana highway spans the entire region, there are still many remote areas where you need a lot of patience in order to reach your destination without losing your mind. This region is off the beaten track, which means less tourism and abundant wilderness.

Other than being the largest city in southern Costa Rica, **San Isidro del General** (population 40,000) offers no spectacular sightseeing. To learn about cultural and environmental aspects of the region, visit the **Museo Regional del Sur** *(Mon-Fri 9am to noon and 1pm to 5pm; inside the cultural centre, which used to house the municipal market, San Isidro, ☎/☎771-5273)*.

San Isidro is an average-sized city whose main advantage is being a good starting point from which to discover the surrounding attractions.

The **Rancho La Botija** *($5, $3 children; 7am to 8pm, closed Mon; 6 km from San Isidro, on the road to Rivas, ☎382-3052, ☎771-1401)* is a small recreation centre housed in an old sugarcane refinery.

The main attraction here is the short path that leads through a series of stones etched with glyphs dating from the Pre-Columbian period. Other objects from the past, such as an old *trapiche* (sugar mill), adorn the main building. In short, a most enjoyable spot for a picnic. The Rivas region features one of the country's most important Pre-Columbian archaeological sites. If you still haven't had your fill, visit **La Pradera** *(on the San Isidro-Rivas road, just before the Albergue Talari)*.

San Gerardo de Rivas *(20 km northwest)* lies just before the Mount Chirripó park, right on the road to the country's highest and most daunting peak. Although most people breeze right through it, San Gerardo is worth a stop because it is one of the most enchanting villages in Costa Rica. Before the bridge, turn left on the road to Herradura and follow the signs to the **Aguas Termales**, less than an hour away on foot. You pay the one-dollar entrance fee to the farmer on whose land the hot springs are located. You could just relax here forever, especially after walking here or conquering the Chirripó.

At the **Parque Nacional Chirripó** *(entrance just past San Gerardo)* you can hike some 3,400 metres along a picturesque and well-marked trail to the *Base Crestones* shelter. The trail zigzags through a misty tropical forest before entering a wasteland of burnt trees devastated by forest fires over the past 40 years. Depending on your experience, it takes 8 to 12 hours to hike the (difficult!) 16 kilometres to the shelter. After a cold night's sleep (bring a good sleeping bag or rent blankets from the shelter), you hike the last 6 kilometres to the peak, which is at 3,819 metres. Leave at sunrise to beat the clouds to the summit and get a clear and breathtaking view of both oceans. At this altitude, the vegetation is alpine and many glacial valleys and lakes can be seen. Spend at least two nights here to enjoy the many summits that surround the shelter and give your legs a chance to rest. If you want to hike up the mountain in a shorter amount of time (two days, one night), you can stay in a very rudimentary shelter nestled midway between the start of the trail and the main shelter near the summit.

During the rainy season, you pay the entrance fee *($6/person plus $3/night)* at the SINAC offices at the entrance of San Gerardo. Otherwise (during the dry season from January to May), it is recommended to reserve ahead of time *(☎506-771-3297, ☎506-771-5116)*. Bring warm clothes as the temperature can change drastically at 3,000 metres. Furthermore, start your days at sunrise to avoid cloud covering as well as the sweltering humidity of jungle afternoons. The descent from the Base Crestones shelter takes between four and six hours on average. It is also possible to climb the **Cerro Urán** from **Herradura**, but the

PRACTICAL INFO

Transportation San José: The Vargas Rojas bus company (☎222-9763 in *San José* or ☎771-0419 in *San Isidro*) offers four departures to San Isidro from San José *(6:30am, 9:30am, 12:30pm and 3:30pm; $2; travel time: 3 hours)*. The return trips follow the same schedule.

San Isidro del General/Chirripó national park: A bus from San Isidro *(daily departures 5am and 2pm; $1)* stops right in front of the administrative offices of the park in San Gerardo de Rivas. The trip lasts approximately 1.5 hours. Buses return to San Isidro at 7am and 4pm.

San José: A bus (daily departures 6am and 12pm) goes directly to Puerto Jiménez. The nine-hour trip costs $6 *(Transportes Blanco-Lobo; Calle 1 and Avenida 7, ☎257-4121)*.

Dominical: Buses to Uvita leave San Isidro del General every day at 3pm and stop in Dominical approximately 1.5 hours after departure time. In the opposite direction, buses leave Uvita at 7am and stop in Dominical around 7:30am. You can also take the bus that runs from San Isidro to Dominical before it heads up the coast to Quepos *(return: 5am and 1:30pm)*. Contact Empressa Blanco in San Isidro for local bus schedules *(☎771-2550; cost: $1)*.

Osa Peninsula (Puerto Jiménez): From San José, a bus *(daily departures 6am and 12pm; Calle 12 and Avenida 7)* goes directly to Puerto Jiménez, which is the main town of the Osa Peninsula. The nine-hour trip costs $6 *(Transportes Blanco-Lobo, ☎257-4121)*.

Zancudo: Boats leave Golfito *($2-$3/person; municipal dock)* for Zancudo on Mondays and Fridays at noon. The return trip is at 6pm, generally at high tide. On any other day, you will have to rent a boat at the municipal dock in Golfito *($15-$20/trip, not per person)*. Local boats provide return transportation from Zancudo either via the sea or via a shortcut through the Atrocha, a mangrove swamp populated by myriad birds and some alligators.

Golfito: Departures from San José at 7am, 9am and 3pm *($4.50; Calle 4 and Av. 18, ☎221-4214)*. It is a seven-hour voyage. You can also hop on any Zona Sur bus going to Río Claro, which is where the Interamericana and the road to Golfito meet. The Villa Neilly—Golfito bus, which passes every hour, will then drop you off at your destination *(travelling time; 30 min.)*. Buses to San José leave Tracopa at 5am, 1pm and 2pm *($5)*.

Zancudo: Buses go there from Golfito during the dry season *(travelling time; 2.5 hours)*. Contact Golfito's Pueblo Civil for schedules and bus stop locations.

Pavones: Hop aboard the 2pm bus at the municipal dock in Golfito. The trip goes along dirt roads in very poor condition, and crosses the Río Coto by ferry at one point. The return bus leaves at 5pm.

San Vito: An express bus from San José leaves from the Empresa Alfaro at 2:45pm *($6; Calle 14 and Av. 5, ☎222-2750; travel time: 5 hours)*; buy your tickets in advance. Local buses leave at 5:45am, 8:15am and 11:30am *($4; length of trip: 7 hours)*. The road is paved all the way. Most buses pass by the Botanical Gardens after stopping in San Vito. Ask the driver before leaving. Return trips are at 5am (express), 7:30am, 10am, and 3pm. The Alfaro office in San Vito is located near the city hall (Municipalidad).

Buses from **San Isidro** to **San Vito** leave at 5:30am and 2pm, and return at 6:30am and 1:30pm. To get to the gardens, you can also climb aboard the San Vito-Villa Neilly bus at 7am or 1pm (return at 6am, 1pm and 3pm). A taxi from San Vito costs approximately $2.50.

Money : Banco Nacional de Costa Rica, north of the Parque Central.

Post Office : Calle 1, south of the park.

path is unmarked and you must be accompanied by a guide. Finally, it is also possible to hike along a 35-kilometre loop that links the two summits. However, this hike is very difficult and is more suitable for expert mountain climbers.

Buy provisions to eat and drink in San Isidro because San Gerardo doesn't have much in the way of stores or restaurants.

Dominical *(30 km west of San Isidro)* is the perfect place to visit if you are not fully refreshed from the thermal waters after hiking up the Cerro Chirripó. Dominical offers leisurely walks on the beach and picture-perfect sunsets. Avid surfers also flock to Dominical, whose waves can be tackled year-round. The best beaches are 20 kilometres south of the village. You can also admire spectacular 45-metre-high waterfalls located between Dominical and San Isidro.

Hacienda Barú *($2; north of Dominical, follow the Dominical beach, ☎787-0003, ☎787-0004)* is a superb private national wildlife reserve. The vast 336-hectare expanse of land harbours various ecosystems such as primary and secondary forests, pastures, mangroves, an old cacao plantation, and a wonderful beach on the Pacific full of trees and plants. Paths cover only six kilometres of the area but go deep enough into the reserve that they give you the impression of being totally immersed in the wilderness. If you've got money to blow, rent a kayak, go on a camping expedition in the reserve, or take part in one of the many activities organized by the reserve. The preservation of the flora and fauna of the region and history of the hacienda are the main focus of the reserve. Travelling north you will arrive at the **Terciopelo Falls** *(on horseback; reserve with Selva Mar,* ☎*771-4582,* ✆*771-8841),* a 40-metre three-tiered waterfall in the heart of the Amazonian jungle.

The **Osa Peninsula** *(8 to 10 h from San José)* is attracting more and more visitors every year and is gaining a reputation as being the Costa Rica's "other" peninsula. Tourists disappointed by the less than abundant wilderness of the Nicoya Peninsula are now turning to **Osa** and its **Corcovado park**, which preserves the only primal forest on the Pacific coast of Central America. Primal as in "wild" and difficult to access. In addition to many hours of bus transportation, trails teeming with tropical wildlife (macaws, jaguars, toucans, snakes, sharks, etc.) await the hardy adventurer.

The main city on the peninsula, **Puerto Jiménez**, features many hotels and restaurants, public phones, transportation (buses, ferries, taxis, airport), food shops, a post office, a tourist information centre near the airport which you must contact to enter the park and reserve your accommodation in a shelter *(Proyecto Osa Natural, main street,* ☎*/*✆*735-5440),* excursion agencies, a medical clinic, a national bank, a gas station and the administrative offices of the Corcovado national park. **La Llanta Picante** *(*☎*/*✆*735-5414)* rents mountain bikes and offers cycling excursions. Their bikes are top of the line and in excellent condition.

This town is relatively quiet except for all the tourists rushing around planning the next day's itinerary (fishing, kayaking, scuba diving, hiking, touring a gold mine, horseback riding, mountain biking, etc.). As the afternoon fades into evening, nothing beats relaxing on the **municipal beach**, situated northeast of town, and taking a dip in the Golfo Dulce.

Parque Nacional Corcovado *($6; 8am to 4pm,* ☎*735-5036,* ✆*735-5282)* is undoubtedly one of the most captivating parks in Costa Rica. A 4X4 taxi goes there every morning at 6am from the *minimercado* El Tigre in Puerto Jiménez *($6)* and returns at 8:30am. The park's humid tropical forest receives an average rainfall of 5.5 metres every year, allowing for a unique wealth of flora to flourish. An estimated 500 varieties of plants grow here, some of which reach 40 to 50 metres or more. Among these is the *ceiba pentandra*, which can grow to an amazing 70 metres! Once you set foot in the sometimes suffocating humidity and heat amidst the trees laden with moss, epiphytic plants and lianas, you will certainly feel worlds away from civilization.

Anyone accustomed to long hikes and sleeping in tents or shelters will thoroughly enjoy Corcovado national park. It is one of the only parks in the country that offers such an extensive network of trails, as well as camping areas, shelters, meals, etc. However, before venturing off into the park, stop first at the park's administrative offices in Puerto Jiménez (near the airport) to get information and make reservations if you plan to spend the night.

The park has five shelters, four of which are especially popular with hikers (La Leona, La Sirena, San Pedrillo and Los Patos). During the dry season (from December to April), the trails are especially busy and it is quite common for 30 hikers to converge at one spot, often at the busy La Sirena shelter.

The Corcovado national park has a large network of trails (80 km total) and three main entrances: **Los Patos, San Pedrillo** and the most popular, **La Leona**. Over 60 kilometres of footpaths, most of which run along the beach, link the various shelters. Other trails fan out around the shelters and plunge into the forest or lead up to a viewpoint. How many kilometres you plan to hike depends on several factors including the weight of your backpack, the heat and humidity, and the desired length of your stay.

Although most hikers spend three or four nights in the park, many come for a day, usually to the La Leona sector, whereas others spend over a week to observe the flora and fauna of the park and give themselves ample time to rest. It is best to arrive in the evening and spend the night at the perimeter of the park before undertaking strenuous hiking in the jungle or along the Pacific coast. You will have to cross several rivers.

The city of **Golfito** *(150 km south San Isidro)* is tucked away in a small gulf that opens into the larger Golfo Dulce, separated from the ocean by the Osa Peninsula. Thus, the most practical way of getting to the Osa Peninsula is to take a ferry from here. The city itself is rather dreary and is filled with taverns frequented by ex-employees of the United Fruit Company, which closed in the 1980s (practically shutting down the whole city along with it). The town's surrounding area is now part of a wildlife reserve and is accessible by a number of paths, notably from the Zona Americana. The paths vary in length so you can decide how far you want to venture.

A number of beaches across from Golfito line the piece of land that juts into the bay. **Playa Cacao,** which has a great view of Golfito, is foremost on the list. **Playa Gallardo** and **Playa San Josecito** are a little to the west. The black sand of the **Zancudo** beach stretches for several kilometres southeast of Golfito, at a point where the Coto Colorado river empties into the Pacific Ocean. This beach is popular during the high season but quiets down during the rainy season. A good place to swim and practice some easy surfing. The beach is also popular with local fishermen. The **Pavones** beach welcomes the more serious surfers.

The **Wilson Botanical Gardens,** in the Las Cruces biological station *($5 half day, $8 full day, half-price for children aged 6 to 12, guided tours cost $35 and last 2 hours; 5 km from San Vito on the Ciudad Neilly-San Vito road; closed Mon; ☎240-6696, ☏240-6783),* has the largest botanical collection in all of Central America. Its many noble missions include studying new plants, mainly for horticultural purposes, and prevent plant species from being destroyed in their natural habitat. As you wander through the gardens, you will encounter thousands of different plants (including over 700 varieties of palm trees), as well as hundreds of birds, reptiles and mammals. Over 3,000 butterfly species reportedly flutter within the gardens — which is reason enough to come!

The vast **Parque Internacional La Amistad** *($6; 6am to 5pm; ☎771-3297, ☏771-3155)* is like no other place in the world. There are no trails (at least not yet) through this untamed wilderness, so you must rely on your basic survival skills. Most visitors to the park prefer the **Las Tablas** area, a protected zone located northeast of San Vito close to the Panamanian border, for the many hotels, restaurants and excursions available. Regardless of which of the three sectors you go to (Tres Colinas, Estación Pittier or Altamira), we strongly recommended that you first contact the National Parks Service *(☎283-8004, ☏283-7343)* or the Fundación de Parques Nacionales *(☎257-2239, ☏222-4732)*, both located in San José, to get the latest information on park conditions. When we visited, there were still no detailed maps of the park or any other documentation available.

San Isidro	# SWEET DREAMS
	Small, rustic but clean wooden rooms are found at the slightly ageing one-storey **El Jardín Hotel** *($7; ☎771-0349)*. Good restaurant.

San Isidro

RÊVE

Hotel Chirripó *($8; close to the Parque Central, ☎771-0529)* and **Hotel Amaneli** *($11; ☎771-0352)* offer basic and clean rooms. Both have a restaurant on the ground floor.

Rooms in the new **El Valle** hotel *($12; above the Núñez hardware store, ☎771-0246)* are basic and fairly clean, and each has a tv.

Dominical

SWEET DREAMS

The **Cabinas Rocas Verde** offer the best value for your money.

Puerto Jiménez

SWEET DREAMS

Travellers on small budgets will find the cheapest rates in town at the **Pensión Quintero** *($8; ☎735-5087)*, which provides spacious, clean and pleasant accommodations.

There are many *cabinas* available in town, **Marcelina**, **Carolina** and **Jiménez** are recommended for their excellent value for the price.

Camping is permitted in certain areas.

San Gerardo de Rivas

SWEET DREAMS

El Descanso has the friendliest and most affordable accommodations in San Gerardo *($8; cross the bridge and turn right, ☎771-1866)*. Host Francisco Elizondo and his family are very courteous and attentive. If you are interested, he can give you a tour of the nearby *finca* where he grows coffee as well as other produce used in the preparation of meals served in the hotel's restaurant. He can also tell you all about the nearby mountain, since he has won many races to the summit — quite a feat!

Golfito

SWEET DREAMS

You can rent a comfortable room, with or without a private bathroom, at the **Hotel del Cerro** *($10; between Pueblo Civil and Zona Americana, ☎775-0006)*.

Parque Nacional Corcovado

SWEET DREAMS

Five kilometres from La Palma and 500 metres from the northwest entrance to the park, the **Cabinas Corcovado** *($10; ☎775-0433, ⌐775-0033)* offer camping sites *($4 for 2 people)*. The restaurant, reserved for clients of the *cabinas*, serves three typical *Tico* meals for a mere $10 per person per day. The owner, Luis Angulo, is an experienced guide who knows a lot about the region and especially about the native Guyami community *($8/hour or $80/day)*.

The park's shelters provide rudimentary but cheap accommodations *($2/person/night)*. You must bring your own sleeping bag, and a mosquito net is recommended. If you plan on camping *($1.25/person/night)*, pack all the necessary equipment (tents and camping equipment can be rented at the tourist information centre in Puerto Jiménez). Meals are available at the shelters but you must reserve them ahead of time. Breakfast *(6am)* costs $4; lunch *(11am)* and dinner *(5:30pm)* cost $6.25. If you want to prepare your own meals, bring your own cooking equipment (portable stove, drinking containers, utensils, etc.).

San Isidro

BON APPETIT

Restaurants in the **El Jardin** and **Chirripó** hotels serve savoury dishes at very affordable prices. Open all day.

Hong Kong *(near the park)* serves Asian food.

The **El Tenedor** *(main street)* has a varied and reasonably priced menu featuring pizza among other dishes.

▐▌▐▌▐ Like its neighbours, Panamá has an incredibly diverse population and varied landscape. However, unlike the others, these are found on a stretch of land that runs east-west in the serpentine shape of a sideways "S." High mountains, paradisiacal islands, impenetrable jungles, sunny beaches and a canal that divides it in two are only some of its landmarks. Until the year 2000, the world-famous canal is under joint supervision with the United States whose presence is felt especially in the capital where the wealthy and the poor live side by side. The contrast is perhaps more visible here than in the capital cities of neighbouring countries.

▐▌▐▌▐ It is not really surprising that Panamá's biggest claim to fame these days is its canal, since the country has always been influenced by its strategic position at a cross-roads of economic trade. Originally a part of Colombia which claimed its independence from Spain in 1821, the notorious pillaging conquistadors stopped here on their way from Perú to Spain when this "new" continent was first discovered. The region then made big money off the railroad which connected the two oceans and allowed Americans to get to California for the Gold Rush of the 1850's. The canal was only constructed at the beginning of this century, although a French group had been interested in this project since 1882. The initial attempt went belly-up in 1893 after 22,000 died of tropical diseases. A few kilometres of canal were the only thing they had to show for the effort. The United States took up the challenge in 1903 — just after they had encouraged the province to separate from Colombia. They assured the supervision of a 5-mile (8 km) zone on each side of the canal, and began work by sending in a biologist to carry out the world's biggest extermination project; to get rid of insects carrying the most dangerous diseases in this American Zone. The canal was inaugurated in 1914, and since 1979, Panamá has taken more and more control of this gem that brings in 100 million annually (each ship pays at least $30,000 to pass through). Today, 95 percent of the canal employees are Panamanian.

▐▌▐▌▐ The population is a mix of Amerindians, Spanish colonists and African descendants. The country is not as well adapted to tourism as its neighbour to the west (Costa Rica), but this means that the floods of tourists stay away, and your trip is likely to be more pleasant since you're not just one more *gringo*.

holidays and festivals

January 9: Martyr's Day.
Maundy Thursday and Good Friday (2000: 20 and 21 April; 2001: 12 and 13 April).
May 1: Labour Day.

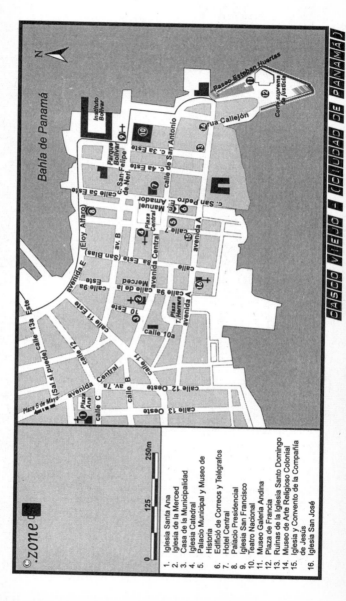

CASCO VIEJO - (CIUDAD DE PANAMÁ)

© zone

0   125   250m

1. Iglesia Santa Ana
2. Iglesia de la Merced
3. Casa de la Municipalidad
4. Iglesia Catedral
5. Palacio Municipal y Museo de Historia
6. Edificio de Correos y Telégrafos
7. Hotel Central
8. Palacio Presidencial
9. Iglesia San Francisco
10. Teatro Nacional
11. Museo Galería Andina
12. Plaza de Francia
13. Ruinas de la Iglesia Santo Domingo
14. Museo de Arte Religioso Colonial
15. Iglesia y Convento de la Compañía de Jesús
16. Iglesia San José

October 12: Día de la Raza (arrival of Columbus).
November 3: Independence Day (separation from Colombia).
November 10: Declaration of Independence Celebration.
November 28: Independence Celebration (separation from Spain).
December 8: Mother's Day.

⏭ CIUDAD DE PANAMÁ ⏮

Ciudad de Panamá's cosmopolitan character might take you by surprise, and its diversity and size are sure to impress. Built on a small bay, the view from the centre of town is fantastic. On one side is the colonial area with its splendid architecture and brightly coloured buildings, while the modern section with its many apartment towers and head offices of foreign banks lies on the other. Ciudad de Panamá has more than 100 banks, not including branch offices, and countless skyscrapers that tower more than 40 storeys. About half of the country's population — 1.3 million people — live in this city. Walking from one section to the other is to go from colonialism to postmodernism, a journey that is as enchanting as it is unusual.

The recent past is also vividly alive, and the 1989 American attack on General Noriega, a former CIA member, is hardly a faded memory. The head of the CIA at the time, George Bush, ordered the attack which took the lives of between 400 and 3,000 people, depending on whom you talk to, about twenty of whom were American soldiers. Traces of this conflict, which left 20,000 Panamanians homeless, are still visible in the western part of the city, especially in El Chorillo. These areas are not safe and you should only go there in the daytime and as a group. You can pass through by bus if you want to get a general idea of the place.

The American influence is certainly omnipresent here. For example, there seem to be more McDonald's per square kilometre than in the most plastic of United States. Nevertheless, the city is very well maintained and flaunts its cosmopolitan and Latin character everywhere!

Ⓩ **Plaza Central** *(in the heart of the Casco Viejo area)*. Old churches, narrow cobblestone streets, pedestrian passageways, bargain markets and the old theatre — all these historic marvels are found just a few metres from the Plaza Central! Walk through these narrow streets to get a sense of another era. Cheap hotels are also situated near the Plaza. In the evening you must return by taxi, even if security has improved in Ciudad de Panamá in the last few years. Casco Viejo and El Chorillo are still unsafe areas, particularly after sundown.

PRACTICAL INFO

Transportation: The bus terminal for travelling in the city is Plaza 5 de Mayo on Avenida Central. The destinations are written on the windshields and most trips cost 15¢. To get to the airport, take the Tocumén bus and count on an hour of travel time (three if you take the bus between 6am and 9am during the week). At the far end of Avenida Balboa is the station for buses going to **David**, $11 ($15 for the express bus). Buses leave every 1.5 hours between 5:30am and midnight, and the trip takes about six hours. For **Colón**, go to the corner of Avenida Perú and Calle 30. Buy a ticket for $2.20 between 5am and 7pm, then jump on one of the buses that leave every 20 minutes. The trip takes two hours at the most.

Money: There is no problem finding a bank here. However, the services offered vary considerably. Most banks are situated in Caledonia, on Via España. A special mention goes to the Banco del Istmo at the corner of Calle 50, which cashes travellers' cheques for free.

Tourist Information: Instituto Panameño de Turismo (IPAT) is situated in the Atlapa Conference Centre opposite Caesar Park hotel, the huge tower on Avenida Balboa by the water. Take bus 2. Open during the week until 4pm. Good information and useful maps.

Mail and Telephone: Plaza Central and Calle San Pedro; the main office is open from Monday to Saturday until 5 pm.

Internet: There is a **cybercafé** behind the Panamá hotel on Véia España, but it is often jam-packed (ah! new technologies). We suggest you go instead to the **Computer** office on Calle Samuel Lewis, slightly south of Véia España and opposite the yellow sign. It is in the same building as Cable and Wire and charges $3.50 an hour.

ⓩ **Avenida Central** *(at the westernmost edge of Plaza Central)*. A great place for shopping and an interesting cultural mix to people-watch. You will see everything here: a little old man leaning on a fire hydrant selling *crazy* glue, dozens of huge clothing stores that sell just about everything for next to nothing, a small park where old people play checkers, Indian shops with draperies and incense, camera and electronic equipment at rock-bottom prices (bargain for half price at least), fashionable watches for $10 — and at least three McDonald's.

Panamá Viejo *(take the "Panamá Viejo" bus at Plaza 5 de Mayo)*. This old part of town was the city in 1671, when buccaneer Henry Morgan invaded it. This well-maintained site contains the ruins of old convents and a beautiful tower. Interesting and not too busy; the police officers that patrol the ruins even have time to give you a detailed history of the city! It doesn't cost anything to explore, and as you'll be inspired to stay on the move since you'll be swarmed by insects if you loiter too long under the trees. Put on insecticide.

Canal de Panamá *(take the old red Balboa bus that dates from 1950 in Plaza 5 de Mayo)*. Get off at Avenida Almador and take another bus or walk for 15 minutes to reach the Yacht Club Balboa. If you walk, you can pick a few incredibly tasty mangoes on the way! At the yacht club, head to the bar where the crews from the various yachts wait their turn to pass through the canal. Since all crews need four people to attach the moorings that hold the boat in the locks, you can usually find someone willing to let you on board and pass through the canal for free, in exchange for a little of your labour. It takes one or two days to make the trip, and it is no doubt the best way to see the famous waterway. However, the amount of traffic depends on the time of year, so you may end up having to wait several days. No problem — here's a chance to socialize and have a drink with the sailors. The busiest time is November and December. Passing through on a cruise ship is prohibitively expensive *($99)*, and your only other option is to go see the Miraflores Locks from the Paraíso bus that leaves from Plaza 5 de Mayo. Go only if you have never seen locks, because although it is a big tourist attraction, the sight is nothing special.

Ciudad de Panamá	**SWEET DREAMS** We deliberately suggest only hotels situated in Casco Viego because they are less expensive and lie in a superb part of the city. For safety reasons, you must take a taxi *($2-3)* when returning in the evening. **Hotel Foyo** *($4; Calle 6 and Avenida A)*. ▶ Very well situated near Plaza Central. The rooms have very high ceilings and fans that don't always work. They are reasonably clean with shared bathrooms. No curfew. **Pensión Panamá** *($5; opposite Hotel Foyo)*. ▶ If the Foyo is full, you can stay here. The rooms are smaller, but very clean.

Ciudad de Panamá

$

SWEET DREAMS

Hotel Herrera *($9; Calle 9 and Avenida A)*. ▶ The same owner as the Hotel Foyo, but a little more expensive because there are more services: private toilets, air-conditioning, refrigerators, restaurant. The prices vary according to the services offered in each room.

Hotel Colonial *($15; Plaza Bolívar and Calle 4)*. ▶ A little more expensive, but very pleasant with its fine old architecture and balconies overlooking the Plaza. A century ago, the higher authorities stayed here when they were working on the canal.

Ciudad de Panamá

$

BON APPETIT

Restaurante Nápoli *(Calle 16 and Avenida Estudiante)*. ▶ Excellent pizzas made with many different kinds of toppings. A complete Italian gourmet menu and at a reasonable price.

The following restaurants have cheap food and are situated in the Casco Viejo and near Plaza 5 de Mayo:

Restaurante San Martín *(Avenida Central and Calle 4)*.
Restaurante Herrera *(Plaza Herrera, Calle 9)*.
Buen Sabor *(Avenida Central and Calle 9)*.
Santana *(Avenida Central)*.
La Viña *(Avenida Central and Calle 6)*.

▶▶ EASTERN PANAMÁ ◀◀

To the east of the canal lies a vast undeveloped region, with two features worth mentioning. One is the Colón region, which has a rich historical past that it tries to recapture, though not always with success. The other is Kuna territory, which you reach by following the Atlantic coast towards the Colombian border. The Kuna Indians make up the majority of the population living on the coast. An archipelago of some 365 heavenly islands also belongs to the Kunas, and it's worth heading out there for a few days, even if it is expensive.

On going further inland you enter the thick of the Darién jungle, the last stretch of Central America before Colombia. In fact, the jungle is so dense here that this is the only place where the Interamericana Highway is interrupted. You can only get to Colombia by boat or else on foot after several days walking (even Indiana Jones would be hard-pressed here). The difficulty in getting to this region certainly discourages many, but its riches are that much more stunning because of it, and it's definitely worthwhile coming here to experience the animal diversity and the human isolation.

Colón

The city grew in leaps and bounds in the second half of the 19th century, when streams of passengers passed through to catch trains to the other shore where they boarded boats bound for California to look for gold. This era was immediately followed by two periods of canal construction beginning in 1880. The city flourished, becoming one of the finest international ports.

This prosperity dropped off dramatically in the 1980s. A severe economic crisis has had disastrous effects on Colón: 50 percent unemployment and a rising crime rate. Add this to the fact that the capital with all conceivable services is only one hour away, and you have all the factors necessary for the decline of a city.

In order to stimulate growth, a free zone was created. Here you can buy a vast array of goods for a little less, but often you must buy a large quantity to get your money's worth. The transfer of goods in Colón is phenomenal because this free zone allows imported cargo from Europe and Asia to be divided into more varied and well-organized lots ready for distribution in their destined markets.

Be careful when visiting Colón, because it has a serious crime problem. Stay only as long as you have to, and do not walk around alone or at night (even in a group). If you have to overnight it here, stay close to the bus station to minimize your travelling. Walk on the main streets because they are guarded by armed men.

You can hitch a ride through the canal from here in a similar way as from the capital, by going to the Yacht Club de Cristóbal and talking to the different crews to see if they need people to help moor their boats in the locks. And if you want to avoid Colón you can take a bus going east to the little village of **Sabanitas**, located 15 kilometres before Colón on the highway from Ciudad de Panamá.

PRACTICAL INFO

Transportation: The bus station is on Avenida del Frente at the corner of Calle 12. Regular and express buses ($1.25 and $1.75) leave every 20 minutes for **Ciudad de Panamá** (1.5 hours of travel). Departures are less frequent on weekends. Buses for **Portobello** leave every hour and cost $2.

Mail and Telephone: Avenida Bolívar and Calle 9. Go there during the week.

Hotel Washington *(at the end of Avenida del Frente on the water)*. This building's history is as interesting as its architecture. Numerous historical figures have stayed at the hotel, including Ferdinand de Lessep, the French engineer with the first team of canal workers, and Juan Perón, the former Argentine dictator who lived here in exile for a time. You can get an idea of the city's former prosperity from what remains of the colonial buildings of this area.

Zona Libre *(enter on Avenida Roosevelt; open from 8am to 5pm and closed on weekends)*. You must show your passport to enter, and hire a negotiator to lower the price of your purchases in return for a fee. You can't take possession of your purchases until you leave the country, since tax-free goods are not allowed into Panamá. The free zone is mainly geared at wholesalers, so unless you plan to make a major purchase, it's better to shop in the centre of town where prices come out to pretty much the same thing.

Ⓩ **Portobello** *(48 km east of the city; take the bus for Portobello)*. Although only ruins remain, this 16th-century Spanish fort was built after Francis Drake attacked Nombre de Dios, further east, which was the departure point for galleons loaded up with gold. The site is very well kept up, with ramparts embedded in the earth and canons pointing at invisible enemies on the calm sea. Leave yourself a day to visit the ruins, which are among the most beautiful in the country.

Playa María Chiquita and Playa Langosta *(halfway to Portobello)*. These two beautiful beaches are very popular on the weekends.

Isla Mamey and Isla Grande *(half an hour east of Portobello)*. Do not come here on weekends because it is jam-packed. These two little islands have picture-perfect beaches with crystal-clear water. To get to the islands, take the bus from Colón towards the coast. Ask the driver to let you off at the boat to whichever island you are going to.

Isla Mamey and Isla Grande

SWEET DREAMS

On Mamey you can scuba dive and stay in little cabins for $25 a night (the **Cabañas Jackson** and the **Cabañas Montecarlo** are the most affordable). Four people can stay in one cabin. Isla Grande is larger and attracts most of the tourists. There are a few scattered hotels, but they are more expensive than the cabins on Mamey.

Colón

SWEET DREAMS

Pensión Acrópolis *($7; Amador Guerreo and Calle 11)*. ▶ There are 16 rooms in this reasonable little hotel, which we recommend only because it is the closest to the bus station.

Pensión Anita *($8; next to the Acrópolis)*. ▶ A little larger than the Acropolis, but just as good of a location.

Colón

BON APPETIT

If your stomach is not too weak at this stage of your trip, try eating in the cheap street restaurants because the others are expensive. There is always the **YMCA** *(Avenida Bolívar and Calle 11)*, which serves good Chinese food; a little pricey, but near the bus station.

Islas de San Blas

This archipelago of 365 islands scattered in the Caribbean Sea is populated and administered exclusively by Kunas Indians. About fifty of the islands are inhabited and the only way to get there is to take a morning flight *(6am)* that leaves Ciudad de Panamá domestic airport from Monday to Saturday. A return ticket costs $50 *(information: Transpasa at ☎226-0932, or Aeroperlas at ☎262-5363, apflyap@aeroperlas.com)*. The return flight leaves at 8am. The planes land along the coast and a small boat takes you to the island. You should know, however, that accommodations are quite expensive. Nevertheless, the Amerindian culture is fascinating, the beaches are marvellous and the coral reefs are simply fantastic! And speaking of fun in the sun, bring your own mask as they are difficult to find here. Also, bring as much cash as you will need — this really is in "the middle of nowhere"! The Kunas are the native people who have been the most successful in preserving their autonomy and culture in Panamá. A number of them do not speak Spanish, so it is a total change of scene for the traveller.

Islas de San Blas

S

SWEET DREAMS AND BON APPETIT

Hotel San Blas *($25 with meals; Isla Nalunega, ☎262-1606).* ▶ This is the cheapest of the island getaways! The price includes all the meals of the day (often fresh fish) and transportation by boat from the airport in Porvenir (contact Luis Burgos when you arrive from the capital). The floor of the room is the sand of the beach and hammocks are available at the water's edge. All in all, a beautiful, peaceful haven for swimming and reading in the shade of coconut palms.

Darién

This really is the jungle, every bit as wild and mysterious as you've imagined it! The Darién is for anyone who loves the outdoors, adores camping and is not bothered by tropical rain. After much deliberation, we decided that the rainy season is the best time to visit this area. During the dry period (December to April), ticks take over the area and can cause serious problems. The dry period is also when the local farmers burn new fields, so a foul smell looms over the area. And finally, the colours of the forest are never as luminous as after a good tropical rainfall!

To get there, take the Interamericana Highway as far as you can. This should take you to **Yaviza,** but double check this in the rainy season. One thing is certain: you can get to **Metetí,** or even **Canglón,** all year long. Buses leave from Terminal Piquerá in Ciudad de Panamá every two hours between 6:30am and 3:30pm. The ticket to Metetí costs $11.20. The road ends here. To continue, you can either hitch a ride, paying a passing 4X4 for a lift, or take a pirogue (dugout canoe) that goes down the waterways (very slowly). Count on at least $20 for a day in a pirogue with a motor.

It's evident that anyone who has come this far certainly wants to venture into the jungle! While this is completely understandable, you should be aware that this area of the jungle is used for trafficking drugs from Colombia. This means it is better to hire a guide who knows which areas to avoid. Plan on spending $8 a day for a guide and food.

There are some great hikes around Yaviza. It is, of course, possible to cross the jungle to Colombia (8 days walking), but this is not advisable because of the danger this region represents for the average tourist. Recently, gangs have systematically captured travellers and held them for ransom. Although this is rare, keep on your guard and never travel alone. Take a guide along!

Yaviza *(at the end of the Interamericana)*. A small town at the end of the road, it is one of the last places to buy food. You can sleep at **Tres Américas** *($8)*, of dubious comfort and rather noisy: but this is the jungle, after all! From Yaviza, cross the river and walk for two hours to the next village, Pinogama.

Pinogama *(10 km from Yaviza)* is a primitive village even deeper in the "no man's land" of Darién. At this point, count on your tent or the hospitality of the people. You could also continue walking along the Río Tuira to Vista Alegre (3 hours), and then cross the river and go for another half hour to Unión del Choco.

Unión del Choco *(near Vista Alegre)* is another little village where you can hang up your hammock or look around for what serves as the town hall. Here you must wear a mosquito net all the time. Go up river for one kilometre and you will find **Yape;** four hours further is **Boca de Cupe.** Beyond these villages you enter very dangerous territory close to the Colombian border. If you do not already have a guide and you plan to continue, the time to find one is now or never.

⏮ WESTERN PANAMÁ ⏭

The diversity of Central America is very evident in western Panamá. There are mountains, beaches, coral reefs, carnivals, bananas plantations, and the list goes on. Much more accessible than the eastern part of the country, this region also has the country's highest mountain: the Volcán Barú at 3,475 metres. The Interamericana runs through this area as far as Costa Rica, providing an efficient access route.

Central Panamá and the Peninsula de Azuero

For budding ethnologists or even for someone looking for the local equivalent of the famous carnival in Rio, the Peninsula de Azuero is just the place. The country's largest carnival, with costumes, traditional music and the whole works, is held here for four days preceding Mardi Gras. Some villages seem to think that the carnival does not last long enough, so they start the festivities a week earlier. Shopkeepers close their stores so they can participate in the fiesta, and the hotels are crowded like never before. In Las Tablas, two streets have a competition to see which one has the most beautiful decorations. The carnival atmosphere is something like winning the Stanley Cup — except that it's a sure thing, every year!

The rest of the year Azuero is a sleepy town, slumbering between the harvests on its ranches and the waves of the lovely Pacific coast beaches. These waves are sometimes large enough for surfers to take them on.

The centre of Panamá is less developed, but this does not mean it is less interesting; in fact, it is all the more so because there are no tourists. There are mountains that keep it pleasantly cool, and flowers and exotic animals are abundant. It is worth stopping for a few days in El Valle to appreciate the countryside and the sumptuous nature.

El Valle

A verdant town where you can breath easily, El Valle is situated in the midst of the mountains only two and a half hours from the capital. You can walk in the surrounding area and climb mountains near the village. It is above all a beautiful place where you can feel at ease and where you can walk around in the evening without fear of attack; a nice change from the capital, where you have to take a cab in the less reputable districts. Try to visit El Valle during the week when there are even less people. All the attractions are easily reached on foot, and you can ask people in the streets for directions.

Petroglyphs *(Barrio La Pintada)*. If you only want to see petroglyphs, don't miss this place. So far, no one has been able to break the code or date them, but the images are eloquent just the same (animals, landscape, etc.). The contour of a sleeping Amerindian can be seen on a mountain ridge near the petroglyphs.

Ⓩ Agua Termales *(Río Antón)*. These thermal springs are situated at the foot of the mountains, in the most peaceful surroundings imaginable. The water is believed to have healing properties, and the temperature is a warm 40°C.

Chutes El Mocho *($1; on the Río Guayabo, 500 m after the Doña bridge on the road to Pueblo La Mesa)*. These 35-metre-high

PRACTICAL INFO

Transportation: Buses leave from the centre of town. Departures are throughout the day at regular intervals for **San Carlos** *($1)* and **Ciudad de Panamá** *($3.50)*.

Money: Change your money in San Carlos or in the capital.

Horse rental: Victor Muñoz rents horses for $3.50 an hour *(☎993-6330)*. He can also find guides for you.

waterfalls create a natural pool which is rumoured to be enchanted. The surrounding nature is always very luxuriant. There is another beautiful waterfall on the Río Antón.

Mercado Artesanal *(in the centre of the main street)*. This market is one of the best in the country. However it is open only on Sunday from 6am to 2pm. Everything is sold here: pottery, clothes and hats, as well as the usual fruit and vegetables. The handicrafts come from as far away as Ecuador, and the prices are reasonable.

Ⓩ **Vivero y Zoológico el Nispero** *($2; to the right after the police station coming from San Carlos)*. If you do not have time to take a jungle safari, no problem! About twenty years ago, two villages started creating zoological parks where you can admire an impressive number of animals and a large variety of tropical plants including monkeys and orchids.

El Valle

SWEET DREAMS

Pensión Niña Dalia *($9; Avenida Principal after Calle Los Millonarios)*. ▣ The budget choice in the village. Take your own supply of soap and toilet paper because the owners are a little stingy with these things.

Hotel Greco *($18; to the right of the main street, at the entrance to town)*. ▣ Clean and simple, this friendly place has individual little cabins in a quiet garden. There is also a small, affordable restaurant.

El Valle

$

BON APPETIT

Café Las Mozas *(to the right when entering town)*.
▶ Succulent food at a reasonable price.

Restaurante Santa Librada *(between Intel and the post office coming from San Carlos)*. ▶ Panamanian dishes and courteous service.

Santiago

There is nothing special to say about this town, except that it is halfway between Ciudad de Panamá and David, and you can buy superb macrame bags here. In short, it is an area of fields and you should stay here only to rest between buses. It is also the gateway to the Peninsula de Azuero.

PRACTICAL INFO

Transportation: Take the bus that leaves Ciudad de Panamá every hour and stops in Santiago before continuing on to **Las Tablas** *($2)*. Buses for **David** stop at the Piramidal hotel *($6)* every hour and a half.

Santiago

$

SWEET DREAMS

Pensión Central *($8; Avenida Central)*. ▶ Clean and with shower. Sometimes noisy.

Hotel Santiago *($12; Calle 2 behind the church)*. ▶ A little more expensive, but certainly quieter. Private bathrooms and sometimes even a TV and air-conditioner.

Santiago

$

BON APPETIT

Aire Libre *(opposite the Pensión)*. ▶ You can get all kinds of good food here. Inexpensive.

Las Tablas

Las Tablas is an ordinary little town 98 percent of the time. The exception is its week-long carnival, which is the country's largest fiesta. If you plan to visit during this time, make sure to reserve in advance. The village also has a church dating from 1789, as well as a museum devoted to an important political figure from the turn of the century. Another smaller festival is held around July 20. Las Tablas is also a good place to stay if you want to visit the various beaches along the coast.

PRACTICAL INFO

Transportation: Buses do not have a fixed schedule. Get the scoop at the hotels or from other travellers. Hitchhiking in this region is quite difficult.

Las Tablas

SWEET DREAMS

Pensión Mariela *($8; Avenida Central opposite the hotel Piamonte).* ▶ Nothing special but you will have a fan, a lock and a bed.

Piamonte *($15; in the centre of town).* ▶ The most comfortable hotel in town, with an air-conditioner in every room.

Las Tablas

BON APPETIT

Restaurante Aida *(Avenida Central).* ▶ Always open, this typical eatery serves Panamanian food.

Playa Venado

Many backpackers recommend this place, which is known primarily as a surfer's paradise. Humungous waves break on the long beach and you can see dozens of people way out in the water every weekend. Fortunately, the beach is large enough that you can easily get away from the crowd. Come here to relax, sunbathe,

---

PRACTICAL INFO

Transportation: One bus a day leaves **Las Tablas** at 1pm and returns the next day at 7am. However, the bus *($3.20)* only departs if there are enough passengers, so be cool. Avoid weekends, as Venado is a little too popular.

---

read and go surfing. *La dolce vita*, indeed! Playa Venado is a little like Montezuma (Costa Rica) was a few years ago, with a group of ex-hippies-turned-"beach promoters" in this tiny haven far from the material world!

Playa Venado

SWEET DREAMS AND BON APPETIT

There is only one establishment here — it is both a restaurant and hotel but we always forget its name. In fact, there are only five or six *cabañas* at $11 a night that can sleep three people. The food is good and traditional. If it is full, you will have no problem pitching your tent in the superb landscape, with roaring waves to lull you to sleep.

David

David is the third largest city, with a population of a little over 100,000. It is hot and humid and is the entry point to the mountains, the much more agreeable climate of the high Chirriquí. Nevertheless, David is still a big city so keep your eyes open, especially around the parks and marketplace. What is reassuring is that most of the people you meet on the street will greet you with a *buenos dias*.

Parque Central Cervantes *(in the western part of the city).* Walk around the square and appreciate the remnants from colonial times, like the Iglesia de San José and the Palacio Municipal.

Museo de Historia y de Arte José de Obaldia *(25¢; Calle 8 Este and Calle A Norte).* Open every day except Sunday and Monday. This museum is located in the house of the founder of Chirriquí province, whose son was the second president of Panamá. The collection of assorted objects trace the different periods from pre-Columbian times to this century, including the colonial era.

Balneario Majagua *(a few km north of the city; take the bus for Boquete and ask the driver when to get off)*. Here, you can bathe in a lovely river below magnificent waterfalls. You can also go rafting, but with some experience and a fat wallet *($90 minimum; ☎236-5281, hsanchez@panpna.c-com.net)*.

PRACTICAL INFO

Transportation: Catching a bus in David is pretty simple, since most departures are from the same bus station *(Avenida del Estudiante and Obaldia)*. The destinations are:

The border with Costa Rica: Buses leave every 10 minutes between 4:30am and 10pm, $1.50 for 1.5 hours of travel.

Ciudad de Panamá: about every hour and a quarter between 6:50am and midnight and costs $11 or $15 depending if it is an express bus which takes 5.5 hours to get to the capital, or the regular bus that stops in numerous towns and takes an hour longer.

Boquete: every half hour between 6am and 9pm, $1.20 for one hour travelling, depending on the driver.

Money: A few banks and exchange offices are spread out around the park. We suggest the **Banco General** because it does not charge a commission to change travellers' cheques (this is very rare).

Tourist Information: Ipat has an office to the left of the church, on the second floor of the Galherma Building, local 4. Not very useful.

Mail and Telephone: Calle C Norte and Avenida Bolívar. Open every day.

David

SWEET DREAMS

Pensión Fanita *($6; Avenida 5 Este and Calle B Norte)*. ▣ Very central and cheap, these rooms are worth the little that you pay. They can be noisy and the floor is not always solid but who can complain at $3 per person. Breakfast and lunch are served.

David

SWEET DREAMS

$

Pensión Costa Rica *($6.50; Avenida 5 Este and Calle A Sur)*. ▶ Near the park and in a pleasant neighbourhood. What is more, the building's façade is impressive and the rooms are simple but comfortable.

David

BON APPETIT

$

La Cacerola *(Avenida Obaldia and Super Barú)*. ▶ Excellent charcoal-grilled and à-la-carte food. A Creole buffet of amazing variety and typical food that is inexpensive.

Restaurante y Cafetería Jimar *(Calle C Norte and Avenida Bolívar)*. ▶ The quality of the food is good for the nominal price. For $2 you can have a fine meal, choosing from a good selection of dishes. Very popular and sometimes noisy, but also interesting for the cultural mix.

Boquete

Love at first sight is how most people remember discovering Boquete. And it's no wonder: arriving in the mountains after the suffocating heat of David, you are instantly intoxicated by the heady perfume of the city's profusion of flowers. You can take all sorts of different trips from this charming little town. Arriving from David, the imposing silhouette of Volcán Barú towers over the countryside at 3,475 metres on your left. The annual flower fair takes place at the end of January to the beginning of February, and is a real feast for the eyes and the nose!

 Pozos de Aguas Termales *(15 km before Boquete, a 45 min. walk near Pueblo Caldera on the same river)*. Hitch-hike or take a taxi from Boquete, and walk along by the river until you come to private land where the friendly owner will ask you to pay a nominal fee of 50¢ and explains the rituals the Amerindians performed at these baths. The baths range from warm to boiling temperatures, and are completely natural. Be sure to bathe in the turbulent water of the Río Caldera rapids. If you can say more in Spanish than *gracias*, this same man will show you a 5-metre cliff overhanging the Río from which you can dive in.

PRACTICAL INFO

Transportation: Buses leave for **David** *($1.20)* every half hour between 5am and 6:30pm from Avenida Fundadores next to the park. On weekdays, there is also a small grey bus that goes by at noon in the direction of **Caldera** *($1)*.

Money: the **Banco Nacional** *(Avenida Fundadores and Calle 5 Sur)* cashes only American Express cheques. For other cheques, go to **Super Centro Boquete** *(Calle 3 Sur towards the Río Caldera)*, but you must spend 10 percent of the cheque on their merchandise.

Tourist Information: Enrique Boutet and his brother started up the one tourist agency in Boquete (☎720-1342) a few years ago. They offer a variety of tours that are quite expensive. However, they give judicious advice on interesting itineraries. Do go and say hello, and show them this book because their help was invaluable.

Mail and Telephone: on the east side of the park. Open every day until 5pm.

Café Ruiz *(to the north on Fundadores on the left side of the Río)*. There is no charge to visit this small company that processes coffee beans gathered by the local Amerindians. It's best to go in the morning, since that's when the place is really hopping. Don't miss this chance to visit one of the only places in the country where they really know how brew good coffee.

Mí Jardín es Sú Jardín *(50 m after the Finca de Café)*. A rich American owns this huge estate, but rarely comes here so he has opened the gardens to the public. The place is fabulous, with flowers and fruit trees as well as a small chapel and a pool with goldfish — all worthy of a famous movie star!

Conservas de Antaño *(take the street by the park, cross the bridge, turn right and go 100 m on foot)*. Here is another small company where they make jam in large vats. You can visit and taste anytime. The mango jam is fantastic!

Volcán Barú *(a taxi will take you to the park where the path begins)*. It's a 14-kilometre climb to reach the summit. Lazier types can hitch a ride with the country's telecommunications employees who make the trip in a 4X4 every second day at 8am. If not, it takes a good five hours to get to the 3,475-metre peak, and three hours to come down. Bring extra clothes because it can get very cold on top. To get a good view, we strongly recommend

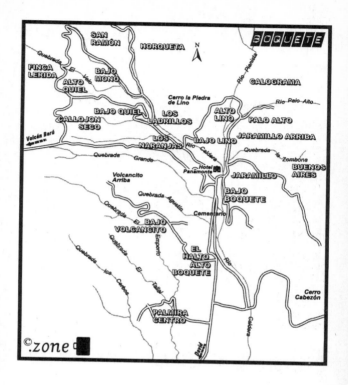

that you go at night, leaving about 1am (arrange the trip with a taxi or ask Enrique of Expediciones Tierras Altas agency to help you). Do not go alone and do not forget your flashlight. Generally the mountains have less clouds in the morning, so leaving at night means you have a better chance of getting there before they do. And it's worth the extra effort! On a clear day, you can see both oceans and the sunrise is spectacular. On the Pacific coast you can easily see the Peninsula de Punta Burica, which is the boundary with Costa Rica.

Boquete *SWEET DREAMS*

Pensión Virginia *($11-$15: the pale blue façade on the south side of the park).* ▣ This place has nothing but good things going for it: the least expensive and the best situated, it has a small restaurant and a piano, and the rooms are decent but sometimes noisy (and less expensive) on the ground floor.

Pensión Marilos *($15: Calle 6 Sur, two streets east of Avenida Fundadores).* ▣ A little more expensive. There is always hot water and the place is much cleaner than the Virginia. It is a little further away and has a kitschy decor, but is still pleasant.

Boquete *BON APPETIT*

Restaurante El Sabrosón *(Calle 1 Sur and Avenida Fundadores).* ▣ Typical Panamanian food: beans, rice, pork *platanas fritas*, meat, carrot juice, milk, etc. Very cheap *($2)* and good. All the daily meals are served.

Volcán

Another little village, perhaps more rustic than Boquete and with a European flavour. Many pioneers from the old country have settled here since the beginning of the century, and this is noticeable in its adornments. Buses for Volcán are frequent, but you must go through David to get here. You can climb the Barú from this side, but the path is less well marked and you must count on at least 8 to 10 hours of hiking. We suggest you hire a guide, and crossing the mountain to Boquete. Though you miss visiting David twice, you will have seen both Volcán and Boquete!

Las Lagunas *(a half hour walk on a road that passes by the police station)*. It is said that the water in these lagoons is ominous and that a few swimmers have been pulled under and drowned. It is for you to decide.

La Fuente *(25¢; halfway along the same path)*. This park does not have the same reputation as Las Lagunas and is much more accessible. It is a playground with swimming pools filled with water from a mountain spring.

Volcán

$

SWEET DREAMS

Cabañas Señoriales *($14; at the entrance to the village)*. ▶ Basic comfort with original decorations inside the cabins. Bathrooms and hot water. There is also a friendly bar nearby.

Motel California *($18; on the main street)*. ▶ Welcoming and clean. The owner comes from central Europe and speaks English. The cabins are good if you're travelling in a group.

Volcán

$

BON APPETIT

All kinds of little *comedores* are spread out through the village. Fish is served as well as local food, and sometimes even the pizzas are good.

Bocas del Toro

 This province is an intense banana production area. Most people get here by boat, so it's a bit isolated from the rest of the country. The population is mainly composed of Amerindians and descendants of slaves who came from the Caribbean Islands. Only the little village of Bocas del Toro on the Isla de Colón has any kind of tourist amenities.

Most of the island's population is black and speaks English, and lives off tourism and fishing. Because it is not very big, you can easily tour the whole island on foot or by bicycle, which takes about a day. Simply a must, with lots of stunning scenery and attractions which include some incredible beaches and perfect spots for scuba diving. But you don't necessarily have to strap on an oxygen tank to get a look at the coral, since this is also a wonderful place for snorkelling.

PRACTICAL INFO

Transportation: Go to **David** and take one of the numerous daily buses for **Chirriquí Grande** *(\$6 for 3 hours travelling)*. Buses leave the same bus station as all the others. From there boats leave each morning for the island between 7am and 2pm, and cost \$3 for a one-hour trip.

Bocas del Toro $	# SWEET DREAMS AND BON APPETIT

Bahía *(\$20; the old United Fruit Building)*. ▶ Overlooking the bay. It also has a restaurant and a laundry service. A few of the rooms have hot water.

Bocas del Toro *(\$25; on the water)*. ▶ There are a few cockroaches and the walls are a little too thin. However, there are fans, baths and a restaurant, and you can rent snorkelling equipment, bicycles and boats.

⏭ GLOSSARY ⏮

Greetings

Goodbye	*adiós, hasta luego*
Good afternoon and good evening	*buenas tardes*
Hi (casual)	*hola*
Good morning	*buenos días*
Good night	*buenas noches*
Thank-you	*gracias*
Please	*por favor*
You are welcome	*de nada*
Excuse me	*perdone/a*
My name is...	*mi nombre es...*
What is your name?	*¿cómo se llama usted?*
yes	*no*
no	*sí*
Do you speak English?	*¿habla usted inglés?*
Slower, please	*más despacio, por favor*
I am sorry, I don't speak Spanish	*Lo siento, no hablo español*
How are you?	*¿qué tal?*
I am fine	*estoy bien*
I am American (male/female)	*Soy estadounidense*
I am Australian	*Soy autraliano/a*
I am Belgian	*Soy belga*
I am British (male/female)	*Soy británico/a*
I am Canadian	*Soy canadiense*
I am German (male/female)	*Soy alemán/a*
I am Italian (male/female)	*Soy italiano/a*
I am Swiss	*Soy suizo*
I am a tourist	*Soy turista*
single (m/f)	*soltero/a*
divorced (m/f)	*divorciado/a*
married (m/f)	*casado/a*
friend (m/f)	*amigo/a*
child (m/f)	*niño/a*
husband, wife	*esposo/a*
mother	*madre*
father	*padre*
brother, sister	*hermano/a*
widower widow	*viudo/a*
I am hungry	*tengo hambre*
I am ill	*estoy enfermo/a*
I am thirsty	*tengo sed*

Directions

beside	*al lado de*
to the right	*a la derecha*
to the left	*a la izquierda*
here	*aquí*
there	*allí*
into, inside	*dentro*
outside	*fuera*
behind	*detrás*
in front of	*delante*
between	*entre*
far from	*lejos de*
Where is ... ?	*¿dónde está ... ?*
To get to ...?	*¿para ir a...?*
near	*cerca de*
straight ahead	*todo recto*

Money

money	*dinero / plata*
credit card	*tarjeta de crédito*
exchange	*cambio*
traveller's cheque	*cheque de viaje*
I don't have any money	*no tengo dinero*
The bill, please	*la cuenta, por favor*
receipt	*recibo*

Shopping

store	*tienda*
market	*mercado*
open	*abierto/a*
closed	*cerrado/a*
How much is this?	*¿cuánto es?*
to buy	*comprar*
to sell	*vender*
the customer	*el / la cliente*
salesman	*vendedor*
saleswoman	*vendedora*
I need...	*necesito...*
I would like...	*yo quisiera...*
batteries	*pilas*
blouse	*blusa*
cameras	*cámaras*
cosmetics and perfumes	*cosméticos y perfumes*
cotton	*algodón*

dress jacket	*saco*
eyeglasses	*lentes, gafas*
fabric	*tela*
film	*película*
gifts	*regalos*
gold	*oro*
handbag	*bolsa*
hat	*sombrero*
jewellery	*joyería*
leather	*cuero, piel*
local crafts	*artesanía*
magazines	*revistas*
newpapers	*periódicos*
pants	*pantalones*
records, cassettes	*discos, casetas*
sandals	*sandalias*
shirt	*camisa*
shoes	*zapatos*
silver	*plata*
skirt	*falda*
sun screen products	*productos solares*
T-shirt	*camiseta*
watch	*reloj*
wool	*lana*

Miscellaneous

a little	*poco*
a lot	*mucho*
good (m/f)	*bueno/a*
bad (m/f)	*malo/a*
beautiful (m/f)	*hermoso/a*
pretty (m/f)	*bonito/a*
ugly	*feo*
big	*grande*
tall (m/f)	*alto/a*
small (m/f)	*pequeño/a*
short (length) (m/f)	*corto/a*
short (person) (m/f)	*bajo/a*
cold (m/f)	*frío/a*
hot	*caliente*
dark (m/f)	*oscuro/a*
light (colour)	*claro*
do not touch	*no tocar*
expensive (m/f)	*caro/a*
cheap (m/f)	*barato/a*
fat (m/f)	*gordo/a*
slim, skinny (m/f)	*delgado/a*
heavy (m/f)	*pesado/a*

light (weight) (m/f)	*ligero/a*
less	*menos*
more	*más*
narrow (m/f)	*estrecho/a*
wide (m/f)	*ancho/a*
new (m/f)	*nuevo/a*
old (m/f)	*viejo/a*
nothing	*nada*
something (m/f)	*algo/a*
quickly	*rápidamente*
slowly (m/f)	*despacio/a*
What is this?	*¿qué es esto?*
when?	*¿cuando?*
where?	*¿dónde?*

Time

in the afternoon, early evening	*por la tarde*
at night	*por la noche*
in the daytime	*por el día*
in the morning	*por la mañana*
minute	*minuto*
month	*mes*
ever	*jamás*
never	*nunca*
now	*ahora*
today	*hoy*
yesterday	*ayer*
tomorrow	*mañana*
What time is it?	*¿qué hora es?*
hour	*hora*
week	*semana*
year	*año*

Sunday	*domingo*
Monday	*lunes*
Tuesday	*martes*
Wednesday	*miércoles*
Thursday	*jueves*
Friday	*viernes*
Saturday	*sábado*
January	*enero*
February	*febrero*
March	*marzo*
April	*abril*
May	*mayo*
June	*junio*
July	*julio*
August	*agosto*

September	*septiembre*
October	*octubre*
November	*noviembre*
December	*diciembre*

Weather

It is cold	*hace frío*
It is warm	*hace calor*
It is very hot	hace mucho calor
sun	*sol*
It is sunny	hace sol
It is cloudy	*está nublado*
rain	*lluvia*
It is raining	*está lloviendo*
wind	*viento*
It is windy	*hay viento*
snow	*nieve*
damp	*húmedo*
dry	*seco*
storm	*tormenta*
hurricane	*huracán*

Communication

air mail	*correos aéreo*
collect call	*llamada por cobrar*
dial the number	*marcar el número*
area code, country code	*código*
envelope	*sobre*
long distance	*larga distancia*
post office	*correo*
rate	*tarifa*
stamps	*estampillas*
telegram	*telegrama*
telephone book	*un guia telefónica*
wait for the tone	*esperar la señal*

Activities

beach	*playa*
museum or gallery	*museo*
scuba diving	*buceo*
to swim	*bañarse*
to walk around	*pasear*
hiking	*caminata*
trail	*pista, sendero*

| cycling | *ciclismo* |
| fishing | *pesca* |

Transportation

arrival	*llegada*
departure	*salida*
on time	*a tiempo*
cancelled (m/f)	*anulado/a*
one way ticket	*ida*
return	*regreso*
round trip	*ida y vuelta*
schedule	*horario*
baggage	*equipajes*
north	*norte*
south	*sur*
east	*este*
west	*oeste*
avenue	*avenida*
street	*calle*
highway	*carretera*
expressway	*autopista*
airplane	*avión*
airport	*aeropuerto*
bicycle	*bicicleta*
boat	*barco*
bus	*bus*
bus stop	*parada*
bus terminal	*terminal*
train	*tren*
train crossing	*crucero ferrocarril*
station	*estación*
neighbourhood	*barrio*
collective taxi	*colectivo*
corner	*esquina*
express	*rápido*
safe	*seguro/a*
be careful	*cuidado*
car	*coche, carro*
To rent a car	*alquilar un auto*
gas	*gasolina*
gas station	*gasolinera*
no parking	*no estacionar*
no passing	*no adelantar*
parking	*parqueo*
pedestrian	*peaton*
road closed, no through traffic	*no hay paso*
slow down	*reduzca velocidad*
speed limit	*velocidad permitida*

stop	*alto*
stop! (an order)	*pare*
traffic light	*semáforo*

Accommodation

cabin, bungalow	*cabaña*
accommodation	*alojamiento*
double, for two people	*doble*
single, for one person	*sencillo*
high season	*temporada alta*
low season	*temporada baja* bed
	cama
floor (first, second...)	*piso*
main floor	*planta baja*
manager	*gerente, jefe*
double bed	*cama matrimonial*
cot	*camita*
bathroom	*baños*
with private bathroom	*con baño privado*
hot water	*agua caliente*
breakfast	*desayuno*
elevator	*ascensor*
air conditioning	*aire acondicionado*
fan	*ventilador, abanico*
pool	*piscina, alberca*
room	*habitación*

Numbers

1	*uno*
2	*dos*
3	*tres*
4	*cuatro*
5	*cinco*
6	*seis*
7	*siete*
8	*ocho*
9	*nueve*
10	*diez*
11	*once*
12	*doce*
13	*trece*
14	*catorce*
15	*quince*
16	*dieciséis*
17	*diecisiete*
18	*dieciocho*
19	*diecinueve*

20	*veinte*
21	*veintiuno*
22	*veintidós*
23	*veintitrés*
24	*veinticuatro*
25	*veinticinco*
26	*veintiséis*
27	*veintisiete*
28	*veintiocho*
29	*veintinueve*
30	*treinta*
31	*treinta y uno*
32	*treinta y dos*
40	*cuarenta*
50	*cincuenta*
60	*sesenta*
70	*setenta*
80	*ochenta*
90	*noventa*
100	*cien*
101	*ciento uno*
102	*ciento dos*
200	*doscientos*
300	*trescientos*
400	*quatrocientoa*
500	*quinientos*
600	*seiscientos*
700	*sietecientos*
800	*ochocientos*
900	*novecientos*
1,000	*mil*
1,100	*mil cien*
1,200	*mil doscientos*
2000	*dos mil*
3000	*tres mil*
10,000	*diez mil*
100,000	*cien mil*
1,000,000	*un millón*

⏭ INDEX ⏮